D0764269

WIND AND SAILING BOATS

Wind and Sailing Boats

*The structure and behaviour of the wind
as it affects sailing craft*

ALAN WATTS

F.R.Met.S.

David & Charles

Newton Abbot   London   North Pomfret (Vt)

British Library Cataloguing in Publication Data

Watts, Alan, *1925–*
    Wind and sailing boats : the structure and
    behaviour of the wind as it affects
    sailing craft. – 3rd rev. ed.
    1. Sailing   2. Winds
    I. Title
    623.88′223   VK543
    ISBN 0-7153-9032-5

First published by Adlard Coles Ltd 1965
Second revised edition 1973
Third revised edition 1987

© Alan Watts 1965, 1973, 1987

Printed in Great Britain
by Redwood Burn Ltd, Trowbridge, Wiltshire
for David & Charles Publishers plc
Brunel House   Newton Abbot   Devon

Published in the United States of America
by David & Charles Inc
North Pomfret ، Vermont 05053   USA

Contents

Introduction

MOST of the material in this book has been suggested as a result of articles written over the last ten or twelve years, and more recently by small-craft people who have attended the lectures organised from time to time by the Central Council of Physical Recreation.

This experience has shown that there exists a need for more information on the wind as it applies to small craft. This information must be practical. It must be information which can be used, and the uses must be brought out boldly so that they are not swamped by the theory and observations on which they are based.

This practical point of view has been uppermost in my mind while I have been writing, and for this reason some reiteration may be evident from time to time. This is intentional, for it is sometimes tedious to have to refer back to previous pages. Such references must be made, but they have been kept to the minimum. Further, if the basic conclusions are restated in several places their paramount importance becomes evident. It is sometimes difficult for a layman to hoist in what to the professional is second nature, and so restating the case helps to push the points home.

I have been aided in this approach by now being a layman who was once a professional. The years since forecasting have been sufficient for me to look at meteorology with a layman's eye. There is a whole world of difference between the met. men talking to their public and talking to each other. In the former case they are usually talking down, while in the latter their jargon is often quite unintelligible. Yachting people stand between these two extremes, and they need wind information which, while it is accurate and qualified, is rephrased in their language. This is what I have tried to do here. Many of the articles listed in the works referred to on page 221 are simply stated and can be read by anyone. This is particularly so with articles with the Royal Meteorological Society's magazine *Weather*, which are written for the layman interested in weather. Many of the articles in the Meteorological Office's *Meteorological Magazine* are also capable of being read by the interested amateur yachtsman.

Should anyone feel that the Solent area, and Chichester Harbour in particular, have been especially favoured, it is as well to explain that inferences gained from native waters can be hedged about with more confident detail culled from personal experience and must therefore be more convincing. Also the area is much used and representative of those places throughout the temperate latitudes where nature has conspired to provide safe and delightful anchorage for small craft.

The reader may well notice omissions. There is, for instance, nothing on tropical revolving storms. However, this information is quoted so often that it seemed unnecessary to repeat it. It appears for instance in every Admiralty Pilot as well as many books on weather in general. Other topics are neglected or lightly touched on for similar reasons. The life cycle of depressions and the standard cross-sections of fronts are to be found in many books on weather forecasting so they are left out of this book. Forecasting wave-height from wind is included, but the tactical uses of waves have been fully covered in *Sailing Strategy: Wind and Current* ([9]).*

This is, I hope, a book on the more neglected aspects of wind which will add something useful to the already wide wind information available to sailing people.

In a letter to a friend Uffa Fox once said, "I hope this letter will give you an idea of the winds, which at all times you must study very intently, as they are the only motive power you have to sail with, and the thing to do is to use them sensibly and not stupidly, for like fire they are a good friend but a bad master."

I trust this book will help more small-craft sailors make a good friend of the wind.

Introduction to second edition

ON reading through the book with a view to revising it I found that the alterations I wished to make were so minor that there was nothing to be lost by leaving the book in its original form. That is indeed how it has been left, but the move towards metrication is a rising tide which will not be stemmed. Yet feet and Fahrenheit are still the familiar units to the vast majority of British yachtsmen. Units are only as good as your understanding of them and so this re-printed edition has been left exactly as it was with metric conversions given on pages 210–212. Only lengths are involved as the knot is a nautical mile per hour and neither the nautical mile nor the hour can be, or are being replaced in the new units. In any case the conversion that 2 kt=1m/s is adequate for most purposes. (To convert feet/second to metres/second divide the ft/s by 3.) There is a conversion scale from °F into °C on page 217.

Elmstead Market,
1973.

Introduction to this edition

THE few small changes made to the 1973 edition brought it up to date from the point of view of metric conversions, etc; this latest edition has entailed even fewer alterations. Amongst these, the Beaufort Scale has been extended and modified to place more emphasis on deep-keel yachts and their needs. The diagram on page 207 has been brought up to date as regards the stations whose actual weather reports are broadcast at the end of the shipping forecasts. Apart from these, only minor changes – in my opinion – needed making.

I hope those who read this book some twenty-two years after it was first published will find it as relevant to their sailing as I trust it was then.

Alan Watts
October 1986.

* The small figure within brackets refers to the list on page 221.

Acknowledgements

WHEN so much diverse information has been obtained from so many sources it is difficult to make adequate acknowledgement to all of them. Very few of the diagrams are reproduced exactly as their authors drew them, as often they were needlessly scientific for our purpose. Thus bracketed figures appended to the captions indicate that the diagram in question is based on one in the appropriate reference at the end of the book.

I am grateful to the Director of the Meteorological Office for permission to use much information from official publications. In particular to the Meteorological Office Library for their continuous help and to the Climatology Section for some of the statistics on winds. Also to the staff at Thorney Island who helped with anemograms.

The diagrams marked (MO) are based on Crown Copyright material with the permission of the Controller of Her Majesty's Stationery Office.

The majority of the photographs are from the Clarke-Cave collection, by permission of the Royal Meteorological Society. The others (7 & 14) first saw the light of day appended to articles appearing in *Yachting World* to whose editor, Bernard Hayman, I am especially grateful as he was responsible for piloting them into print.

Charles Curry gave invaluable help with the Firefly performance chart and allowed me to dash some of my ideas against the rocks of his experience.

William Barltrop did the better-looking diagrams, and the author did the rest.

CHAPTER ONE

The Measure of the Wind

As WIND is invisible, all the estimates of it are by inference from some other source. The methods differ with the precision which is desired and their practicality under the circumstances. A dinghy helmsman will not usually take any wind-finding devices with him other than a racing-flag and his cheek. With these he will assess the wind at the dinghy and react accordingly. However, he will not win races by noting the immediate wind and nothing else. He will have to forecast wind changes which he can see affecting craft, flags, smoke, clouds, etc., upwind of him. On his correct assessment of the new wind situation will rest his reaction to it. The correct reaction can well lead to leadership of the fleet, but this may often depend on knowing the cause of the wind change as well as its likely progress. For instance many helmsmen schooled by any book on weather forecasting will act to take advantage of the veer of wind which accompanies the passage of a cold front. Yet during a race in small waters the passage of a front is a relatively rare occurrence. The wind changes which affect dinghy fleets are usually more immediate ones bred in one type of airstream and not due to one great air mass being replaced by another, as happens at fronts. The usual pattern of fronts and their winds and weather are so often described that the reader can find them very easily, and, while Chapter Two gives a sketch of them, it is not the intention to deal with the more usual wind features at great length. It is the smaller features of the wind which help to win or lose races, and these are not normally covered in any detail in books on weather forecasting. This is not therefore primarily a book on forecasting, but forecasting cannot be neglected as the offshore cruising or racing skipper has as friend or enemy the larger-scale weather features.

The dinghy and the deep-keel yacht are sometimes poles apart in their need for wind information. Often the dinghy helmsmen who consistently do well have the ability to produce a mental vector blackboard on which they can chalk in their mind's eye wind and current arrows applicable to the situation as it exists, or is likely to exist, say, round the next mark. Such mental computing is only successful if the wind a quarter to half an hour ahead is correctly forecast. Nearer the mark the prediction time contracts to a few minutes. Sometimes the wind ahead is quite unpredictable, leaving the field wide open for the correct instinctive reaction in the flurry of rounding.

The deep-keel skipper who is racing or cruising for many hours or even days has problems of wind forecasting which are very different. The flux of pressure systems and fronts is his deep concern; the shipping forecasts his ever-present help. Wind is much more a question of isobars deduced from some rough and ready chart or other. He has the time if not the inclination to put his wind forecast on paper and ponder it. The dinghy man must have his in his head.

It is therefore of prime importance to know the general pattern of wind changes to

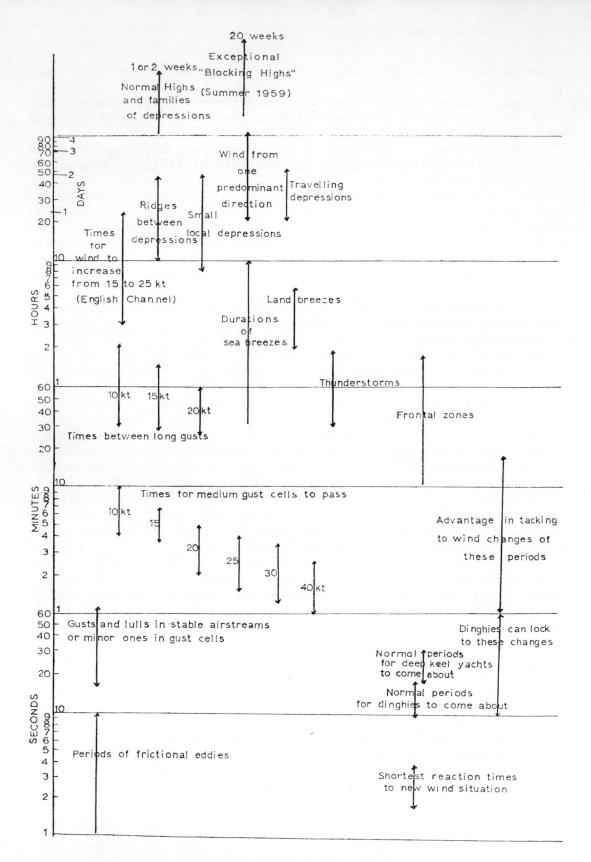

1.1: *The spectrum of the wind.*

be expected, so that small clues can suggest future events. Micro-changes in the pattern of the wind-stream or meso-scale changes in local winds during a day of settled weather are not the usual concern of weather forecasting books, because they are just not important enough. To the small-water sailor they are of paramount importance and their usual periods of recurrence can be assessed from Figure 1.1.

What is important as a wind change to any craft is limited, at the short period end of the chart, by her normal reaction time. This time is defined in Chapter Three and will vary from ten seconds in short dinghies to minutes in very large yachts.

However, the times between gust cells of the medium variety show that even 12-Metres can react to them, and careful study of the wind structure might lead to faster sailing of such craft. Wind structure seems to have been a neglected field in the past, and one of the objects of this book is to attempt to redress the balance. When personal or national prestige is at stake the effort may well be worth a more careful study. There are hundreds of unanswered questions thrown up by any inquiry into the reaction of sailing craft to micro-wind changes, amongst them the peculiar circumstances of catamaran sailing where most of the work is off the wind and the ability of any craft to carry a spinnaker in a gusty wind. These are just two of many topics which spring to mind, but which it has been impossible to cover.

The upper limit to the period of any of the wind features is that over which winds can be considered permanent, and the limits of permanency are set by the duration of the race or passage. For dinghy races taking an hour or two sea breezes and thunderstorms, as well as the long-period gust cells, can become established and pass before the race is over. These are semi-permanent features. Depressions, however, do not normally pass in such short times, neither will the wind increase from Force 4 to 6 during the course of one race. However a meeting can easily encompass such wind changes.

The "spectrum of the wind" which is Fig. 1.1 will help the reader assess what is and what is not an important wind change for him, and he can then if he feels inclined study such changes in more detail.

In order to provide these details and make them convincing it is necessary to take actual examples, preferably from one's own experience, and this may appear to centre attention on the places one knows best. Therefore, if Chichester Harbour and Thorney Island seem to have more than their fair share of publicity, it is only because I was raised in the waters of Chichester Harbour and the Solent and then returned there later as a weather forecaster at the R.A.F. base on Thorney Island. It was inevitable that the weather forecasting experience I acquired there together with the sailing I did at the same time should have become welded into a more than usually intimate knowledge of the wind processes which affect sailing boats—particularly with regard to dinghies. It was so easy to spend a week-end sailing the waters surrounding the Island of Thorney and then to look at the wind one had been sailing in permanently recorded on an anemogram. It was in this way that the germs of some of the ideas put forward in the following chapters were born.

Particularly was this so with the sea breeze, "Hampshire has Hayling but Sussex has Thorney. The isle of the hawthorn, the Isle of the Breeze," says Sylvia Hurd in her poem "Thorney in Winter." And so it is, but the winter breeze is from many directions at the behest of the pressure patterns on a vast scale. In summer that breeze is more often than not off the sea. More than half the summer days find Thorney and its environs blessed with a sea breeze, so that the hawthorns become wind-shaped by them and trail leafy wakes towards the hinterland.

A breeze of such regular occurrence which could sometimes produce swings of 180° almost instantaneously was obviously a fruitful wind to study, especially when one was thinking of winning races. It was something the Air Traffic Controllers were interested in as well, for sometimes aircraft landing into a north wind would find that their head wind had abruptly become a tail wind. Thus an investigation into the sea breeze was indulged in under the aegis of the Air Ministry with a strong sideways glance at its uses in sailing races. The results, while not very precise on timing, are nevertheless useful when sailing inland waters, which include harbours and coastal shallows.

The fact that examples are taken from precise localities should not, however, prove an obstacle. All weather information on the small- and medium-scale winds must perforce be undertaken in one locality, but wherever the general coastwise terrain is the same, *i.e.* a coastal plain backed by hills which are perhaps 10–20 miles inland, then the sea breeze will act as it does at Thorney. There may be small differences in detail, but the general pattern will be the same. The location of Thorney, so near the Solent and in the centre of the South Coast where a vast mass of craft abound, is certain to be familiar to many people. If the reader does not know this area, then the maps and photographs will help him visualise it and so apply the results to his own local sailing waters. In any case, as so many places where sailing is done have environs like Thorney's the results we found there will be widely applicable. Where there are mountains and cliffy places such as in the West Country and Wales or in Scotland then suggestions on how to predict the wind's behaviour will be given.

Also it must be pointed out that, while the examples of all sorts of winds stem mainly from the British Isles, wind will act in the same ways wherever one sails in the temperate latitudes of the northern hemisphere. This is evinced by small-craft helmsmen of all nationalities managing to keep their end up against local competition wherever international meetings are held. Where disadvantage may creep in is when helmsmen of one hemisphere find themselves competing in the other. The results of Chapter Three show that the small-scale features of wind are not impartial when it comes to the two hemispheres. The correct reaction to gust and lull in the temperate waters of the northern hemisphere is the exact opposite of that required in the southern. In any case, to take advantage of the wind shifts, port or starboard tack is often not an arbitrary choice. The wind has a built-in bias towards veering when it gusts and backing when it lulls in the northern hemisphere, while it will back when it gusts and veer when it lulls in the southern hemisphere. Those brought up in Torbay may find it odd sailing in gusty winds at Melbourne or Cape Town. It has obviously been impossible to draw two sets of diagrams for the two hemispheres but as pointed out in the ensuing pages (Chapter Three, "Gusts Down-Under", pages 104–5) the southern hemisphere diagram is obtained from the northern by interchanging veer and back wherever they occur.

HOW THE WIND LOCKS TO THE BOAT For a craft to sail with components of its velocity directed against the wind requires that the action of the wind on the sails be converted into a reaction in a direction different to that of the wind.

This is achieved by the agency of changing the air density on opposite faces of the sail. If the air is considered as composed of molecules in constant motion then (when the

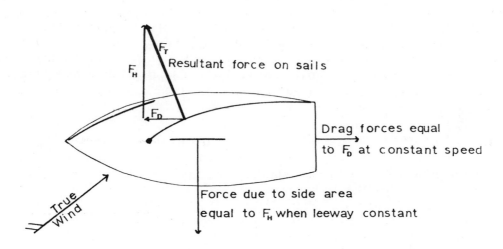

1.2: *The force on a sail is due primarily to different densities of air molecules on its two sides.*

Faster less dense Airflow

SAIL SECTION

Slower denser Airflow

Force on this side exceeds that on the other

Resultant force on sails

Drag forces equal to F_D at constant speed

True Wind

Force due to side area equal to F_H when leeway constant

1.3: *The resultant forces on the craft when on the wind.*

mass of air is at rest) they are in equal number on either side of any sail and, as they all move with the same average velocity, the force they exert as they strike the sail from either side is the same. If however the molecules could be increased in number on the inner side of the sail and decreased in number on the outer side then, as each continues to strike the sail with equal force, there will be an excess of force directed from the inside of the sail to the outside.

This is achieved in practice by slowing up the air on the inner side and speeding it up on the outer side. As air density is the mass in unit volume then, considering two equal volumes on either side of the sail (Fig. 1.2), the volume with the greatest number of molecules in it will exert the greatest force. This force is directed perpendicularly to the sail, and in the diagrammatic representation of a small area of sail the excess force is depicted for sake of argument as one unit. This is merely to illustrate the point and bears no relation to any actual forces exerted on actual sails.

If the effect of such forces is summed over the whole sail, then they can be compounded into a resultant force F_T which acts through the centre of effort of the sail and has a driving component F_D which is directed forward. If the useless heeling force F_H is cancelled by an equal force, due to side area of hull and keel, then the force F_D remains to provide motion for the craft (Fig. 1.3). Thus a wind flowing with components apparently against the direction of motion can, through the agency of sail, exert forces in the fore-and-aft direction.

This explanation has been included because it is evident from continuing correspondence in the yachting press that there is still doubt about the mechanics of sailing against the wind. I think this stems from the inability to see where the actual force comes from. It might be worth pointing out that the molecules in air at normal temperature and pressure are moving amongst themselves at speeds akin to those of the fastest jet aircraft, and the force each exerts depends on the square of the velocity with which it strikes the sail. Each individual collision of molecule with sail material provides an extremely small force, but then there are an immense number of molecules striking any small area at one moment so the force becomes relatively big. As already pointed out, if the number of molecules is changed on opposite faces then an excess force acts from the side with most to the side with least molecules striking the sail. Therefore the function of sail is to change the air densities. Only by streamline flow can this be achieved and if there were some other way of changing the densities, other than through the medium of letting the air stream past the sail at different speeds on its opposite faces, then this could also be used to provide a driving force.

It would seem when beating into, say, a Force 4 wind that the really big forces are due to the airstream impinging on the sail along its streamlines, but this speed is only about one-hundredth of the speed of the molecules amongst themselves. The wind is the drift velocity imposed on an immense number of molecules moving very fast indeed in all directions and, as stated before, the force exerted depends on the square of the velocity. So while the pressure forces exerted by the molecules moving at very high speed amongst themselves nearly cancel each other it only needs the numbers on opposite sides of the sail to be changed by a relatively small amount for there to be a sizeable force exerted across the sail. This is comparable to, and larger than, the drag exerted when they drift in streamline flow (or turbulent flow) against the sail itself.

It therefore appears that any agency which will increase the difference in air density on opposite sides of the sail must increase the driving force. So the beneficial effect of a foresail is to speed up the air-flow over the outer side of the mainsail by the compression of the slot effect. Recent work at the University of Southampton has shown that the optimum sheeting is with overlapping portions of mainsail and foresail neither converging nor diverging thus providing a parallel slot. This still provides a compression which the air must alleviate by increasing its speed.

The other prerequisite for producing drive from most of the sail area is that the flow should be more or less streamline over the whole of the outer face of the sail, whatever it does on the inner face. Streamline flow means that there must be no turbulent eddies.

Experiments with wool tufts on both faces of the sails of my National Firefly have revealed some rather unsettling facts concerning the airflow over the outer face when off the wind. On the wind the wool tufts obediently trail aft on the outer face as they should, but on a reach those nearest the mast refuse to do anything but stream forwards, whatever the sheeting of the foresail. This indicates that the mast is producing a strong turbulent back-eddy just behind it where one would like smooth streamline flow in the other direction. Undoubtedly similar results would be found for many other dinghies and yachts. Thus do theoretical ideas fall down when put to the test. Yet we are happy to put up with imperfection for the lack of complication and cost, and prefer to make our craft alike in their imperfections. Still, able helmsmen in strictly one-design classes such as the Firefly can still beat able helmsmen in restricted classes such as the National Twelve. Modern Nationals certainly have the edge over Fireflies, but the margin is not so great as to preclude some degree of competition when the two classes are raced together. Yet the National has been developed and the Firefly has not. The moral of this story is that whatever you do to craft of the same general design and accomplishments to make them faster, superior helming can always overcome the disadvantages. A major factor in such superiority is the ability to predict and then handle the wind changes which come along. A few false moves and no amount of careful design work can redress the balance.

THE FORCE OF THE WIND Finally a word about real craft in real winds. In the appendix it is shown that the pressure exerted by the wind varies as the square of its strength. This is in practice not quite true as there are edge effects to be taken into account when considering the pressure of the wind on a relatively small thing like a sail.

On the wind, for example, the wind pressures at 15 knots and 25 knots should stand in the ratio of 225:625, *i.e.* 1:3·6 and it can be seen from Fig. 1.4 the ratio is a little less than 1:3.

However the simple rule that the pressure of the wind increases as the square of the wind speed is good enough for practical purposes.

This means that a wind which suddenly gusts to twice its former speed is exerting a heeling moment which is four times greater than it was before. It is not surprising that in the stronger gusts associated with Force 4 (say when under the influence of the land) dinghies will have to spill wind. A wind which suddenly gusts from 14 kt to 23 kt increases the heeling moment by a factor of three, as can also be seen from Fig. 1.4. These factors assume that no change of direction also occurs in such a short time interval that the helmsman cannot react to it. However a sharp veer may often accompany a gust. Thus, if you are beating on the starboard tack the gust is not only stronger but more from the beam and so increases the heeling moment on two counts. The reaction is instinctively to check sheets and then make up, hardening in as one does so.

On the port tack the stronger wind comes more from the bow. The tendency is for the foresail luff to shiver at this imposed low angle of attack but the heeling moment is still there; not as great as on starboard, but not capable of being met by checking sheets as on starboard, and therefore more difficult to combat. Pulling up the helm would seem to be the wrong thing to do in a sudden blow, but on port tack it must be the fastest way to keep moving through a heading gust. (In the southern hemisphere the effects described for starboard occur on port and *vice versa*.)

Going from beating to other points of sailing, as for instance after a thrash to a windward mark followed by a reach off to the next mark, the yacht making 5 kt to windward in a 20 kt wind experiences an apparent wind speed of 23–24 kt, *i.e.* Force 5 becomes apparently Force 6. On bearing away to make 7 knots or so the apparent wind strength falls to Force 4, and all is calm and collected.

A further point to be made concerns the state of sea, which by throwing all manner of craft about can increase the apparent heeling power by having a wave-induced heel

B

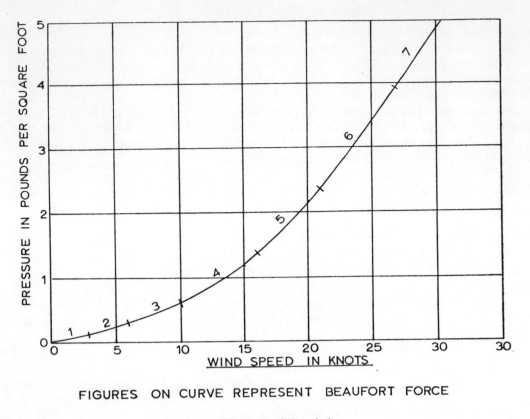

FIGURES ON CURVE REPRESENT BEAUFORT FORCE

1.4: The force of the wind.

coupled to a gust-induced heel. Other combinations of these factors make the planning of tactics difficult, for wave frequency is too rapid to be in any way predictable over periods of more than a few seconds. Each wave and gust or lull has to be met at the time and on its merits.

Force 4, which does not in general produce much seaway, would seem to be the best dinghy breeze. Survival is not paramount as it may be in stronger winds. Most dinghies will get some exhilarating planing and not be overpowered for much of the time as occurs with Force 6 if not Force 5. The gusts in the unstable airstreams can give occasional sit-her-up-and-hang-on planing sprees without overworking the rescue boats or covering the lee shores in struggling masses of sails and crews.

Other writers have also suggested that for deep-keel yachts this same Force 4 is that wind which produces the best working in the various conditions of sea which it generates. Of course it must not be lost sight of that even Force 4 against a strong tidal set can produce quite a nasty seaway whose shortness is difficult to meet adequately.

CHAPTER TWO

Pressure Systems and Wind

THE prevailing wind for the British Isles is westerly. This is because these islands lie in the path of that part of the planetary wind circulation which is called the prevailing westerlies.

The mechanism of the earth's wind circulation is not fully understood, and, apart from the main features shown in Fig. 2.1, the small-craft helmsman need not concern himself with it. His interests are more local. Stepping down in the scale of size from planetary winds we come to pressure systems. This is a general term for depressions and anticyclones and their attendant pressure features (Fig. 2.2).

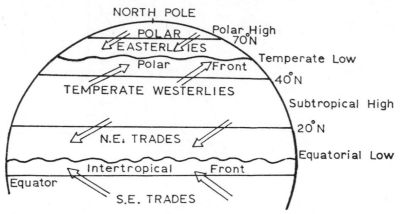

2.1: *The prevailing winds of the northern hemisphere. Those of the southern hemisphere are a reflection of these in the equator.*

The winds which form these systems stem primarily from large-scale differences in temperature between various parts of the earth's surface. Land areas are warmed by the sun while sea areas are not. This is a general rule with many exceptions. Ocean currents may bring warm water into cooler seas, much as the Gulf Stream does in our latitudes. Or, like the Labrador Current off the east coast of Canada, a cold stream can bring cool water into contact with warmer water farther south.

This advection of sea temperature is often accomplished against the normal situation in which the sea surface isotherms increase in temperature from poles to the equator.

There will also be land areas covered by anticyclones which are reservoirs of cold air. The Siberian High is such a system in winter. It produces Polar continental (cP) air which is dry and very cold (Fig. 2.3).

Anticyclones over the tropical land areas are breeding grounds of dry warm winds which, if fed to us in summer, produce our most delectable weather.

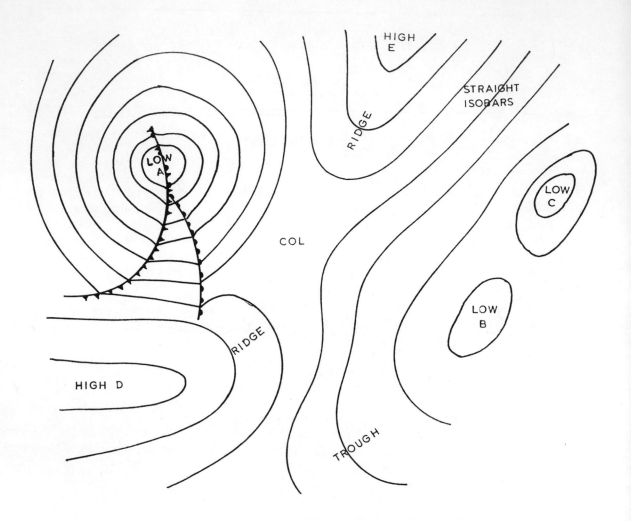

2.2: *The major pressure systems and features of the weather map.*

Anticyclones over the oceans, on the other hand, produce humid air-masses. The Azores anticyclone (or high) for example sends us wet, warm, cloudy air. It is called Tropical maritime (mT). Photo 16 is typical of this airsteam.

A similar quasi-stationary anticyclone system over northern waters leads to a cold, relatively wet air stream and such air is called Polar maritime (mP) (Photos 6 and 8).

The two most prevalent airstreams over the British Isles are Tropical and Polar maritime in origin. Sometimes a long sojourn over the Atlantic will leave a once very showery Polar maritime airstream relatively dry when it arrives over the western approaches, and such air is termed Returning Polar maritime. It is cool, but not unpleasant, and often produces a lot of cotton-wool cumulus clouds which do not grow sufficiently to produce showers (Photo 9).

On these airstreams the pressure systems feed. More especially, the depressions (or lows) use the temperature difference between the Polar and Tropical airstreams to

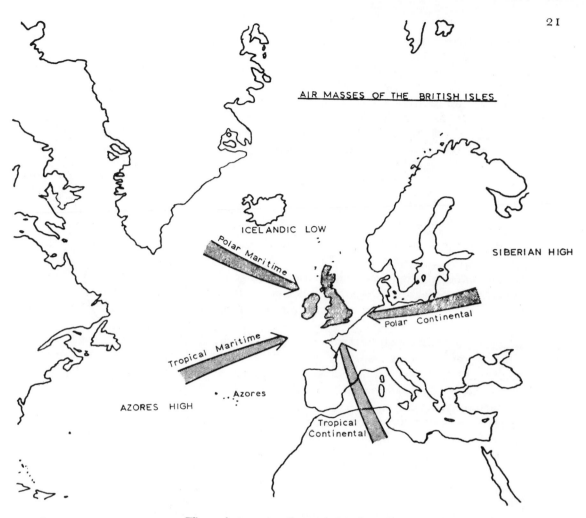

AIR MASSES OF THE BRITISH ISLES

ICELANDIC LOW

SIBERIAN HIGH

Polar Maritime

Polar Continental

Tropical Maritime

Azores

AZORES HIGH

Tropical Continental

2.3: The major sources of our wind and weather.

energise their very strong winds. On the whole a depression with unmodified Polar air in its northern quadrants and similarly unmodified Tropical air in its southern warm sector will be a very vigorous disturbance.

Depressions are like heat engines—they work best when the difference in temperature across them is greatest.

It is a very curious fact, which has become second nature to us through the advent of TV and newspaper weather charts, that the winds do not flow as one would expect, that is straight out of high pressure regions into low ones. Certainly when a low pressure region first forms then the winds do blow straight into it in an attempt to fill it up, but this simple effect is soon modified by the fact that the air is not fixed in any way to the earth's surface, except near the ground or sea, and will, like all bodies possessing mass, continue to travel in a straight line while the earth turns round beneath it.

A simple experiment will make this fact plain. First let us take a wind which is suddenly initiated. For instance a sea breeze sets in on the South Coast from south to north. Represent the breeze by a ruler pointing along a line drawn on a sheet of paper. Mark the line north and south. Now, keeping the ruler fixed, slowly rotate the sheet of paper underneath it in an anti-clockwise direction remembering that the paper with its line represents the rotating earth. What has happened to the sea breeze which remained fixed in space? It has veered with the earth's rotation. How quickly the wind veers depends on the latitude. At the North Pole the rate of rotation of anything fixed to the earth is at its maximum value, and anyone standing there will rotate with the earth at a rate of $15°$ every hour. On crossing 'The Line' the rate of rotation on one's own axis is zero. In between these extremes the angular velocity of anything fixed to the earth is given by $\omega \sin \theta$ where ω is the angular velocity at the pole ($15°$ per hour) and θ is the latitude angle. Thus at say a latitude of $60°$ the rate of rotation on one's own axis as you stand on the earth is $13°$ per hour and in lower latitudes, at say $30°$, then it has fallen to $7\frac{1}{2}°$ per hour.

Therefore the tendency for the earth to rotate under any newly initiated wind increases from zero at the equator to $15°$ per hour at the poles. In the northern hemisphere it is an anticlockwise rotation while in the southern it is clockwise. The apparent change in such a wind to an observer who has reference points fixed in the earth (as we always have) is for the wind to veer with time in the northern hemisphere and to back with time in the southern.

Hence sea breezes which start off blowing perpendicular to our coasts in the morning will be found to be blowing from a veered direction in the afternoon. The sea breeze has been mentioned as it is a wind which can be observed from its inception. Winds on a much larger scale have had this force acting on them for days, weeks or even months, so its effects are fully developed.

It therefore occurs that winds which start off blowing from the Azores towards the North Pole, for example, will develop into westerly winds while those that start off blowing from the polar regions towards the warm southern seas will develop easterly components (Fig. 2.1). They move initially at the behest of a pressure gradient. That is a pressure fall divided by the distance over which the fall is measured.

The gradient is greater when pressure falls rapidly with distance. Such a steep pressure gradient should initiate a strong wind, and this is so, but the tendency for the earth's rotation to make the wind appear to veer as it flows from high to low pressure looks to us earth-bound mortals like a new force on it. This force is called the geostrophic (or Coriolis) force, and it sets up in opposition to the pressure gradient force. Without going into detail, we can say that the geostrophic force depends on the wind speed, V, and the winds are in equilibrium and flow between the two opposing forces when the geostrophic force equals the pressure gradient force. The relation for equilibrium is:

$$\text{Geostrophic force } 2\,\omega\,\text{V} \sin \theta = \frac{\text{pressure gradient}}{\text{density of air}} \qquad \textbf{2.1}$$

An experiment simple to describe but not so easy to do will illustrate the balance which exists between the geostrophic force X and the pressure gradient force Y.

Take a dish with a smoothly sloping inner surface and put it on a gramophone turntable the speed of which is under control (Fig. 2.4). Put a small ball in the dish and speed up the turntable so that the ball remains balanced on the sloping face of the dish. The ball represents a parcel of air in motion. Its tendency to roll into the middle is analogous to the pressure gradient force while the centrifugal force outwards is analogous to the geostrophic

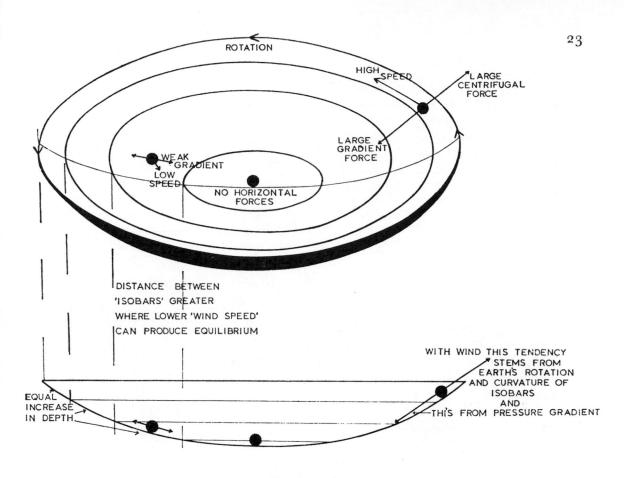

2.4: *An analogy to illustrate the balance between geostrophic and pressure-gradient forces, and the reason for the relation between isobar spacing and wind strength.*

force. The speed of the ball represents the wind speed. Slow up the rotation (the wind), and the ball comes to rest where the gradient is not so steep. Speed-up the rotation, and the ball will only find equilibrium where the gradient is steeper.

If circles are described symmetrically on the inside of the dish (akin to contours), so that every interval between one circle and the next represents an equal increase in depth, then the circles will be widely spaced in the middle and become progressively closer towards the sides of the dish. The rate of rotation to keep the ball between any pair of these contours will be inversely proportional to their distance apart.

The contours are analogous to lines of equal pressure (isobars) in the atmosphere, and where the isobars are closest there the pressure gradient is strongest and the wind is strongest as in the model.

Thus close isobars will indicate strong wind, and wide open spaces on the weather map will be areas of calm or light variable winds.

The model is a good analogy, but it must not be stretched too far. For instance we

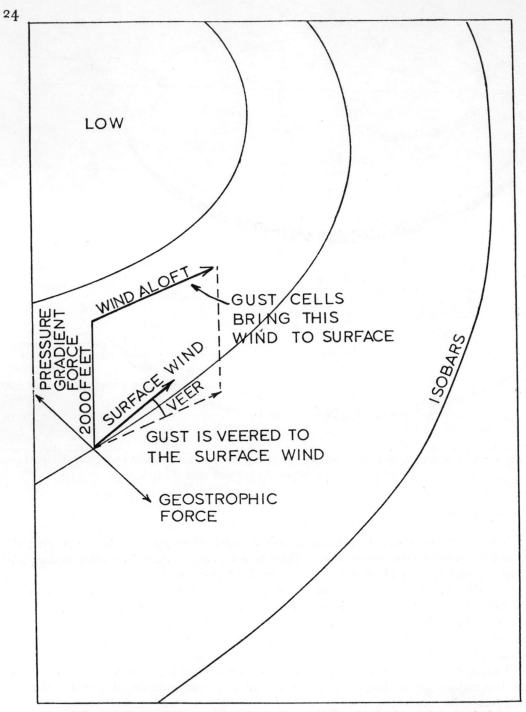

LOW

PRESSURE GRADIENT FORCE

2000 FEET

WIND ALOFT

SURFACE WIND

GUST CELLS BRING THIS WIND TO SURFACE

VEER

GUST IS VEERED TO THE SURFACE WIND

GEOSTROPHIC FORCE

ISOBARS

2.5: *Why gusts are normally veered to the surface wind direction in the northern hemisphere.*

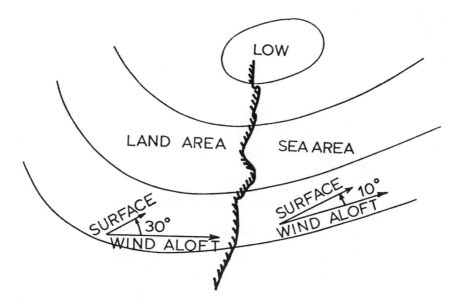

2.6: *The relation of surface wind to wind along the isobars over land and sea.*

could rotate the table both ways and produce the same balance but in the northern hemisphere the well established wind always flows to keep *Low* pressure on its *Left*.

This fact is annunciated in the famous law due to Professor Buys Ballot of Utrecht and called Buys Ballot's Law. "Stand with your *back* to the surface wind in the northern hemisphere and *Low* pressure is on your *Left*." The law will hold in the southern hemisphere if one *faces* the wind when low pressure is again on the left.

This law only holds with any degree of certainty in the temperate latitudes of either hemisphere. In the tropics the value of sin θ tends to zero, and so there is little to balance the pressure gradient forces, and near the equator winds do tend to flow directly from high to low pressure.

Returning to temperate latitudes there is one highly important factor which slightly upsets the geostrophic balance. This is the frictional drag of the surface on the wind. In any given latitude equation **2·1** shows that the wind speed is proportional to the pressure gradient, but this only holds at a level above where the frictional drag of the earth is felt. In Chapter Four values are quoted for the depth of this "friction layer", but for now it can be taken that it is less than 2000 feet deep under normal circumstances. Thus **2·1** only holds above the friction layer, or say at 2000 feet and above.

The rougher the surface over which the wind blows the more it is slowed down, *i.e.* the smaller V in **2·1** becomes. Slowing the wind at the surface does not upset the balance which exists at 2000 feet, and so the pressure gradient force is not altered, and at the surface it becomes bigger than the geostrophic force. It can then haul the wind at the surface across the isobars in towards low pressure (Fig. 2.5). It can be seen immediately that over the sea, whose frictional effect is small, the wind will only blow at a relatively small angle to the isobars (10° on the average), while over the rougher land it will blow at a greater angle (30° on the average) (Fig. 2.6).

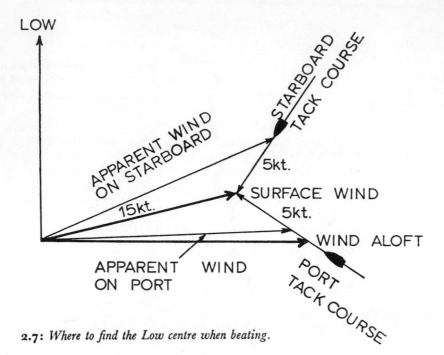

2.7: *Where to find the Low centre when beating.*

If the mean wind speed over the land is V then it is usually 2V over the sea and 3V aloft above the friction layer. These results have important consequences and will be considered more carefully in Chapter Three.

Having introduced Buys Ballot's Law, which is an extremely useful rule-of-thumb law for finding depression centres, let us add a few refinements based on the above. Standing with your back to the surface wind on land is easy, but the centre of the low is more likely to be about 2 points forward of your immediate left.

At sea it would be useful to have a rule which did not entail a lot of vectors being drawn, and Fig. 2.7 illustrates it. The centre of the low is abeam of the wind aloft. The true surface wind is backed 10° from this, and the close-hauled courses are at 45° to the surface wind. Taking a surface wind of 15 kt, and assuming a speed through the water of 5 kt, then the apparent wind on port is parallel to the wind aloft and that on starboard is backed 20° from it.

Thus we can say that when beating and sitting with your back to the apparent wind the centre of the low *is* indeed on your left hand on port tack but that it is two points aft of this direction when on starboard.

On other points of sailing it is more difficult to give specific rules as the offwind performance varies greatly from craft to craft.

STABLE AND UNSTABLE WINDS Large scale winds can be divided into two main types. Those that are stable and in which little convection occurs and those that are unstable. The most familiar convective airstream is the unstable north-westerly so characteristic of spring and giving rise to the March winds and April showers. This is a wind which accompanies well-washed skies which become visible between great heaps of shower cloud (Photo 6). It is a blustery wind, and when established can last in the same direction for days, only gradually becoming less showery and showing a marked diurnal variation. The nights in the eastern half of the country are largely clear with stars and moon being conspicuously bright. The mornings start clear and gradually cloud up to build into showers by the afternoon, this activity dying out with evening. On the western coasts the showers may go on all night and penetrate inland, expending their energies on the mountain slopes and not surviving the encounter. Often all that penetrates the area beyond the mountains are cloud heaps.

The wind by day and night is blustery, but the mean speed falls over the land with nightfall. Over the open sea there will be little variation between day and night, although off a windward shore the wind variation over the sea will follow that over the land.

In Chapter Three details of gusts and lulls are given, but at this stage, when looking at the wind as a whole, we can state that the gusts are usually up to $1\frac{1}{2}$ times the mean wind speed and occasionally up to twice the mean wind speed. This fact should be allowed for at night by putting in a prudent reef, for gusts cannot be seen coming. Over the open sea the ratio of gust speed to mean speed will be less than over the land, but it must be remembered that the gust speeds will be roughly the same over both land and sea, while the mean speed is something like twice as great over the sea as over the land.

Stable airstreams are usually either very cloudy or cloudless. This is because if the airstream is wet enough to form cloud then the cloud will spread out under the attendant thermal lid (inversion) and cover the whole sky. Such skies occur in the depths of winter anticyclones, and they may be present on summer mornings, but by then the sun has normally enough power to "burn-off" the cloud cover leaving a stiflingly hot day. The wind must only be light to moderate for such inversions to persist. When the wind is stronger and cloud cover persists, then it must be a very deep cloud layer, and a front is usually the reason for the cloud. There is however one very important area of a depression which can have strong winds and a low cloud cover. This is the warm sector where deep stratus and stratocumulus cloud will hide the sun for long periods even in the height of summer. The air in warm sectors is Tropical maritime, and its trade marks are eight-eighths of stratus or stratocumulus (Photo 16).

The wind in stable situations is damped down and the gusts and lulls are small variations on the mean speed. This is because the stability does not allow the eddies in the wind to grow to such proportions that they can fetch down very much stronger wind from aloft as happens in unstable airstreams.

WIND SEQUENCES The birth, life and death of the frontal depression is covered in most books on weather forecasting and here we are going to omit a lot of the details to bring out the main facts about the winds in depressions.

Briefly the two main air masses of these islands (the Tropical maritime and Polar maritime airstreams) meet along a line of demarcation called the Polar Front which stretches from eastern North America right across the Atlantic at many seasons of the year. For the reasons given earlier the Polar air has easterly components and the Tropical westerly (Fig. 2.1 page 19).

Waves form in this Polar Front and some of these develop into depressions. A wave in this case is a northward kink in the surface of separation between the two air masses. Because such waves initiate a pressure fall at their tips the tip becomes a low centre and

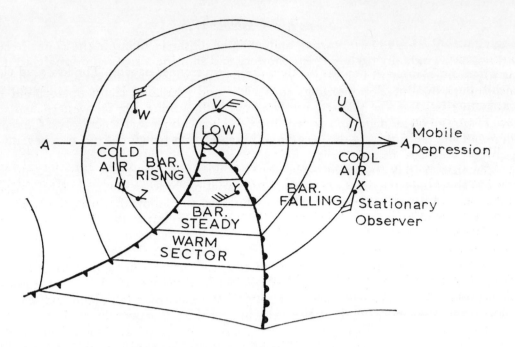

2.8: *Wind changes as a depression moves over.*

after a day or so there is a frontal depression in being. These are called frontal depressions because there are other kinds in which no fronts develop. Such frontless whirls of air may sometimes be produced by areas of very strong convection. In winter they are "Polar lows" and in summer "heat lows" often producing thundery activity. The importance of the fronts from the point of view of wind is that savage changes may occur at them and particularly at cold fronts. The winds in a developed depression can be gauged from Fig. 2.8, because at the surface they flow inwards to the isobars at the angles mentioned earlier and do so to keep Low pressure on the Left.

Such depressions tend to move in the direction of, and with the speed of, the wind in their warm sectors, so that this depression is moving a little north of east at perhaps 25 kt. The latter is a representative speed of advance although small depressions may skip along at something approaching 60 knots and large ones spanning thousands of miles can be to all intents and purposes stationary. The latter type of depression produces persistent nasty weather for days or even weeks on end. The weather is not really foul, it is just unpleasant, with periods of rain and a few—very few—sunny spells, but the wind persists in say the south-west quadrant and will not move.

The mobile depression (which is the most prevalent) carries its circulation with it and so, to the south of the line of advance AA of the centre the wind veers as the depression passes. At X the wind may be from the south or even east of south and Force 4. At Y, say 10 hours later, the depression centre will have moved so that the wind at point X has changed to that depicted at Y. It is now strongly from the south-west and Force 7, for example. At some time in between X and Y a warm front has passed over the observer bringing with it a change of cloud type and a moderately abrupt veer of wind. The warm front is preceded by a falling barometer and a belt of rain, but normally when the rain ceases and the barometer steadies off then the warm front is passing. The low scud cloud beneath thick nimbostratus may give way to more extensive low stratus or perhaps somewhat lumpy but just as extensive stratocumulus which has a rather higher and firmer base. The rain may be replaced by driving drizzle, and it may seem noticeably warmer. You are in the warm sector (see the warm front sequence, Photos 1–4).

The next major wind change to expect is at the passage of the cold front. Any lightening of the windward horizon should be suspected of heralding the cold front, for the latter often has sharply ascending air currents in its clouds, and these up-currents must have some compensating down-currents somewhere. One place for them is in advance of the front, which helps to dry out and evaporate some of the cloud just ahead of the front itself. Thus a temporary clearance may precede the cold front. When it arrives the clouds will become thicker and blacker. There may well be sharp showers, and this is one way of telling a cold front (or occlusion) as warm fronts seldom produce showers. The barometer will kick up, but careful observation of all these things may be precluded by the antics of the vicious gusts which accompany the more vigorous cold fronts. There is often a sharp veer to north-west from south-west as the cold front moves over and while sometimes the wind may decrease it is more normal for the wind to gust strongly and stay strong. The warm frontal rain may last for hours, but the cold frontal precipitation is over much more rapidly (Photo 5).

When the front itself has gone the wind should settle down to a gusty north-westerly, and as the sky opens overhead one must expect showers building into the cold air wedge below the front. These will produce their own micro-wind changes, rather as described for gust-cells in Chapter Three. The sharpest gusts will be under the leading edges of the shower clouds as they sail up in the wind. For a while, say 10–15 minutes, all will be wet and windy, but the shower passes, and the wind which has veered as it gusted will back in the clear space behind the retreating shower.

This sort of wind will be with the observer at X some eighteen hours after he has the wind depicted there. Now the mean wind is typically about Force 6 from the north-west and more gusty than at either X or Y.

It will be noted that throughout the period in which the depression centre passed to the north the wind has consistently veered. If it goes on veering then no other depression is following this one in, and one can expect a ridge of high pressure, especially if the showers die out. Then the wind will lighten and may back a little. Such a back should be suspected, for strings of lows are generated along the Polar Front and these are called a "family". If the wind begins to go back and the barometer steadies off, or even begins to fall, then the most likely event is another depression, and the next one's centre should be farther south than the last. So this time, as the wind goes back through south-west and begins to pick up again, it could be that the observer will be at a position such as U with respect to the centre. In this case he is to the north of the depression centre, and one way he can detect this is to note the wind direction and use Buys Ballot's Law.

The other thing he will note is that the wind will go on backing through east to become perhaps north-east when he is closest to the low centre. The wind at V has been purposely angled to the isobars, as this is what sometimes happens near the centre. There are other forces besides the balance of forces which gives the geostrophic wind. A term depending on the curvature of the isobars should have been included in equation **2·1** which makes the wind depart from its isobaric tramlines where the curvature is strongly about lows (cyclonic curvature) or highs (anticyclonic curvature). Normally the curvature is too small to make the complications worthwhile, but weather maps will often show winds, which are close to a tight little low centre, blowing almost directly into it. Similarly the wind will blow rather more directly out of highs where anticyclonic curvature is strongest. This wind is called the Gradient Wind.

Eventually as the low centre moves away to the south-west of him the observer will have a northerly or north-westerly wind. The weather on the line UVW will be that of high or medium level cloud at U, low cloud with rain or drizzle at V and possibly showery at W, although there are no true fronts shown to divide these weather types. But troughs of deteriorated weather occur to the north of depression centres and may look like fronts as they produce temporary increases of rain or showers. Very often, however, the region to the north of the centre is one of dull leaden skies with light winds and very little change until the centre gets away to the east.

The usual wind changes in moving depressions can be gauged from Fig. 2.8. The other main divisions of the weather map are highs, cols and regions termed "straight isobars" (Fig. 2.2).

Anticyclones or highs are regions of sinking air and outflowing winds. It is not the downward motion of the air which produces the high pressure but the fact that the air column as a whole over the high is colder and therefore more dense than over a depression. This might seem odd from the earth-bound viewpoint of a bare-backed dinghy sailor coaxing his craft through a warm anticyclonic wind. The fact remains that while the lowest strata of the atmosphere are warmer than normal in summer anticyclones, the air miles above is colder than the average. The concentration of warmth in the lowest layers can be traced to the sinking air warming-up and producing strong inversions of temperature lapse within a few thousand feet of the ground. Where the inversion occurs it effectively separates the air decks above and below it, and incidentally separates the winds above and below it as well. This point will be returned to. The heat of the sun is thus concentrated in the surface layers and the temperature shoots up.

In general the winds in anticyclones are light and their angle of outflow to the isobars is normally greater than it is in depressions. Because of the lack of cloud and the lightness of anticyclonic winds these are most likely to be modified by land and sea breezes and mountain and valley winds. See Chapter Five.

A col is the saddle-backed pressure region between two lows and two highs (Fig. 2.2). Because the wind directions on diametrically opposite sides of the col are opposed to one another there must be a region of calm in the middle. However cols, unlike lows and highs, are rather negative features of the weather map, being due, one might say, to the lack of a definite pressure system at that point. Lows, for instance, tend to move into the col ahead, and where the col is today a low may be tomorrow. In general the highs are relatively static compared to the much more mobile lows, which therefore tend to move through the "pass" of the col with the edges of the highs giving way to them.

"Straight isobars" are what they say, a region over which the isobars are to all intents and purposes straight. In such regions there is little tendency for weather development, and what the weather is today should be tomorrow as well. On the whole regions of straight isobars are rare. They sometimes occur over the British Isles when a big depression has slowed up over Scandinavia, or its local waters, while a high sits poised over the Atlantic waiting to come in when the low has made up its mind to fade away or move over. Then the wind may persist in the northerly quadrants for many days on end.

The other main features of the weather map are ridges and troughs. These are analogous to spurs and valleys on ordinary maps and can be recognised with mnemonics of the same kind as one uses for contour maps. V-shaped contours towards high ground indicate a valley on contour maps and V-shaped isobars towards high pressure indicate a trough (pressure valley) on weather maps.

The winds in ridges are anticyclonic and normally light, while troughs are regions of cyclonic winds, and their axes are the centres of deteriorated weather. It may be an air-mass trough, in which case the weather on either side is the same while the wind veers during the passage of the trough. Such troughs are often showery with local increases in gust intensity under the shower clouds.

Frontal troughs may contain warm fronts, cold fronts or occlusions, the latter being a mixture of the warm and cold fronts with weather which is also a mixture of that associated with the two fronts. Thus it may be said that in general warm-frontal troughs produce relatively gentle veers of wind on their passage, while cold fronts and occlusions may produce strong wind veers.

WIND CHANGES AT FRONTS Before we leave fronts and troughs it would be useful to look at some actual cases of wind changes at fronts so as to know what to expect.

An analysis of 36 fronts which passed over Cardington in the years 1927–30 shows very clearly that almost every front produces a veer of wind. These 36 were analysed because they showed the greatest wind changes on the passage of the frontal squall. The wind never backed. It always veered, the average being 63°. The strongest veer was 150° when a wind from 190° 19 kt went to 340° 9 kt. In almost a third of the cases the wind veer was 80° or more and these fronts occurred at all times of the day and night.

In the vast majority of cases the wind decreased with the passage of the front, and only once was there a dangerous increase, which was when a wind from 190° 29 kt went to 240° 42 kt.

In the other cases where the wind grew as it veered the increases were either very small ones or the wind before the squall was less than 10 kt, and the increase, even of 10 or more knots, could be met without real danger.

The lesson is clear. If a cold front is expected then a wind veer is also to be expected.

As the squall of the front passes the wind must be expected sometimes to increase by 15 kt in periods of a minute and the direction to veer by as much as 80° in this relatively short interval of time, but while the wind will go on veering as the squall passes the speed will decrease very rapidly in many cases.

One word of warning must be sounded. Fronts which do not produce much change of direction can have stronger winds behind them than in the front. This is true of both warm and cold fronts when they are well wrapped up as part and parcel of depressions.

The above are frontal squalls with changes of direction, but occasionally there are squalls in which no direction change occurs. They usually occur in association with gale force winds, and in apparently homogeneous airstreams, yet, while they are rare, they might conceivably encompass the destruction of a yacht at sea which was already hard-pressed by the wind. One such was a south-westerly wind of 31 kt mean speed which suddenly, without noticeable change of direction, increased its speed to 57 kt in 3 minutes. Such wind increases must be brought down from aloft by some super-sized eddy in the airstream, and luckily they are very infrequent, at least at this intensity.

Another disturbance which causes strong vector wind changes (a vector wind change is one which includes a change in both direction and speed) is the line squall (Photo 3). This consists of dark masses of cloud, very often with thunderstorms embedded in the cloud mass, which stretch in a line athwart the wind. The wind increases sharply under the leading edge of the cloud line and heavy rain may occur for about 20 minutes with hail and thunder. Then the rain eases and the cloud lifts and the wind dies down somewhat but usually remains veered from its direction before the disturbance.

The thunderstorm is the other main disturber of the winds, but it is such a potentially dangerous system that it (and its winds) have been given a section to themselves in Chapter Five.

THE GATHERING OF THE WIND   There are three main ways in which the wind can increase. The first is due to a steepening pressure gradient. The second is due to faster wind being fetched from aloft on to the surface, and the third to the reinforcement of an existing wind by a local wind such as a sea breeze.

For a pressure gradient to steepen then the pressure difference across a given distance must increase with time. As this will tend to put more isobars between the two points in question forecasters talk of "tightening" the gradient. To illustrate this, let us consider the situation in Fig. 2.9*a*. Along the line ABCD the gradient must be tightening, for pressure is falling at A and rising at D, so over this distance the difference in pressure must increase. Twelve hours later the depression centre has moved over A while the high has gone on building at D. The average gradient has steepened, and there are more isobars between D and A than there were before (Fig. 2.9*c*).

The winds, however, at B, which were not strong in the first instance, will have increased. The sections drawn in Figs. 2.9*b* and 2.9*c* show the strongest winds where the slope is greatest. There was little slope at B at first, but twelve hours later this is the area of greatest slope and highest winds. Over the area of C where the winds were strongest the pressure has risen sharply, as it must do to squeeze the low forward towards A, while the high itself at D has slowly intensified. The result is a general slackening of the gradient between C and D, and this area is developing the light winds and clear skies which a rising barometer often herald. The average gradient, however, has steepened so that the winds in general over the area ABC have increased in the twelve-hour period. For instance, winds which were strong at B could have become gale force.

To a lone yacht or other single observation point the flux of the pressure systems is not often apparent. Unless a crew are keeping a careful check on the synoptic situation as given in the shipping forecasts then all they see are the risings and fallings of the barometer or barograph. The subtle interplay of rising and falling pressure over thousands of square miles is impossible to assess, and therefore, while a falling barometer normally heralds wind increase, it need not always do so. There is only one situation where professional forecasters issue gale warnings on pressure change alone and that is when the barometer at some reliable station is falling (or rising) at a rate of 10 mb or more in three hours. In this case a gale must invariably result, for 3–4 mb per hour is an above-average tendency and pressure in surrounding areas will not be falling so fast. Thus the gradient

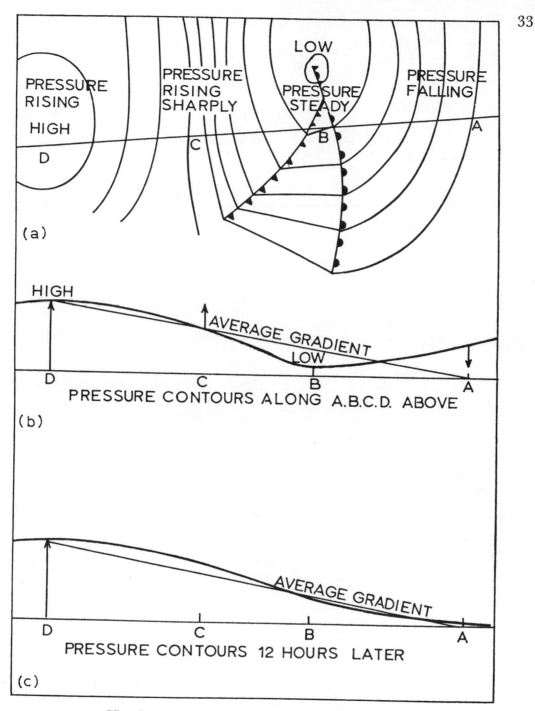

(a)

PRESSURE RISING

HIGH

D

PRESSURE RISING SHARPLY

C

LOW
PRESSURE STEADY

B

PRESSURE FALLING

A

HIGH

AVERAGE GRADIENT
LOW

D   C   B   A

PRESSURE CONTOURS ALONG A.B.C.D. ABOVE

(b)

AVERAGE GRADIENT

D   C   B   A

PRESSURE CONTOURS 12 HOURS LATER

(c)

2.9: *The effect of the "gradient" as pressure systems build and decay.*

C

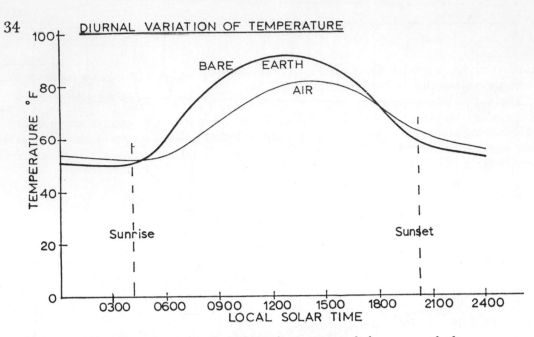

2.10: *How the earth and air change in temperature during a summer's day.*

must tighten between the surrounding areas and the place where the pressure is tumbling so steeply.

At other times gales can only be forecast if you know the tendencies over wide areas, and a single lone barometer reading is not enough.

The link between falling barometer and wind rests on the normal situation where highs tend to remain inert while lows tend to change rapidly. The example of Fig. 2.9 is one of these situations. A falling barometer often heralds a depression on its way and the winds tend to be strong between its periphery and centre but not *at* these extreme points. As the low moves into a region of falling pressure so the winds must increase, but the wind system can often be thought of as shifting with the depression and therefore remaining constant in strength. Point A will then have largely the same wind as B had 12 hours ago.

Only when the depression is itself developing will its winds become generally stronger with time. In a developing depression the central pressure must be falling. The one depicted in Fig. 2.9 is a depression just beginning to occlude. The central pressure in this case is temporarily stationary and will soon start to rise. A depression with a rising central pressure is one which has seen its best days and is on the way to filling-up.

DIURNAL VARIATION OF WIND The gales and strong winds of moving pressure systems are entities which only vaguely know what time of day it is. Without a doubt the strong winds of a vigorous depression will, when given a reasonable land fetch, show a diurnal variation, being less gusty during the hours of darkness and showing a maximum gustiness during the afternoon. Their mean speeds, however, under similar conditions will not vary greatly with time of day.

The diurnal variation of wind follows, and is linked to, the diurnal variation of temperature. Thus this variation is one associated with land areas because there is no diurnal variation of sea surface temperature except very close to the coasts or in a tidal stream which has stemmed from some area of tidal creeks and has brought a reflection of the temperature of the flats and banks with it.

The temperature of the air over the land varies as shown in Fig. 2.10. With it is a corresponding variation in the temperature of bare ground. The temperatures shown are those associated with clear weather in summer, but the general form of the curves will be the same at most seasons of the year. Thus, while the ground heats to its maximum temperature in the middle of the day the air temperature is at its greatest some two hours later. This is because the temperature is governed by the difference between the incoming radiation from the sun and the outgoing radiation from the earth. Although the former is a maximum at midday the balance between loss from the ground and gain from the sun is not struck until after local noon.

The wind also follows the same pattern, being greatest in the mid-afternoon and a minimum about dawn. Thus, in a wind system without any marked changes of pressure, the wind will pick up in strength from early morning until the afternoon and will then begin to decrease (Fig. 2.12, page 39).

INVERSIONS For the greatest number who will sail within the land's influence in fair weather this pattern is the normal one, and it occurs because of temperature inversions.

The average rate at which air temperature falls off with height is about 3°F per 1000 feet of ascent.* Like all averages this figure is seldom realised, and near the ground such a "lapse-rate" is rare, being either greater by day or less by night. In the first hours of the sun's heating of the land the air immediately over the warmed surfaces cools off at the Dry Adiabatic Lapse Rate. This rather formidable title is that given to the normal lapse rate of unsaturated air. An adiabatic change is one which takes place without gain or loss of heat. Thermals which push off from the ground in the morning cool at this natural rate and they mix up the air above in steadily increasing depth. They are phantom balloons of warmth which rise as long as they have not cooled to below the temperature of their surroundings. Therefore if they cool at a constant rate, and their starting temperatures increase, each succeeding one will forge somewhat higher in the wake of the one that went before (Fig. 5.24, page 170).

Usually due to overnight cooling there exists over land a temperature stratification of the air which can be regarded as three decks. The lowest of these is where the air is mixed by thermals, and large wind and temperature differences tend to iron out. Above this is the inversion layer. Here the remains of yesterday's heating has left a warm stratum, and as this reverses the normal tendency for the temperature to lapse with height it is called a "temperature inversion". Above the inversion the air resumes some sort of normal lapse rate. Let this latter deck be called the "upper layer" (Fig. 2.11).

As the first thermals rise to meet the inversion they mix stronger wind from above with that below and so the wind begins to pick up. As the heating proceeds the thermals will find themselves trying to rise through the inversion which is warmer than they are. They will thus tend to sink back and the only layer which can be mixed is below the inversion.

These inversions are sometimes found within a few hundred feet of the ground

* (5° per kilometre)

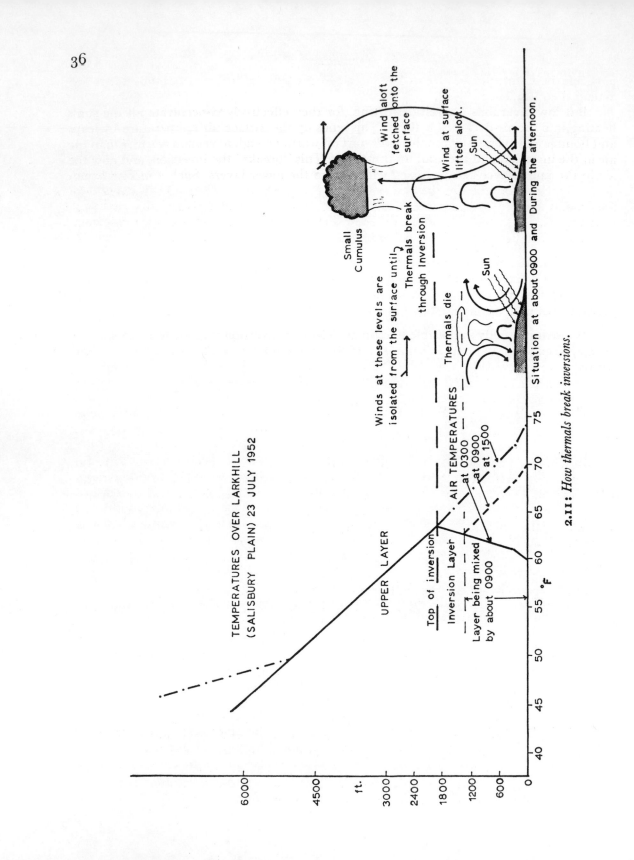

2.11: *How thermals break inversions.*

particularly in anticyclones where sinking air from aloft also helps to maintain them and extend their influence.

But low inversions are self-destroying, for they effectively concentrate all the sun's heating into the air-deck below them. This sends up the surface air temperature by leaps and bounds and eventually the thermals start off warm enough to remain warmer than the air in the inversion and they sail up through it. This "breaks" the inversion, and now the air in the upper layer can be mixed with that in the lower layers. Such a mixing brings down the wind from the upper layer. Before this the upper layer wind was as isolated from the ground as if the inversion were a solid barrier, but now it finds its way to the ground as bigger puffs. These are usually in a different direction from the wind below the inversion.

The attributes of days with strong inversions are:

(i) rapid rise of air temperature,
(ii) slow increase in wind speed in spite of a lot of sun,
(iii) sometimes an early-morning cloud layer, the cloud being around the inversion height (Photo 9).

While it is usually impossible to estimate when an inversion is going to be broken it is normal to expect it to break in summer and thus the sudden arrival of strengthened wind, with a more or less wide variation in direction between puffs and lulls, can be attributed to such a cause and can be expected to be *the* wind, for a while at least. It is rare for inversions once broken to re-form again before evening.

A word of warning, however. The breaking of a summer-morning inversion helps the onset of sea breeze and thus the new wind due to the former cause can soon be succeeded by another even newer wind from seaward.

In Chapter Four the way the wind increases in speed with height is given. Here it is sufficient to say that normally the wind will veer and increase with height in the first 2000 feet of ascent. Therefore in the hours when the wind is being established by the mixing of wind above with that below the tendency will be for it to be light and backed to the direction of the isobars when it first appears and gradually to veer and increase as time proceeds.

The sort of thing that happens at a coastal place like Thorney Island in the early forenoon of a summer's day is illustrated in Fig. 5.2a (page 132). The nocturnal wind, which has meandered softly off the land during the night, picks up from the west so gently as not to disturb the speed recorder and then, before it is nine by the sun, the sea breeze takes over for the day.

If 2 June 1959 was a day of almost total calm before the sea breeze arrived then 13 June was different (Fig. 5.2b). Here the wind above the night's inversion was easterly, for a high was centred over the Hebrides and the isobars were east-west over southern England. The speed trace shows clearly how the easterly wind picked up during the morning due to mixing with stronger true wind from above and then once again the very prevalent sea breeze took over to give an onshore wind for the rest of the day.

Inland the wind increase will not normally be bedevilled by local winds. However, Chapter Five reveals how far the sea breeze creeps inland on warm, unstable days.

In the evening of any gentle summer's day, whether it develops a sea breeze or not, the wind will lighten and may well fall calm. This is due to the re-establishment of the inversion and is in evidence in all the six examples of Fig. 5.2.

It cannot be too strongly stressed that the air is warmed and cooled from the surface upwards. Thus as the land temperature falls with the setting of the sun the air temperature follows suit. But if the wind falls light this cooling is restricted to a shallow mixed layer and becomes confined near the ground. Night inversions may be within a hundred feet of the ground although higher inversions are more normal. What happened to the wind at Cardington on a late September afternoon (Fig. 3.9, page 62) shows the normal mode when the inversion sets in. The wind immediately becomes much less variable and usually changes direction. It will normally back by ten or more degrees and the speed will decrease. It will seem like an even lighter wind for the more noticeable stronger puffs are damped out. The wind trace after 1700 is typical of a summer evening—gentle, solid wind.

But near the coast the tendency for land breeze to replace sea breeze may easily cause the evening to be calm under an anticyclone, and very often sun-bronzed day-sailors are to be found punting, paddling or rowing home in the total calm following a day of sea breeze.

What happens in brief is that the surface wind becomes cut off from that above by the inversion which extends upwards slowly with the onset of night, leaving the surface wind quite isolated and destroying what momentum it had in useless friction with the obstacles in its path. Abandoned it dies of loneliness.

In the above ways a diurnal variation occurs. Wind grows with the day's heating (deeper mixing) and falls with the evening's cooling.

Such a variation will even extend to stronger winds than those discussed above, but in general the diurnal variation in strong winds is very much less noticeable than in lighter ones.

HOW STRONG IS THE WIND   In Chapter Three a theory of gusts is given which helps to explain many of the features of large-scale winds. It is not, however, necessary to know the mechanism of gustiness in any great detail to recognise its important features.

What any small-craft skipper wants to know is whether the wind is going to be too strong for his comfort or that of the weakest link in his crew. Weather forecasts normally give mean wind speeds to be expected and on top of this there will be the gusts. A mean speed of 15 kt may not sound too bad, but when it frequently gusts to 25–30 kt then the apparent wind speed may seem very much more. For yachts the best average to take as a criterion would seem to be the average of the mean wind and the wind speed in the gusts. Thus one would arrive at a *yachtsman's wind speed* more in keeping with the feel of the wind experienced. Often when a well-reefed yacht seeks the thankful shelter of a harbour the conditions, as given by the mean wind speed, are not anything like as unpleasant as the crew knew them to be outside. Of course seaway and morale are also factors in assessing the advisability of shelter, but still it is amazing how often quite intrepid skippers make estimates of the wind which are substantially above the true mean speed. The reason may not be far to seek, for the strongest wind which regularly occurs is the one which has to be fought. This is what we may call the "mean gust speed". On an anemogram the mean gust speed will be a line through the tops of the regularly recurring gusts. The *yacht's mean wind* speed will be taken as an average of the *mean speed* and the *mean gust speed*. Thus we shall arrive at a fairer estimate of the true strength of the wind as felt by the yacht, and such derogatory terms as "a yachtsman's gale" will take on a nobler meaning.

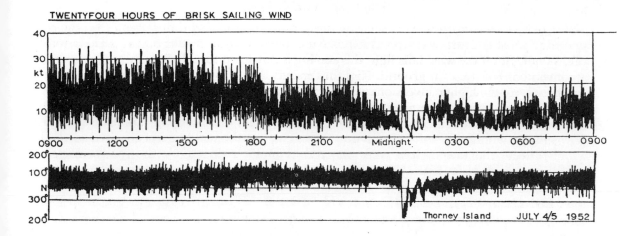

2.12: *A day's wind at a coastal station* (MO).

In Fig. 2.12 an anemogram of a strong sailing wind is reproduced. This record was taken at Thorney Island on 4 and 5 July 1952. The record really splits into three parts. The daytime portion between 0900 and 1830, the evening portion from 1830 to midnight and then the night's wind. The first is typical under unstable day conditions with no temperature inversion, while the second is the sort of thing which happens when, in spite of the wind speed, the airstream begins to stabilise with the onset of evening. This wind would have been found over the inshore waters, creeks and harbours away from windward coasts. It illustrates the points about the yacht mean speed being greater than the true mean.

Take the day-time hours. The mean speed was 18 kt, but the mean gust speed was almost 30 kt. There were some gusts to 35 kt, and the safety of a yacht lies in its ability to ride the worst that the wind can do. By our criterion the wind we have called the yacht mean speed was 24 kt. Thus while the mean wind was Force 5 the more representative mean was Force 6 and was gusting into Force 8.

Using Ian Proctor's Beaufort Scale for dinghies as given in his book *Sailing Wind and Current* this wind, if taken at its true mean, would have entailed the easing of sheets to the stronger gusts in International 14 footers (Table A.A, page 214). Taking the yacht mean speed as a criterion this same dinghy might well have done better with a reef to the bottom battens. Any hard-sailed racing dinghy is always overpowered in the strongest wind. Often it is a case of holding on, while the wind worries the life out of the craft and then hurries on to harry someone else. Therefore helmsmen who are not out to fight the last fraction of a knot from their craft could well take the yacht mean speed as their criterion. Before giving some rules for the assessment of the latter look at the evening wind in Fig. 2.12. The fall with evening is very marked, and, while the direction trace showed a little kick to the east when the fall set in, there was nothing to suggest that this drop in speed was anything more than the normal diurnal variation of wind speed. It was not, for instance, due to a front passing by at the time.

The mean speed for the evening portion is 12 kt while the mean gust speed was 20 kt

giving a yacht mean speed of 16 kt. The mean speed was well within Force 4, yet the re-
petition rate of the gusts was such as to make it appear much more like Force 5. There were
occasional gusts to 25 kt, *i.e.* the top of Force 6.

Another feature of constant occurrence is that the ratio of maximum gusts to mean
speed is greater at night than by day. This is because the wind above the earth is not
greatly affected by friction with it and tends to retain its speed, while that nearer the
surface is slowed by the evening inversion setting in. Thus eddies will continue to bring
down strong wind from aloft by both day and night, but the wind nearer the ground (and
which affects the mean speed very acutely) is much reduced by the meteorological
conditions which occur in the evening.

ASSESSING THE YACHT MEAN SPEED If the forecasts give mean speeds,
and these are unrepresentative, then some way of obtaining a more useful figure must be
sought.

To obtain the maximum gust speed under normal day-time conditions the mean
speeds can be multiplied by a factor of 2. But this large factor of 2 applies only to winds
of Force 3 and 4. Table 2.A gives the factors by which to multiply the mean wind speed.

TABLE 2.A

Wind speed range	Factor for maximum gust speed	Factor for mean gust speed	Factor for assessing yacht mean speed
Daytime			
Force 3–4	2	1·6	1·8
Force 5–6	1·8	1·5	1·25
Force 7–8	1·6	1·5	1·25
Night-time			
Force 3–4	1·9	1·5	1·5
Force 5–6	1·8	1·5	1·5
Force 7–8	1·7	1·5	1·5

The reason why the yacht mean speed has been taken as the same as the mean gust
speed at night is that at night the gusts cannot be seen coming and it is prudent to allow
the mean gust speed to be the best criterion. Also it must be reiterated that these values
are for sailing under the influence of the land.

Over the open sea the ratio of the gust speeds to the mean speed will be lower than the
above, being more like the 1·5 of the stronger overland winds. However the mean speed
itself goes up by as much as 2 compared to wind over the land, so the result over the sea is
a stronger overall wind with less gustiness than over the land.

The forecasts of winds over the sea given in the shipping forecasts will take into
account the lower frictional drag of the sea on the wind, so in the following table the given
wind strength is that forecast for the sea areas and not for the land areas as in the previous
table.

TABLE 2.B

THE WIND SPEED TO ALLOW FOR WHEN THE FORECAST OR
ACTUAL MEAN SPEED IS KNOWN

Beaufort Force	Knots	Yacht mean speed	Mean gust speed	Maximum gust speed
Day-time index under influence of the land				
3	7–10	9–13	14–16	14–20
4	11–16	14–21	17–25	21–32
5	17–21	22–26	26–32	30–38
6	22–27	27–34	33–41	40–49
7	28–33	35–41	42–50	45–53
8	34–40	42–50	51–60	54–64
Night-time index under influence of land				
3	7–10	10–15	10–15	13–19
4	11–16	16–24	16–24	21–30
5	17–21	25–31	25–31	31–38
6	22–27	33–40	33–40	40–49
7	28–33	42–50	42–50	48–56
8	34–40	51–60	51–60	58–68

TABLE 2.C

THE WIND SPEED TO ALLOW FOR WHEN THE FORECAST
(OR ACTUAL) MEAN SPEED IS KNOWN

Given wind strength

Beaufort Force	Knots	Yacht mean speed	Mean gust speed	Maximum gust speed
Day-time or night-time index on the open sea				
3	7–10	8–12	10–15	The size of the
4	11–16	14–20	17–24	maximum gusts is
5	17–21	21–27	26–32	not in general very
6	22–27	27–34	32–41	much greater than
7	28–33	35–42	42–50	the mean gust speed
8	34–40	42–50	51–60	over the open sea.

WINDS OVER THE COAST   The foregoing tables were either for areas solely of land or solely of water, but an investigation at Gorleston near Great Yarmouth on the coast of East Anglia throws some light on the effect of the coastline on winds which flow either off it or on to it. No account is taken here of winds which lie in the two southern or two northern octants, as with a north–south orientated coastline they lie too close to it to be considered either as onshore or offshore. Thus the conclusions are for winds from any of the four octants which lie about the perpendicular to the coast.

Broadly the conclusions are:

(i) Onshore surface winds are about $\frac{4}{5}$ of the wind at "isobar height" (about 2000 ft aloft) in winter and $\frac{2}{3}$ in summer.

(ii) When the wind at isobar height is Force 5 or less the onshore wind in summer can become stronger at the surface. This is not surprising, for the surface wind is reinforced by the sea breeze while the wind aloft is not.

(iii) Offshore winds are about $\frac{1}{3}$ of wind at isobar height in winter and about $\frac{2}{3}$ in summer.

(iv) These offshore winds tend to be relatively weak on summer nights but relatively strong during summer days. Again this might seem surprising until it is realised that the sea breeze force, which acts against offshore winds, will turn the winds of less than Force 4–5 into onshore winds whenever it can during summer days. This leaves the stronger offshore winds to predominate in the statistics of day-time offshore winds.

YACHTSMEN'S GALES   Now that we have seen that for yachts a mean wind speed greater than the forecast or actual mean speed is a better criterion, it is possible to reassess the results of some past observations.

In *Weather*—the Royal Meteorological Society's magazine—I found an article "Yachtsmen's Gales at Cowes" where J. R. D. Francis of Imperial College reported his analysis of winds around Cowes Week to see if a remark in *The Times* had any foundation in fact. *The Times* correspondent said something to the effect that by ending up with a gale in 1957 Cowes Week was running pretty true to form. So using the records of wind at Calshot, Thorney and Tangmere he analysed the winds of Force 4 and more which occurred during Cowes Week in the Solent area between 1919 and 1957. The following were his results:

Wind Strength	In week before	In Cowes Week	In week after
Force 7–8	4 occasions	1	0
Force 6	13	7	16
Force 5	31	37	45
Force 4	83	94	74

The record shows that winds of Force 7–8 are relatively rare and that on the whole it is windier in the weeks before and after Cowes Week. However assuming that these high winds had occurred during the day when sailing was in progress let us compute the yacht mean speed for the above occasions.

As Force 6 is usually considered to be the wind at which many able yachtsmen baulk, from the point of view of the pleasure rather than the necessity of the thing, if we take Francis's results as they stand and divide them into Force 6 and above and below Force 6 then we have, using the yacht mean speed as a criterion:

	In week before	*In Cowes Week*	*Week after*
Winds of greater than Force 6	48(17·5)	45(16·5)	61(22)
Winds less than Force 6 but more than Force 4	83(30)	94(34·5)	74(27)

As there were 273 days in each of the above weekly periods (7 days and 39 years) then the brackets give the percentages of this total, and these figures really give the relative chances of any day in one of the three weeks spanning Cowes Week being blown out with a yachtsman's gale.

Bearing this example in mind it would be interesting to see what sort of winds the English Channel experiences in summer.

WINDS IN THE CHANNEL AND GALES ELSEWHERE It cannot be disputed that the English Channel and its environs are one of the main strongholds of small-craft sailing in the British Isles. These small waters, where craft can be sailed safely and easily, and where a handy haven is never far away, attract the greatest number of craft both big and small, so it is not unreasonable to give some more detailed wind statistics for the area. Thorney Island, with an anemometer which has recorded continuously for 22 consecutive years, provides a representative place in the middle of the South Coast. It is a well exposed coastal station so its winds should be very much those which are experienced by yachtsmen in the Channel.

What do its statistics show? They show first and foremost that in the sailing months of April to October there has only been one brief hour of wind with a mean speed of 39 kt or greater in any of these months over the whole time since records began in June 1942. That was in April 1947. Obviously no statistics can be done on one hour of wind so the highest speed bracket in Fig. 2.13 is 25 kt or over mean speed. This presupposes that gusts may be 40–50 kt so they are no mean winds. April provides the longest spells of such winds, and April 1947 was excessively windy, giving no less than 68 hours of 25–38 kt wind during the month. This is exceptional, and actually nine of the twenty-two Aprils have had no winds of this severity at all. It seems that if April is going to be windy in the Channel then it is often very windy for a considerable period.

May tends to have a few hours of this sort of wind per month, but on the whole it is less than 10 hours. June and July have the least of the strong winds with over half the years

44

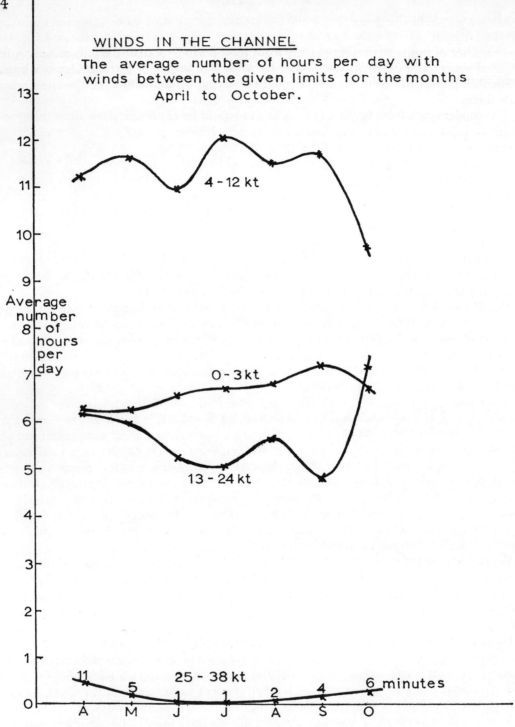

WINDS IN THE CHANNEL

The average number of hours per day with winds between the given limits for the months April to October.

2.13

showing no winds of this strength at all. In August the stronger winds begin to increase again, but August is less windy than May. September is also remarkably quiet, the increase in the number of hours stemming mainly from long periods of strong winds in only a few individual years separated from each other by periods of from 3 to 7 years. October begins the downhill plunge into winter and the month of laying-up shows few years with no winds of gale force.

The moderate to fresh breezes (13–24 kt), as would be expected, show their minimum in June and July, but September provides an even quieter month for these winds, thus making windy August look more windy than it is known to be.

A word about the statistics may not come amiss. The graph shows the number of hours of such winds averaged over the 30 or 31 days of the month. Thus an average of 5 hours per day does not mean that every day will have to find its quota; rather the statistics give the relative chances of finding winds of the given speeds on any day of a month.

Returning to Fig. 2.13, the most prevalent winds in any month lie between 4 and 12 kt, and while the hours of darkness may account for a lot of them, it is still evident that light and gentle breezes are the rule rather than the exception. This must be so, for remarkably few regattas are cancelled because of too much wind.

Finally, light airs are more likely in summer than moderate to fresh breezes, except in October when people are packing up anyway.

The curves of probability of Force 8 gales at Southport, Lerwick and South Shields (Fig. 2.14) point to the fact that while west-facing Southport has most summer gales and east-facing South Shields least, this is what would be expected when the British Isles stands in the path of the prevailing westerlies.

The comparable figures for Thorney Island are just too few to appear on Fig. 2.14. Between 1943 and 1963 there were no winds exceeding 34 kt mean speed in any of the following months; May, June, August, September and October. April 1947 produced just one hour, July 1956 two hours, and even November has only produced a total of five hours (three in 1954 and one each in 1957 and 1959). Thus it is obvious that the English Channel is very gale-free in the summer months, and this has nothing to do with Thorney being a land station. It is remarkably well exposed with an anemometer whose effective height above ground level is over 40 ft. This is, however, small consolation if a "gale" for small craft starts at Force 6 (22–26 kt).

HOW LONG BEFORE IT BLOWS? One of the great worries when one is caught coastwise in a gathering wind is how long will it be before it really blows up. Obviously there are certain limits which can be set on the time even without investigation.

For instance it is rare for a wind of Force 4 to become Force 6 in one short hour and this is particularly true in summer. But the rise from Force 4 to Force 6 would appear to be in a time span of less than 10 hours. For if a representative speed of approach of a depression is taken as 30 kt then in 10 hours its centre can move some 300 miles. If one is to be worried about the approach of a depression there must be some of the indications that it is coming. The wind must be back in the south to south-east quadrant (if south of the centre) and the cirrus plumes must be giving way to milky cirrostratus, thus ringing the sun or moon with a halo. The barometer must be showing a falling tendency, and on top of these indications there is a rising wind. Thus if these portents are there, and after

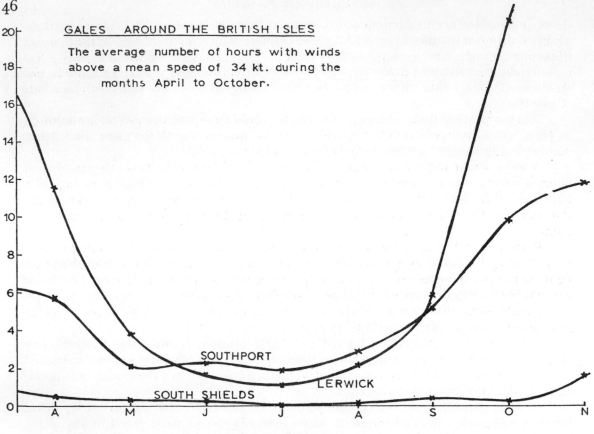

GALES   AROUND THE BRITISH ISLES

The average number of hours with winds
above a mean speed of 34 kt. during the
months April to October.

SOUTHPORT

LERWICK

SOUTH SHIELDS

2.14

ten hours the wind has not greatly increased, then, being 300 miles nearer the centre, it cannot be much of a depression—perhaps an old one filling-up.

Therefore we can compress the rise of wind from say 15 kt mean speed (Force 4) to 25 kt mean speed (Force 6) into somewhere between one and ten hours' duration. But this is not of much practical help, so, to answer the question of the sort of times involved, the records at Thorney were checked for definite depressions whose winds before the storm were in the direction bracket of 100–200° and really looked like the winds due to depressions in that they increased and veered with time and then, still veering, died down. Taking the 40 examples found in the years 1959–1961 the shortest time that it took the wind to rise from 15–25 kt mean speed was 3 hours and the longest was a day. On breaking down the times into four-hour periods the following pattern resulted:

Time of rise (hours)	3–6	7–10	11–14	15–18	19–21	22–24
Number of occasions	15	17	3	2	0	3

Average (excluding the very long times) $7\frac{1}{2}$ hours. If we take just the sailing months of April to October inclusive an even more interesting picture emerges:

Time of rise (hours)	3–6	7–10	11–14	
Number of occasions	4	5	2	Average 7·7 hours

Over the whole year by far the most likely rise-time for wind in the Channel as a depression comes in is between three and ten hours, 75 per cent of the occasions falling within this span.

When we consider the sailing months all the long-delayed increases drop out, and again most of the relatively few occasions when such winds occur fall in a time of less than 10 hours.

Therefore we can say that with a gathering depression one can stay at sea until the wind is a mean of 15 kt and then there will be at least three hours to make port before the wind is 25 kt mean speed. In many cases there will be an interval of up to ten hours of slow wind increase and on the average there are $7\frac{1}{2}$ hours.

THE WIND AND HIGH TIDE The great summer gales that I remember are imprinted on my memory by the necessity to don waterproofs and rush to the creek wall in order to rescue, or attempt to rescue, craft that had given up the unequal struggle with their too short moorings. One of the things which stands out, however, in the jumble of impressions of flying spray and tossing wreckage is the way the wind seemed to be less strong after the tide turned. I investigated this effect for my own native waters by taking the Thorney wind records for the period May to August inclusive in 1960 and 1961 and found the following:

With all the winds of 18 knots or greater in this period of two succeeding summers (and there were only seven of them!) the wind came up with and went down with the tide. The anemograms of speed looked like bridges spanning the time of high water. Further, the highest gust, which was between 35–40 kt, occurred within 30–40 minutes of high water (as predicted). It might, of course, have occurred more or less close to the actual time of high water. Representative figures are 18 kt before high water, 21 kt at high water with a single gust to 35–40 and then a fall to 15 kt after the tide has turned.[20]

These strong summer winds occurred at all times of the day although there were none at night. This does not mean that the effect does not occur at night—I know from experience that it does—but that there were no really strong winds after dark in the two-year period chosen.

Thus for strong winds of Force 5–6 in summer the wind tends to come up and go down with the tide. When I mentioned this fact to one of the meteorological assistants who kept the wind statistics at Thorney he said he was not surprised, for he had noted independently that when strong winds persisted for days in the same quarter then the time at which the maximum gust occurred appeared roughly one hour later each day.

The effect may occur for less strong winds, but it is difficult to unravel it from other effects, and, while lighter winds do show an overall tendency to come up and go down with the tide, the effect is not consistent as it is with the Force 5–6 winds.

Frankly I can offer no conclusive explanation. It may be that the "flattening" of the surroundings leads to the increase and yet you would think that the surroundings were equally flattened by the tide for an hour or two on either side of high water. Also it cannot be any tide-borne effect for the waters are slackest for a considerable time about high water. Yet longshoresmen will tell you that the wind comes up with the tide and others that it goes down with it. They both seem to be right, but the reason is obscure.

WINDS ABOVE THE EARTH The sailing layer is a very shallow stratum of air.

It is the comparative thickness of one page of Tolstoy's *War and Peace* to the whole book, the latter representing the depth of the troposphere. The troposphere is the shell of air in which most weather processes occur and whose mean height is around 50,000 feet in these latitudes. Its boundaries are the earth's surface and the tropopause, which is a large and permanent inversion which becomes visible when the cirrus anvils of thunderclouds push and spread under it (Photo 12).

The layer above is the stratosphere and is of no interest to us at present. Most of the winds which have some direct and observable bearing on the wind at the surface occur in the troposphere, and these are the only ones to be considered.

The wind at around 2000 feet has already been discussed, and the direct communication of winds in the first few thousand feet with the sailing layer is by means of gust cells and other eddies as will be explained in Chapter Three. In general the height to which convection currents can extend is the depth through which wind above the earth can be fetched on to the surface. When there are shower clouds or other cumulus about, then normally the cloud tops will show the depth of convection. This may be upwards of 10,000 feet. When the cumulus (Cu) grows into cumulonimbus (Cb), then the wind from very far above the surface can be brought down in vicious gusts such as those that are found just ahead of advancing thunderstorms. The mechanism of this can be followed in Fig. 5.18 (page 160). Suffice to say here that thunderstorms reach upwards to very high points for their strongest winds. Normally the wind at the surface is a mixture of wind from the first few thousand feet and true, lighter surface wind.

It is found that at all heights isobaric maps can be drawn which look like the surface ones we are used to but are generally much simpler. The winds at all levels obey Buys Ballot's Law in that they flow to keep Low pressure on the Left. The isobar spacing, however, is on the average closer showing that the wind aloft is in general stronger than the wind at 2000 feet, which it will be remembered is the wind defined by the surface isobars.

Often an isobaric map, at say around 10,000 feet aloft, will show the lows and highs in roughly the same places as the surface ones, and this will indicate that on the whole there is not a great change in the wind with height. This is true of developed systems like highs and lows which have had time to become organised and whirl up to considerable heights. Sometimes the winds about lows will exist without much change like a vertical shaft of solid winds right up through the first 20,000 to 30,000 feet. When this is the case then the lows are old semi-permanent ones, often of the "two fried egg" variety, which persist for days or weeks in roughly the same place. (Right-hand side of Fig. 2.2, page 20.)

From this we see that if the winds stay the same with height then little change is to be expected in the weather pattern. What we have today may well be what we have tomorrow.

It is when the winds change with height that the weather is on the change as well. If the wind veers with height there is warmer air coming in, and if it backs there is colder air approaching.

Thus winds will veer with height ahead of an approaching depression as a warm sector is on its way. Conversely in the direct rear of cold fronts the winds will back with height as colder air is on its way. When the air is mild and of the Tropical maritime variety it may well burn off in the summer sun to reveal upper clouds. These will give the direction of the wind aloft. These should be roughly parallel to the lower winds, for in

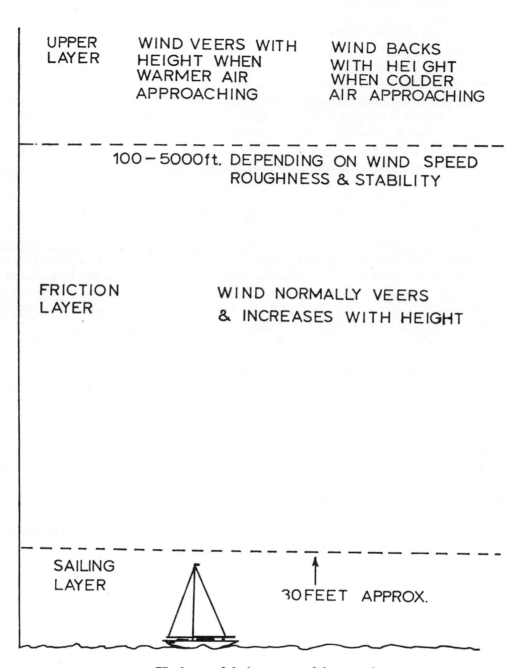

UPPER LAYER

WIND VEERS WITH HEIGHT WHEN WARMER AIR APPROACHING

WIND BACKS WITH HEIGHT WHEN COLDER AIR APPROACHING

100 – 5000ft. DEPENDING ON WIND SPEED ROUGHNESS & STABILITY

FRICTION LAYER

WIND NORMALLY VEERS & INCREASES WITH HEIGHT

SAILING LAYER

30 FEET APPROX.

2.15: *The layers of the lowest part of the atmosphere.*

D

large blocks of warm Tropical maritime air the winds should be roughly the same direction at all levels.

This illustrates a principle which can be stated thus:

Upper and lower clouds (and winds) in the same direction: no change in the weather.
Upper wind veered from lower: then expect a warm front or warmer air.
Upper wind backed to lower: then expect colder air.

The wind strength aloft is revealed by the cirrus clouds. These are the mares'-tails of weather lore, and when they are a great set of flying plumes from the horizon they denote a jet-stream. Jet streams are very high velocity "pipelines" of wind at around 40,000 feet aloft and are a more or less permanent feature of the winds above the temperate latitudes of either hemisphere. They and depressions are linked as the fronts of the latter form just to the south of the jet-stream axis, which runs roughly parallel to the direction of motion of the depressions themselves. In general the stronger the wind aloft the stronger the wind at the surface in the accompanying family of depressions, and thus a jet-stream banner of cirrus mares'-tails is well allied to the incidence of strong wind at the surface later (Photo 2).

While the jet-stream wanders north and south of its mean position and sometimes breaks up altogether (as happens when a big high intervenes), it is still a useful forecasting tool for wind. Sometimes the actual cirrus filaments can be seen moving and then the winds aloft are approaching 100 kt. Such violent wind will not appear at the surface, but a Force 8–9 gale can well blow up half a day to a day later. Other indications of strong upper winds are shredded cirrus and contrails (Photo 1). When the latter become rapidly blown apart (as opposed to fading) the winds aloft are strong. Other indications are the long veils of ice which precipitate out of cirrus clouds and fall backwards into the less strong wind below (Photo 1). The angle which these ice showers make is revealing. If they are sharply angled back then expect strong wind. If they are almost vertical there is little wind shear (change with height), and any developing wind may not be very strong. Incidentally, cirrus fall-streaks always point towards the warm air, *e.g.* towards the approaching warm sector of a depression.

How the wind can be expected to change with height is summed up in Fig. 2.15.

CHAPTER THREE

Gusts and Eddies

WHEN the wind blows it is never steady. The most stable weathercock kicks and turns to
its movements. Birds flying into the eye of the wind twist and dive out of the strong gusts
to seek parts of the wind field which are less forceful. In the restlessness of a night of high
wind the alternate soughings and intermittent quiet periods tell one's ear of the wind's
changes of mood.

These are just some of the ways in which, on all but the rarest of occasions, one can
recognise that the wind is variable in both speed and direction. They are, however,
evidence by inference, and while they may be stored in the mind's eye, in the cine-
camera, or on a tape-recorder they are, like the wind on the cheek, largely incapable of
measurement in any truly permanent way.

The most useful permanent record of the wind is obtained by using an anemograph

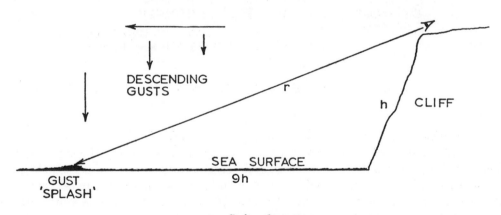

3.1: *Seeing the gusts.*

(which will be described later) but before we think of instrumentation let us consider more
direct evidence of gusts and eddies.

Take a vantage point overlooking a fluid surface which is being acted on by the wind.
Two such surfaces spring to mind. One is a cornfield on a hillside and the other is the
surface of the sea in the lee of a cliff. The cliff must not be too high or the details will be
lost in distance. The size of the object decreases as the square of the distance from which it
is viewed. This means that what is perfectly visible and observable from a cliff 100 feet
high is perhaps invisible from one of 300 feet.

Allowing for this fact, and having chosen a cliff which is not too high, and off which
the wind is blowing, one can see the gusts chasing one another across the surface (Fig. 3.1).

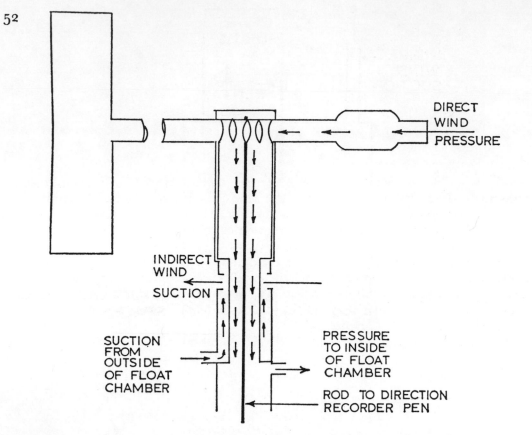

3.2*a*: *The business end of a Dines Pressure Tube anemometer.*

Such observation is revealing, for the gusts are seen to remain as entities for a very long distance, and the overall pattern of gust cells can be visualised using the splash-marks as evidence of the gust fronts, *i.e.* the gust-cell leading edges. The ideas which will be put forward can be understood with more confidence when they can be tied to personal observation of something visual like gust splashes hurrying across water, and it is worth an hour of anybody's time to sit on a cliff or promontory and watch what the wind does with the surface.

Having looked at the gusts as well as we can, we are still in doubt about many aspects of them, and thus more permanent instrumental records must be obtained which can be studied in the quiet of an armchair or laboratory rather than in the teeth of a howling gale or driving rain. The actual records of winds which are reproduced in this book are all taken from the charts (anemograms) of various Dines Pressure-Tube anemometers. This device is illustrated in Fig. 3.2 and works in the following way.

The wind vane shown in Fig. 3.2*a* has an open ended tube into which the wind blows. The carefully designed vane makes the tube look directly into the eye of the wind. Holes in a central tube communicate the pressure differences via pipes to the inside of a specially designed float-chamber in a room below. This operates like the old-fashioned diving-bell

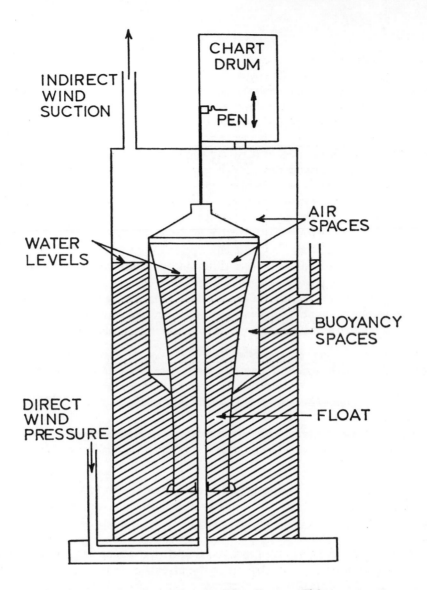

3.2b: *The speed recording device of a Dines Pressure Tube anemometer.*

and, as the air pressure rises in the air space above the water in the float, the latter rises taking the speed pen with it. As the wind gusts so the float rises, and as it lulls and the pressure is relaxed, so the pen falls again. In this way the wind speed traces are produced. At the same time as the wind is blowing into the pressure tube it is also blowing past some holes in the vane body so producing suction. Air is thus drawn from the space above the water on the outside of the float. This also aids the float in rising as the wind gusts but does not hinder its fall as the wind dies away again. Careful design has ensured that what the chart says the wind has done at any one moment is what it was actually doing at that moment. Meteorologists who wish to make calculations from these records will obviously make strenuous efforts to ensure the least possible errors in speed and direction, so the anemograms may be believed. The direction is communicated from the shaft on which the vane is mounted to the pen via specially designed cams. There are two pens so that when the wind swings through east beyond north, and would go off the chart, the pen previously resting will pick up from the top of the chart and record down towards west as at 2300 in Fig. 5.2*a* (on page 132).

One must remember when looking at anemograms that they are produced at one point, and that any detail occurred at a given time. They are the spot records of the wind and are made at various meteorological stations throughout this country and the world, for this device is still one of the most effective ways of recording wind speed and direction.

The normal anemogram covers a period of 24 hours being changed once a day at about 0900 Local Time. However, in order to show the features of gusts and eddies the charts can be run faster than this and the upper anemograms of Fig. 3.3 give just 10 minutes of wind on a gusty day. Several different anemograms are produced in this book in order to convince the reader that the conclusions drawn about the micro-structure of the wind are not just based on an odd case or two. Most are taken from Giblett [15]

The conclusions that can be drawn from anemograms and which are of prime interest to racing helmsmen are as follows and will be explained in more detail later in this chapter:

(i) *Gusts are wind which is brought down from aloft where the wind is stronger.*

(ii) *In general the wind will veer from the mean direction as it gusts and will back from that direction when it lulls.*

(iii) *It is advantageous when beating to be on starboard tack when a gust strikes and to revert to port tack when the wind lulls.*

(iv) *In gusty conditions the wind field may be visualised as composed of gust cells which move with the speed of the mean wind and can maintain their individual identity when crossing a dinghy fleet which is not hopelessly spread out.*

These are the normal conditions which obtain in winds typified by unstable north-westerlies. There are also abnormal wind patterns, the characteristics of which will be referred to later.

EDDIES IN THE WIND It has been found that there are, in the wind mass, sets of eddies whose characteristic dimensions in the direction of travel are

(i) of the order of 4000–8000 feet,
(ii) of the order of 5–15 miles.

Both these have with them smaller eddies which are too short in duration to have any helpful effect on sailing. They are the sort to which a helmsman automatically reacts as he noses his way through the wind, but they are not the sort to tack to. These will be called short eddies; the 4000 feet ones will be referred to as medium eddies and the very large ones as long eddies.

The long and medium eddies are due to convection currents and will be found when the airstream is unstable, that is when the surface is warmer than the air above it.

The short eddies are usually due to turbulence when the onward rushing air meets surface obstacles.

A fairly consistent picture of what medium eddies look like has been built up and a

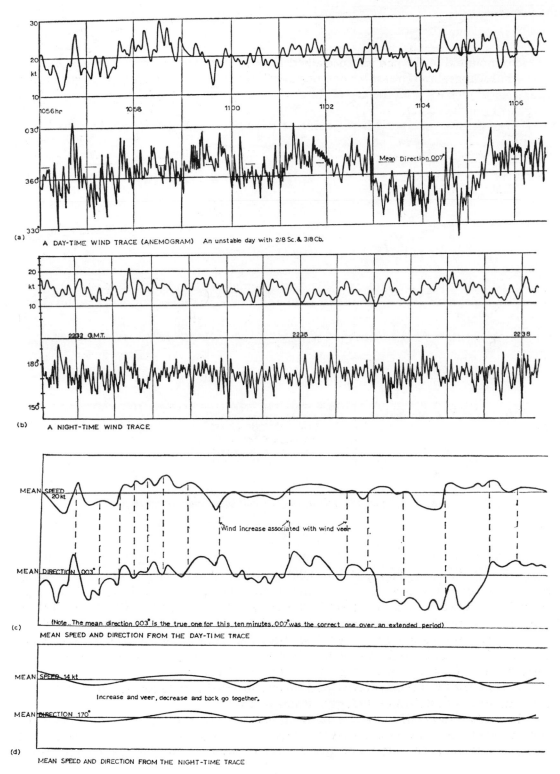

(a)   A DAY-TIME WIND TRACE (ANEMOGRAM)   An unstable day with 2/8 Sc. & 3/8 Cb.

Mean Direction 007

(b)   A NIGHT-TIME WIND TRACE

MEAN SPEED 20 kt

Wind increase associated with wind veer

MEAN DIRECTION 003°

(Note. The mean direction 003° is the true one for this ten minutes. 007° was the correct one over an extended period)

(c)   MEAN SPEED AND DIRECTION FROM THE DAY-TIME TRACE

MEAN SPEED 14 kt

Increase and veer, decrease and back go together.

MEAN DIRECTION 170°

(d)   MEAN SPEED AND DIRECTION FROM THE NIGHT-TIME TRACE

3.3: *Details of typical gusty wind by day and night. When the means are sketched the wind is seen to veer as it gusts and back as it lulls.*

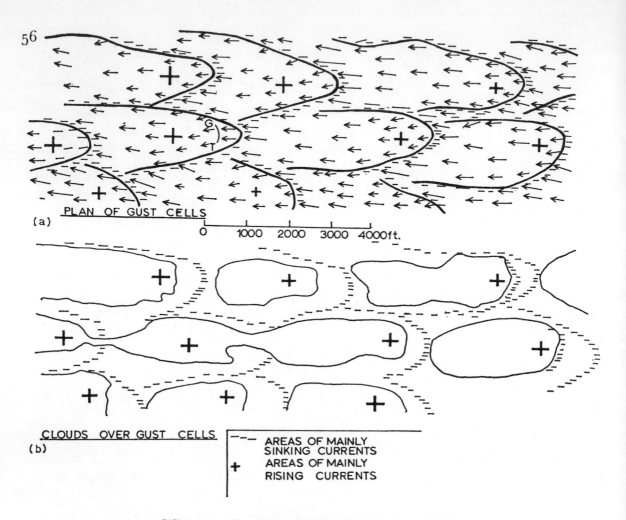

3.4: *What gust cells might look like and how clouds reveal them.*[15]

plan view is shown in Fig. 3.4. The solid horseshoe-shaped edges represent a physical division between warm air rising within the horseshoe $(+)$ and cold air sinking around them $(-)$. Between these two lots of air there is a "gust front" which slopes backward from the trailing edge of the characteristic clouds which form over the gust cells. In general the gust front at the surface is to be found under the leading edge of the following cloud as shown in Fig. 3.5. These clouds are the visible sign of the sort of gust cells which are being described (see Photos 7 and 8). Figs. 3.4 and 3.5 depict the medium eddies, but nevertheless the long eddies also may have cloud edges associated with their arrival, and again the wind increase is to be found under the leading edges.

It is useful to describe what is going on in a typical gust cell. The whole cell and its capping cloud are moving along at the speed of the mean wind, but superposed on this mean motion there is high-speed gust air being brought down in descending currents

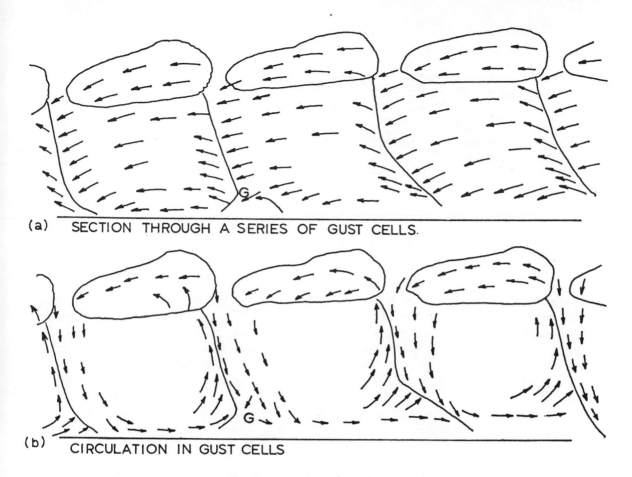

(a) SECTION THROUGH A SERIES OF GUST CELLS.

(b) CIRCULATION IN GUST CELLS

3.5: *Idealised wind flow in gust cells.*[15]

behind the leading edge of the gust front. Often this strong wind breaks through the front proper as it is dragged back by contacting surface obstacles, and a gust tongue occurs (G in Fig. 3.5). This is that shivering stab of increased wind which so often presages the immediate arrival of the gust proper and which has a helmsman crying "sit her out" to his crew. Experience has taught that a gust tongue is indeed the herald of the true gust.

Air which descends like this does so as if it were in a lift and retains the speed and direction which it had aloft. It has already been said in Chapter Two that the wind aloft is normally veered from its direction at the surface and is stronger. Thus the gust is veered from the direction of the mean wind and is stronger (Fig. 3.4*a*).

On contact with the surface this cool fast air from aloft becomes slowed by friction while the rest of the cell drifts by above. Thus the wind at the surface is slowed and warmed by contact, for the ground is warmer than the overlying airstream in unstable conditions. It then finds itself in the rear of the cell, and being warm it must rise. In the after end of the gust cell therefore the air is rising back aloft whence it originally came and will help maintain the cloud. How the air circulates if you take away the mean wind speed is shown

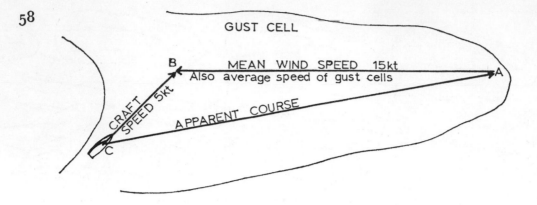

3.6: *The idea of an apparent course.*

in Fig. 3.5*b*. It brings to mind the tracks of those lumbering tanks of the first world war. The track rises at the rear and falls at the front while the whole vehicle moves forwards. The analogy cannot be pushed further, however, because the strength of descent in gust cells is often different from that of ascent, which is, of course, not so with the tank. Even so the visual picture is quite apt, and once again aids seeing the invisible.

This then is the picture of gust cells in the wind. How often will one meet them when sailing?

To answer this question it is necessary to introduce the idea of an apparent course. Imagine riding in a gust cell at A in Fig. 3.6 and observing a dinghy beating towards and across your path. The dinghy's course is an apparent one compounded of your own forward motion and that of the dinghy. Looked at from the dinghy the course through the gust cell is also an apparent one along the apparent wind direction CA and at the apparent wind speed. It can be called an "apparent course".

The cells on the whole are three times as long as they are broad, but supposing a dinghy beats at 5 kt at 45° to a mean wind of 15 kt it will meet a gust front, with an attendant increase and veer of wind, in a time which is on the average

$$T = \frac{\text{length of cell}}{\text{apparent wind speed}}$$

In a representative case this will be

$$T = \frac{4000 \text{ ft}}{27 \text{ ft/sec}} = 148 \text{ secs. or about } 2\tfrac{1}{2} \text{ min.}$$

However, while this is obviously the case for the dinghy sailing the apparent course ABC in Fig. 3.7, another dinghy 300 yards away will meet his own set of gusts at P and Q with a very definite gust at these points while he slices through between the cells at R.

Thus it would be foolish to lay down any hard and fast rules about the time between meeting gusts. Even so it is good evidence for the reality of what has been said that the main peaks of wind speed and direction in Fig. 3.3 do occur roughly every 3 minutes when the mean speed is about 20 kt.

The time of repeat of the wind features will obviously vary both with their size and

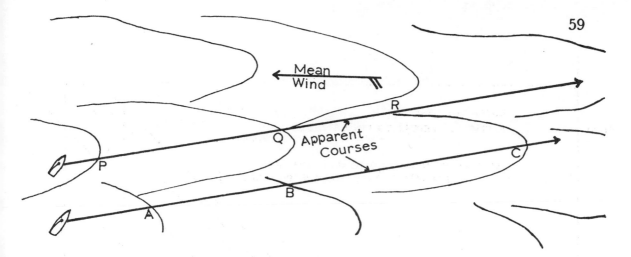

3.7: *The same apparent course will yield different wind patterns depending on position.*

with the mean wind speed and for this reason Fig. 3.8 has been drawn. It is a set of graphs of the length of repeating features against their time of repeat, for wind speeds of from 5 to 25 kt mean speed (Force 2 to 6). On this has been put the average limits to the size of the medium and long types of eddies, although the two sets merge under certain circumstances. The short eddies have been neglected because their time of repeat is too fast for any intelligently anticipated reaction to them. They are features for immediate and very temporary action and no form of prediction can be tied on to them. Not so the medium eddies, as will be shown. The long eddies are more difficult, as it is rare that one can decide that the wind shift now being encountered is due to a long eddy rather than a medium one of more than average size and duration. Sometimes, however, the long eddies can be recognised by cloud lines separating open sky from more densely packed cumulus, cumulonimbus or stratocumulus cloud.

With the medium eddies the time of repeat in wind speeds of less than 10 kt falls between 3 and 20 minutes. Winds less than 5 kt have not been considered as the sort of convection cells we are discussing here do not usually occur in a regular way in such slack airstreams. The long eddies have repeat times of perhaps 20 minutes to half an hour, and it is to be expected that they will be most noticeable in moderate winds when repeat times of an hour or more can also occur.

Returning to the actual examples it will be seen that medium eddies occur in a very much more dampened manner about ever 1 to 2 minutes on the night-time wind trace which is Fig. 3.3*b* on page 53. At the same time if the smooth curves of mean speed and direction are followed in this figure one can see how the wind veers as it increases and backs as it decreases (Fig. 3.3*d*).

Thus in the rear of the gust cells there is wind which is not only lighter than the mean, but which is also backed from the mean direction. This makes the vector wind change, as the gust front sweeps over the craft, even more marked than it otherwise would be, because

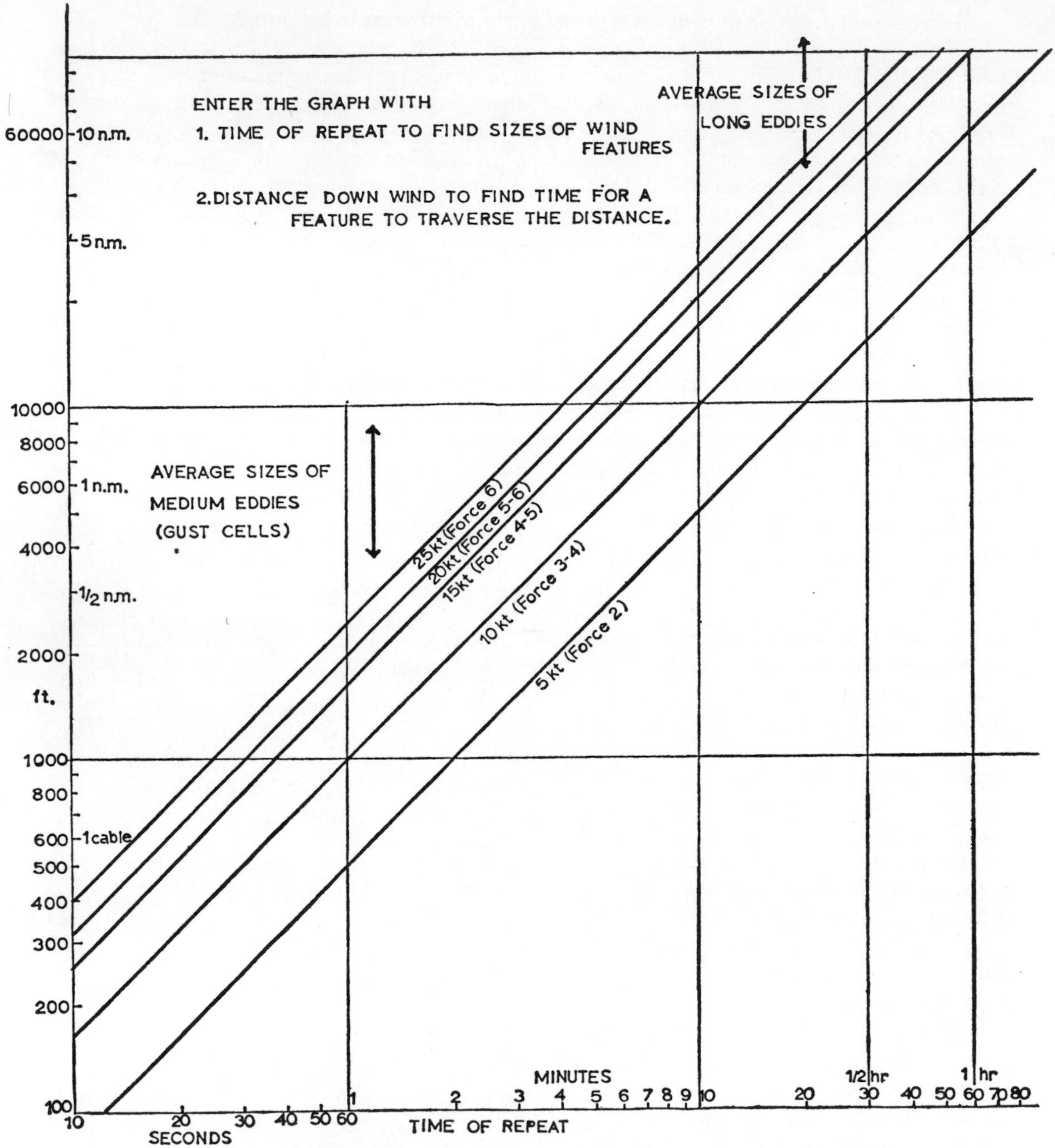
ENTER THE GRAPH WITH
1. TIME OF REPEAT TO FIND SIZES OF WIND FEATURES
2. DISTANCE DOWN WIND TO FIND TIME FOR A FEATURE TO TRAVERSE THE DISTANCE.
AVERAGE SIZES OF LONG EDDIES
AVERAGE SIZES OF MEDIUM EDDIES (GUST CELLS)
60000
10 n.m.
5 n.m.
10000
8000
6000
1 n.m.
4000
1/2 n.m.
2000
ft.
1000
800
600
1 cable
500
400
300
200
100
25kt (Force 6)
20kt (Force 5-6)
15kt (Force 4-5)
10 kt (Force 3-4)
5 kt (Force 2)
10
20
30
40
50
60
SECONDS
MINUTES
1
2
3
4
5
6
7
8
9
10
20
1/2 hr
30
40
50
1 hr
60
70
80
TIME OF REPEAT

3.8: *Graphs to find the time for a wind feature to travel, or the size of features when the time between them is known.*

light wind which is backed to the mean wind is suddenly replaced by strong wind which is veered to it.

In general there are four main types of gusty airstreams to be noted.

Type 1 is associated with cumulonimbus clouds when convection is extending to great heights. In this case there are major gusts of wind every half an hour or so at any one point, but, of course, they will occur slightly more frequently when one is beating towards them. As well as these long eddies which double the mean wind speed (*e.g.* 22 kt increases to 44 kt in a few seconds) there are gust cells of the medium variety whose time periods are of the order of a few minutes. The whole wind field is very variable in both speed and direction. An example is to be found in Fig. 3.15 on page 73. A typical sky is shown in Photo 12.

Type 2 is associated with cumulus and stratocumulus cloud, which is normally well broken and thus the surface may be warmed by the sun and convection maintained. But the convection height is limited to the tops of the lower cloud, and medium cells of perhaps 4000 to 8000 feet in length are formed. The long eddies are not now in evidence. Fig. 3.3*a* (page 55) is a good example, and Photos 6 and 8 are very typical.

Type 3. These gusts set in during the late afternoon or evening when the earth is cooling and becoming the same temperature as the air above. There are then short eddies as in Fig. 3.9 with some changes in direction of about 10 degrees or a little more. The wind speed, however, shows very quick changes with no definite pattern.

Type 4. Later in the evening when an inversion has been established the eddies become damped down to such an extent as to be practically streamline flow, as is in evidence after 1650 in Fig. 3.9. Then the sailing wind is one where the craft weaves a gently undulating course. It is the classic wind of quiet evenings.

As well as the veer and increase which accompany the passage of the normal gust cell, the wind also becomes steadier when it has increased, and only some twenty seconds later does it begin to resume its smaller oscillations. This is very noticeable in Fig. 3.12 page 66. The reason for this absence of small oscillations as the wind gusts is to be found in the fact that the gust is steady upper air which has not been made full of short eddies by contact with the surface. Farther back in the gust cell the wind is surface wind and will have all the superimposed unsteadiness which contact with the surface imparts to wind.

It may be asked how long gust cells last. If a helmsman experiences a gust, how far away, both down wind and across wind, will his opponents be pretty certain to experience the same gust? This is a difficult question to answer, for gust cells are easy to visualise but difficult to record. It has been proved that they can, and do, persist for at least 700–1000 feet down the wind, and it seems likely that they can run on as organised entities for very much farther than this. Watching gust splashes from a handy height reveals that individual gusts run on for considerable distances.

Thus a gust which can be seen striking craft 200 to 300 yards away in the direction of the true wind is pretty certain to be with you in less than half a minute. A dinghy which careens to a gust 100 yards upwind in a 20 kt wind gives 10 seconds warning which is just enough time to crash-tack from port on to starboard to gain the maximum advantage from the veer which goes with the gust. Other cases can be deduced from Fig. 3.8.

The ratio of distance knuckle to thumb tip to its distance from the eye, when held up at arm's length, is about 1:15. This simple yardstick will fit a 20-foot mast at 100 yards (Fig. 3.10).

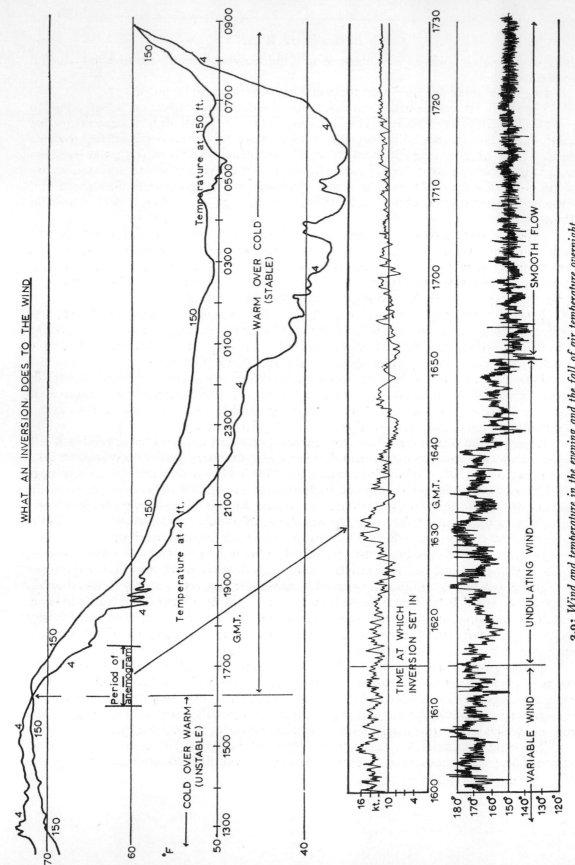

WHAT AN INVERSION DOES TO THE WIND

Temperature at 150 ft.

Temperature at 4 ft.

150

4

150

4

150

4

150

4

150

4

150

4

150

4

G.M.T.

0900   0700   0500   0300   0100   2300   2100   1900   1700   1500   1300

°F

70

60

50

40

COLD OVER WARM → (UNSTABLE)

WARM OVER COLD (STABLE)

Period of anemogram

TIME AT WHICH INVERSION SET IN

16 kt.
10
4

1600   1610   1620   1630   1640   1650   1700   1710   1720   1730
G.M.T.

VARIABLE WIND   UNDULATING WIND   SMOOTH FLOW

180°
170°
160°
150°
140°
130°
120°

3·9: *Wind and temperature in the evening and the fall of air temperature overnight.*

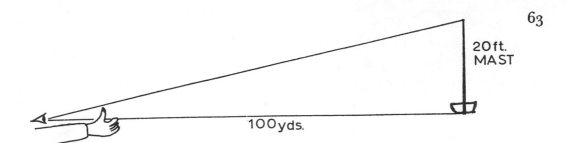

20ft.
MAST

100yds.

3.10: *A practical measure of 100 yards.*

In general any natural length x which comes to hand at y from the eye will measure the distance Y of an object of height X when

$$\frac{Y}{X} = \frac{y}{x}$$

So
$$Y = X \frac{y}{x} \qquad (3.1)$$

If the units of x and y are the same (inches for example) then the unit of Y is the same as that of X. (See Chapter Four for other natural yardsticks.)

It has been found that in a wind of mean speed 34 m.p.h., with cells about 5000 ft long in their direction of travel, then they are about 600 ft wide. The width however will depend on the height to which the convection currents extend.

If an air mass is at rest the pattern of convection is one of square cells with rising air in the middle of the cells and descending air around the outside. Such cells have diameters of $2\sqrt{2h}$ where h is the height to which the convection currents extend. Thus in thundery summer weather with little wind and great cumulonimbus clouds erupting up to the tropopause h is the whole depth of the troposphere—and it may be over 40,000 ft deep—whence the thunderstorms would occur in cells some 20 miles across.

If, however, the airstream is in motion, and the wind increases with height without much change of direction, then the convection currents occur in strips lying down the wind, and their width is $2h$, *i.e.* twice the height of the convective layer. This is the more normal case, and so cumulus and cumulonimbus clouds tend to form in lines along the wind direction. Cumulus cloud streets can often be seen extending along the wind from some good source of thermals. An instance is the cloud street which often streams away from the Isle of Wight when conditions are right (Fig. 3.11). Photo 6 is a very convincing example.

The height of the tops of fair weather cumulus is often 5000 feet, in which case the distance between one street and the next should be 10,000 feet or roughly two miles. Under the cloud line will be found the variable pattern of gust and lull in association with the overlying cloud, while between the streets in the clear strip there will be less variation. The clear air tells of descending currents, but they will be weak, and not like the ones descending between the gust cells under the gaps in the clouds.

A similar type of cloud effect to that of cloud streets will sometimes occur when the wind is blowing parallel to a strip of water which is flanked by rising ground. Such a

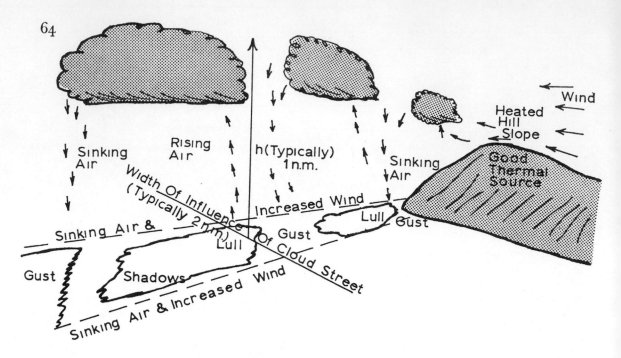

3.11: *How a cloud street forms.*

situation may occur when the wind is from the south-west and blows up the West Solent. With the day's heating the land areas produce convection currents, while the sea may be too cool for the production of thermals. Then a cloudless "street" exists over the Solent while cumulus is very prevalent over the Isle of Wight and the opposite mainland. The air tends to be stable over the water and convective over the land, so that in the land-locked waters from Lymington to Chichester the gust-cell pattern occurs, while over the Solent the wind will be steadier than over the land. It must not be forgotten, however, that the mean wind speed over the Solent will be higher than in the sheltered harbours and this for two reasons. Firstly the water is smoother than the smoothest of land and the surface wind tends to be channeled even by the modest height of the Lymington to Calshot shore. More on the Solent winds will be found in Chapter Five.

If the whole of the troposphere is unstable, with cumulonimbus anvils to be seen, then in summer the clear areas on either side of the thunderstorm cells will lie some 100,000 feet apart, or 19 miles. Or, what is the same thing, the distance between one line of thunderstorms along the wind and the next will be about 20 miles. It is interesting to note that the super thunderstorms which have occurred over England in the last few years and which have been studied in detail have been individually 10 to 15 miles long in the direction of their motion.

Thus the spacing of convection clouds from the small cumulus of fair weather to the awe-inspiring and sometimes death-dealing cumulonimbus of the worst storms does tend to obey the above laws. Thunderstorms, however, are not simple gust cells of the type discussed above. Their winds are described later on pages 158–166.

1 High-altitude clouds – cirrus and cirrocumulus. The streaming appearance of the cirrus is due to "ice-showers" falling into slower wind below and so becoming left behind. The sharper the angling of the "fall-streaks" the stronger the wind is likely to be in any following depression. This is a windy sky.

2 Great bands of "jet-stream" cirrus blow up across the dying cumulus of fair weather. The shape of the cumulus – thick ends upwind – reveals that the surface wind is left-to-right across the picture. Applying the rule on page 50 a warm front must be expected soon – time to consider a likely haven.

3 A few hours later a warm front is confirmed by altostratus, which gives the sun the appearance of being viewed through ground glass. The dark shreds of cloud below are the last vestiges of the cumulus, wasting away now that their heat supply has been cut off.

4 Altostratus over the Solent. The picture is taken from Pilsey Island in Chichester Harbour looking south-west. In the background the Isle of Wight is clear in spite of being twelve miles away. Wave streaming in the stable air aloft produces lens-shaped clouds downwind of the island. The yacht coming in is probably prudent.

5 A cold front passes. The line of the front is marked by the trailing *virga*. Expect a different air-mass and a veered wind in the clear air behind the front.

6 In the cold air behind the front big cumulus can grow. In strongish winds, and downwind of hills, they grow in cloud-streets. The nearer line has formed from a better thermal source than the others and is growing rapidly. The cap of *pileus* over the left-hand heads is a sure sign of strong convection and spells the risk of showers with squally winds.

7 Chichester Harbour from the Downs. Out across the flat coastal plain sinks the nocturnal wind on quiet nights. By day, the slopes of the Downs initiate sea breezes. Thorney Island lies in the middle of the picture. Now, in an unstable northwesterly, cumulus caps grow over gust-cells.

8 Cumulus streets over the Sussex coastal plain in a westerly wind. In the foreground Bosham Channel. In the background the Downs.

9 Cumulus "chimneys" sprout hopefully, but there is an inversion above under which they must spread. Already the cloud spreading out above is shading some of the cumulus below, and as it spreads so gustiness will become damped down.

10 Altocumulus castellanus at dawn. Such a sky presages thunder later. Do not be deceived by the apparent stability of the lens clouds in the lower right-hand corner. Smoke may rise vertically now but winds can be moderate and gusty by evening.

11 This might be the evening of the same day as Photo 10. Beyond the village of Bosham, thunderclouds (in the hail stage) grow over the Downs. Craft are tide-rode in the force 3 south-easterly, but winds may turn towards the storms and then later cascade offshore.

12 Thunderstorms growing down the wind. The great anvil head is the parent and is past its prime. On its cold outflow grows a daughter storm out of whose base heavy rain (and perhaps hail) is falling. Other daughter storms can easily form as the storm area develops.

13 Line-squall cloud stretched across the wind. Embedded in it may be thunderstorms, but it is not wide and if precautions are taken to meet the strong gusts it will soon be over.

14 Cloud along a sea breeze front over Colchester, Essex. The sea breeze from the left was from the east of south, and the off-shore wind from the north-west. The photo was taken looking west. Under the line winds were fitful gusts amid calm patches.

15 A wave-cloud down-wind of a hill-ridge – a sure sign of standing-wave streaming. Under such lenses winds can become retrograde.

16 Stability and low cloud are partners. In tropical maritime airstreams stratus may cover high ground like this and speak of dampened eddies and no organised gust-lull sequences.

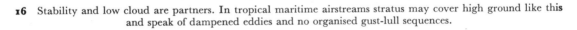

WHY THE WIND VEERS AS IT GUSTS It has already been stated that gusts are brought down from aloft where the wind is stronger, but as well as its increased speed the wind above the surface has a different direction from that which is fully under the frictional effect of the surface. That the wind normally blows to keep *Low* pressure on the *Left* is common knowledge and the reasons for it have been given in Chapter Two. It was also shown in that chapter that when the earth interferes with the natural balance of forces which exist above the friction layer the result is an angling of the surface wind into low, and out of high. Thus the wind will increase and veer with height in the friction layer which is normally taken to be 2000 ft deep, but may be much shallower in stable conditions with light winds, or much deeper in convective conditions with stronger winds. Table 4.A (on page 107) gives the depth of this layer under normal convective conditions, and in stable air, and it will be seen that it may be anything from 100 ft to 5000 ft deep. When the airstream is very unstable, with deep cumulonimbus clouds, the height from which gusts are brought down may be 15,000 feet or more. Here interest centres on the medium eddies whose depths are given in Table 4.A under the heading of "Normal Conditions", and so we can talk of wind above the friction layer and also of that within it.

Above the friction layer the wind flows obediently along the isobaric tramlines under the equal and opposite pulls of pressure gradient force towards low pressure and geostrophic force away from low pressure. When the wind speed is curtailed by surface friction the geostrophic force decreases while the pressure gradient force remains the same as above the friction layer.

Thus, referring to Fig. 2.5 on page 24, when the wind at the top of the friction layer is brought down to the surface as a gust at the head of a gust cell, it will still be flowing in the same direction as above, that is parallel to the isobars. It will replace air in the rear of the previous cell, which has been fully slowed by friction with the surface to a speed less than the mean speed, and which is therefore backed across the isobars to its fullest extent. Hence lull air (as fully backed to the isobars as it can be) is replaced by strong gust air which is as veered as it can be. The effect is then enhanced, and is shown in a typical form in the anemogram, Fig. 3.12. These three minutes of gusty wind were chosen by a team of meteorologists who studied the structure of the gust cell in the late nineteen-twenties. Out of their experience and from dozens of such anemograms they chose the one reproduced in Fig. 3.12 as typical of the gust and lull sequence.[15]

As with all things connected with the wind and weather there is always room for deviations in detail, and thus it will be seen that in this case, as the gust struck, the wind backed for ten seconds or so. However the rule that it veers as it gusts was not long disregarded, for, still at its strongest, it had veered from the mean direction before 20 seconds were up, and it then stayed that way for the next two minutes as the wind decreased into the lull. Note also that between $2\frac{1}{2}$ and 3 minutes the wind has backed to the direction it had before the gust struck.

It may be said that a mean speed of 28 kt gusting to 39 kt is not a very typical wind for most dinghy events, but the same features are known to obtain in lower wind speeds in convective conditions of this kind.

The typical airstream for gust cells is the unstable north-westerly which is normally partly cloudy. But it can happen that a very dry airstream can be full of gust cells without any capping clouds. Usually, however, there are some puffs to be seen somewhere—say over local hills where the wind is pushed upwards more than elsewhere.

E

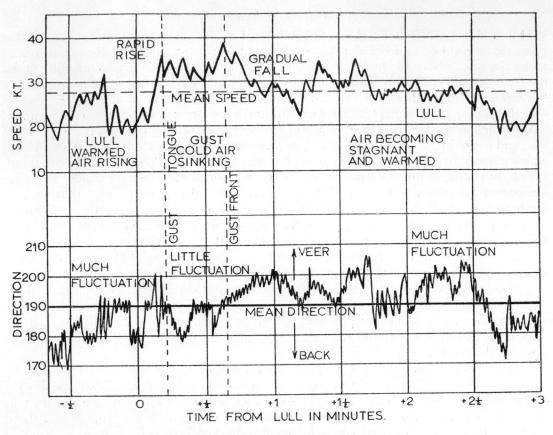

3.12: *A typical gust and lull sequence.*[15]

As a general rule the deeper the convection currents the stronger the gusts, but there are exceptions to this rule. Small cumulus will mean small wind features in direction, speed and frequency, while big cumulus will produce strong gusts well veered from the mean surface wind and with a time of repeat which may be just as rapid as the smaller cells if the wind speed is higher, as it often is.

On the whole it can be said that the slower the wind the more it will tend to seek low pressure and the more it will be backed to the mean surface wind. Sailors on inland waters surrounded by the roughest terrain will experience the most profound effects of gust cells, while those on the open sea will find them correspondingly diminished in the scale of variation.

Evidence that the wind does actually veer with height has been obtained, and it shows some variation with the time of day and the time of year. Again, these figures were taken over level country and the wind speeds were from 8 to 25 kt. The wind above the friction layer was assumed to lie along the isobars and the wind near the surface was that at 150 feet. Larger values might be expected if the lower wind had been measured in the sailing layer.

TABLE 3.A

AMOUNTS BY WHICH THE WIND ABOVE THE FRICTION LAYER
IS VEERED FROM THAT AT 150 FEET

Time of day	0100	0700	1300	1800 *G.M.T.*
March, April, May	35°–45°	30°–35°	15°–20°	25°–29°
June, July, August	25°–29°	30°–34°	20°–24°	20°–29°
September, October, November	30°–34°	25°–29°	10°–20°	30°–40°
December, January, February	30°–34°	30°–40°	20°–25°	30°–35°
Average over the year	30°–40°	30°–35°	10°–14° * 20°–25° †	25°–30°

The most interesting thing about these figures is that during the afternoon, when much of our sailing is done, the wind near the surface is least different from that above in spring and autumn and still below the overall average in summer and winter.

We therefore find that the variations between gust and lull will be least noticeable in the afternoon, but in the evening, night and early morning a considerable difference in direction normally exists between the stronger and the not so strong wind. The reasons are not far to seek, for when the earth is cool the wind is most tightly bound to the surface and becomes slowed down by the greatest amount. The wind above ignores this and continues to blow along the isobars at the same speed and in the same direction as before. The wind below gets angled in towards low pressure more and more as its speed drops, so the difference between the two diverges.

To sum up; the wind is never steady, but at some times it is steadier than at others. It is at its most gusty during the heat of the day and least gusty in the cool of the night. The gustiness is of three main sizes:

(i) short eddies which are too rapid for any more than an immediate and almost instinctive reaction on the part of helmsman,
(ii) medium eddies which tend to veer as they gust and back as they lull,
(iii) long eddies which do the same, but may typically repeat at intervals of half an hour to an hour in very unstable airstreams.

The observations can be tied to a visual picture of gust cells moving in the mean wind and to all intents and purposes remaining entities within the limits of visual observation by a dinghy helmsman. These cells are about three times longer than they are wide in moderate winds, but when the wind falls very light they tend to become squarish cells with diameters of up to 20 miles.

These are the observations. Now to give some ideas on how to react to gustiness.

* Spring and Autumn averages. † Summer and Winter averages.

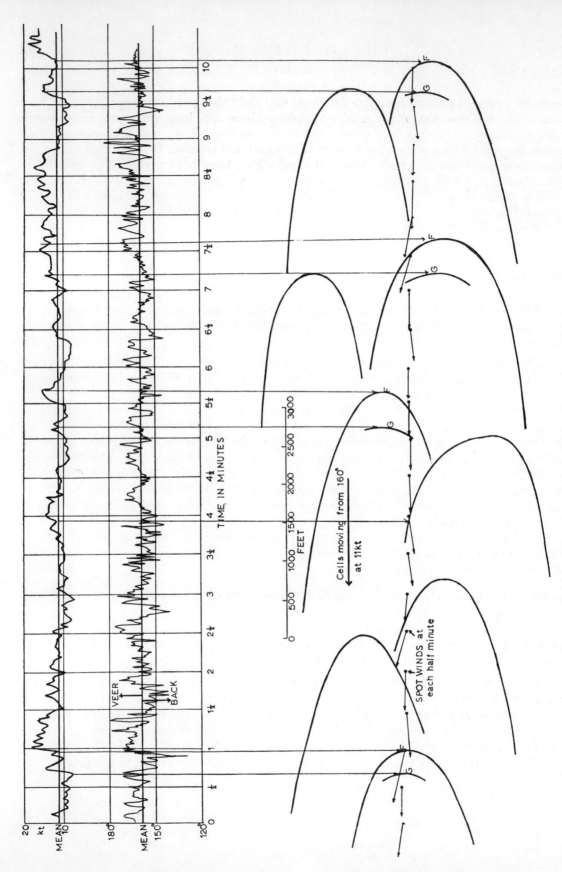

3.13: *Ten minutes of normal wind fitted to a possible gust-lull sequence.*

FITTING THE WIND TO THE WIND PATTERN In order to explain the meaning of an anemogram, Fig. 3.13 shows ten minutes of moderate wind to which the probable gust-cell pattern has been fitted. At first sight the speed trace is not very significant, while the direction trace is very variable. There are, however, some recognisable features. Noticeable increases of wind occur after 1 minute, $3\frac{1}{2}$, $5\frac{1}{2}$, 7 and $9\frac{1}{2}$ minutes. This makes the repeat time somewhat shorter than usual and signifies that the gust cells were some 2000–3000 feet in length. Veers of wind which have been preceded by noticeable and relatively prolonged backing also occur at about these times. When the mean wind speed is about 10 kt the smaller features take on a significance which would not be so apparent in a stronger airstream. This is the case here. A gust-cell pattern can be drawn below these anemograms which answers most of the questions about why the wind did what it did at a particular moment.

The gust at 1 minute is preceded by a gust tongue (G) some 20 seconds before, and others are noticeable at 5 minutes, 7 minutes and $9\frac{1}{2}$ minutes, each with the same time lapse between heralding tongue and actual gust.

The lack of anything very significant occurring for some minutes after the first true gust can be explained by the anemometer sampling the edges of cells and not meeting one head-on.

WHAT IS THE MEAN WIND? This anemogram, like others, poses a question which must worry many a Race Officer. What is the true mean wind direction and how does he find it?

Finding the answer is not easy, but sometimes he must do so, and the procedure would appear to be this: he must sample several gust–lull sequences, and to do this he needs to note the direction associated wih the highest and lowest speeds reached over a period of at least ten minutes. There should be two or three gusts of value approaching $1\frac{1}{2}$ × mean wind speed for a correct assessment, and in very unstable situations (days of big Cu or Cb) the only true assessment can come after 30 minutes or so, as is evident from Fig. 3.15 page 73.

During this time he must note the wind directions from his pennant or by other means. None of these observations is very easy with the usual instruments. The Race Officer may have a cup anemometer or something of this kind, but he rarely has a wind vane. It would seem that committee boats might well fit a mast-head wind indicator in order to be sure of the facts about the day's wind, and race committees running Olympic style events ought to have such a device as a matter of course.

GUSTS AND TACKS As the direction of the wind in a gust is veered from the direction it had in the preceding lull, it is advantageous when one is beating to be on starboard tack when the gust strikes. Conversely, it is advantageous to be on port tack in the lulls.

As the medium gust-cell features usually repeat at intervals of some minutes (two to four in typical cases with a 20 kt mean wind (Fig. 3.8)), then an astute tendency to be on starboard in the gusts, and on port in the lulls, is perfectly possible when one is beating. In unrestricted waters a few minutes on either tack often forms the pattern of a dinghy's progress to the windward mark. It is usually good racing tactics as well, for relatively short tacks help to keep a craft between its opponents and the next mark and also prevent overstanding when the mark is reached.

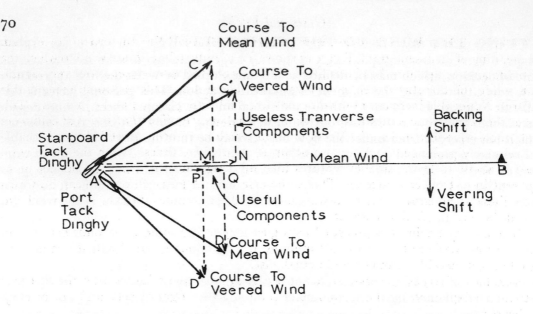

3.14: *When the mark is in the eye of the mean wind a veer aids starboard tack.*

Before going any further let us see why being on starboard is correct for gusts and port for lulls.

Let the mean wind be blowing from B to A in Fig. 3.14 and let the dinghy at A be on starboard tack towards C. Assume a course at 45° to the mean wind. Now let the wind veer as it may do in a gust and neglect the ability to point higher in the stronger wind as this will act equally on either tack. The dinghy on starboard at A now points towards C' and his component of velocity towards B is greater by MN. The useless transverse component is lessened. As he wishes to reach B then both these are to his advantage.

Now consider the port tack dinghy, which passed close across the bow of the other towards D as the wind veered. He will now be proceeding to D' and his component towards B is smaller than before by PQ while his unwanted sideways component is increased.

In a veer therefore, when the course is to windward, being on starboard tack is an advantage while being on port is a disadvantage.

Conversely when the wind backs the craft on port will be aided in the progress to the mark while the other on starboard will be hindered.

Therefore when the normal veer accompanies gusts one should try to be on starboard, while as the wind lulls it is helpful to revert to port tack.

Later it is proved that there is an abnormal set of conditions where the wind veers as it lulls and backs as it gusts.

ANTICIPATING THE GUSTS From a practical point of view it is no use knowing about the structure of gust cells if their incidence cannot be detected in sufficient time to allow for action. As a useful rule one can assume that it takes a second a foot of craft length to tack, that is from the moment of putting the helm down to when she is drawing and settled on the new tack. Thus the tacking times lie between 12 and 20 seconds for dinghies and will be correspondingly longer for larger craft. To this we have to add the time of decision, which may be defined as the time elapsed between the first appreciation of a new situation and the moment of appropriate action. This personal factor is very difficult to assess. It will vary with the individual and the circumstances. It may depend on whether the crew is throwing out water or retrieving unruly but essential equipment which has emerged from under the bow bag. It may be that the helmsman is undecided about what action to take, if any, and he may hold on too long and lose—or sometimes hold on and gain. In bigger craft the sheer weight of the organisation required to go about may make the helmsman loath to tack, or the contents of an open vacuum flask may seem more pressing. There are a hundred and one reasons for variation in the time of decision.

However, in a racing fleet of dinghies people crash-tack, often without regard for their crews, as soon as the stimulus has registered. So in this case perhaps we could take 3–5 seconds as the normal time of decision. That makes the total time between initial stimulus and final result some 15–25 seconds. Consultation with Fig. 3.8 on page 60 shows that in a 15 kt mean wind 400–600 ft of air moves by in this time. In a 10-kt wind some 200–400 ft of air moves by, etc.

Thus big gusts need to be seen coming some 100–200 yards to windward when one is on port tack and wishes to be about on starboard to meet the gust in an efficient and controlled manner.

I submit that this is normally beyond the bounds of possibility, for the line of sight is so close to the sea surface that 50 yards is a more likely distance at which gush splash marks first become truly visible.

Therefore, in general, other criteria must be sought. One is to expect the new gust when intuition whispers that the wind has fallen below the mean wind speed for a minute or more. Then craft to windward can be more carefully watched to see how they are reacting. The ones at 100 yards can be measured quickly by the thumb yardstick given on page 63.

The gust front appears at the surface just under the leading edge of the following cloud but it is often difficult to know quite when the cloud edge has arrived, especially as there may be other more pressing considerations such as starboard tack craft to be allowed for. Even so the leading edges of individual cloud elements do give some indication of a gust, although the message may not be precise (Fig. 3.4).

The incidence of gust tongues can also be useful and in the lee of rough terrain gust tongues can be very prevalent and should be allowed for. A short and not very weighty shiver of wind must be expected to be followed some seconds later by the true gust. The line marked "gust tongue" in Fig. 3.12 is not the true front, but a gust tongue of more than usual intensity, for the wind veered with it and then backed again, after which the true veer set in associated with the true stronger gust some 20 seconds later. It is evident from experience, and also from the instrumental records, that most of the biggest gusts are preceded by gust tongues of veered wind. The wind then backs which makes the true gust hurrying along behind even more marked than it otherwise would be. Thus gust tongues are often reliable precursors of gusts.

THE TECHNIQUE OF TACKING TO GUSTS To illustrate the technique of tacking to the gusts the anemograms of a classically variable wind of moderate strength are reproduced in Fig. 3.15. These fifty minutes of wind are part of the wind record of a day with cumulonimbus clouds about, and while the wind direction was highly variable the speed showed moderate variations about a mean speed of 14 knots. On such days the fleet becomes almost unbelievably spread out, because those who know and care can play the wind shifts to their own advantage while the others forge unhappily on getting farther and farther behind.

It is the sort of day when dinghies delight in the flying spray of controlled planing, but the wind is not so strong that survival must sometimes take precedence over tactics.

The record begins at about 1145, so this is a day-time wind whose variations are generated over level country and can easily be the kind which flows over estuaries and creeks when the wind is routed overland, or any inland water.

It will be noted that the mean direction is 080°, but that the gusts were veered some 25°, approaching 105°, while the lulls were backed by an equal amount, even going back at times to 050°. The wind was therefore variable over some 50°, but the changes were not random. They conformed to the gust-cell idea put forward above.

The time of the main repeating pattern in the direction of the mean wind, to, say, an observer on the committee boat, C, is between 10 and 20 minutes which can be assessed most readily from the smoothed direction trace which is Fig. 3.15*b*.

This makes the long gust cells between 13,000 and 27,000 feet long (2 to $4\frac{1}{2}$ miles). Within these were medium gust cells, whose repeat time was of the order of 2–3 minutes, and were therefore between 2500 and 4000 feet long. Although an astute helmsman could gain advantage from the medium length cells, we shall ignore them in order to bring out the salient points governing the technique of tacking to the longer gusts, and these points will apply to the shorter eddies also.

The evidence available seems to show that these cells are about three times as long as they are wide, which makes the long ones some $\frac{2}{3}$ to $1\frac{1}{2}$ miles across. So, in this case we can assume that roughly the same changes of wind affect boats which tack in a zone 3 cables either side of the mean course from the line CD to the first mark M of the Olympic course. This latter is the recommended $1\frac{1}{2}$ n.m. on the first leg and the course is laid so that the first mark is dead to windward, although it is interesting to note that the officer of the day in the committee boat would have needed to observe the wind continually for at least half an hour in order to have inferred that the mean wind was in fact 080°.

Nothing much will be lost by assuming that at the same moments the same wind affects boats which go off on opposite tacks as illustrated in Fig. 3.15*c*. On the average the wind features will approach craft (which are beating at a mean speed of B knots at 45° to the mean wind) at a speed of

$$Z = \left(V + \frac{B}{\sqrt{2}}\right) \text{ kt where V is the mean wind speed.}$$

In this case V is 13 kt while we will assume $B = 4\frac{1}{4}$ kt (somewhere between the speeds of conventional 12 and 14 footers).

Thus Z is 16 kt, and the times at which the dinghies meet the wind features are computed on this basis.

Between the five-minute gun and the start the wind steadily veers, and this shift makes starboard an even more desirable tack at the start than usual. Thus, take two dinghies who cross the line with the gun and both of whom travel at $4\frac{1}{4}$ knots but are on opposite tacks.

The starboard tack boat S is seen to have an obvious advantage over his port tack

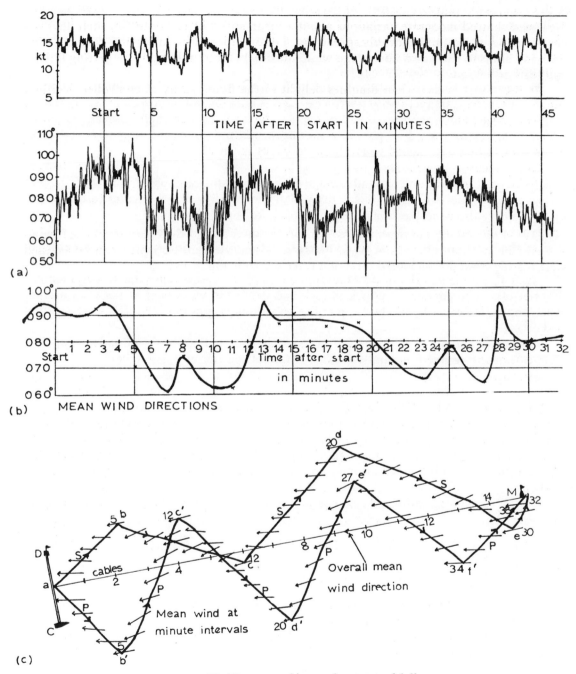

3.15: *To illustrate tacking to the gusts and lulls.*

rival and his tacks have been planned to bring out the maximum advantage. In the stress of the race, with so many factors influencing the moment of tacking, it is obviously unrealistic to expect a dinghy to tack at the exact moment which will give him maximum advantage. The course sailed by S, however, is that unattainable perfection to which the keen racing helmsman aspires. The craft P on the other tack does nothing that is very right and the diagram shows what happens.

Helmsman S stays on starboard until he finds the wind steadily backing and then 5 minutes after the start tacks onto port. The wind is backing still and so S makes excellent progress being some 3 minutes ahead of his port tack rival when their courses first cross. P of course, having started on port in a veering wind, finds himself losing on S and tacks just in time to be on starboard when the wind backs against him at b'.

Craft S senses the wind veering again 11 minutes after the start and prepares to tack so as to be on starboard and take advantage of the veer. Out-of-phase P, however, decides to tack when S does and again this is to his detriment. After this S decides to tack on to port whenever the wind has really begun to back for some minutes.

It is of course not to his advantage to tack to the veer at the 28th minute as he is too close to the buoy, so this part of his course is dictated not by wind but by the necessity of being on starboard at the buoy.

Craft P, who is still doing his worst, manages to tack at exactly the wrong moment (d'), but after that manages by luck to tack and catch the wind veer at the 28th minute on starboard. However he still ends up at the buoy some 7 minutes behind his more canny rival.

These two courses are about the best, and the worst, that could be sailed, and it is obvious that the course in actual fact will be one of the many possible courses which lie between these extremes.

GUSTS AND SAILING FREE   The question of sailing off the wind on a gusty day is very much more complicated than that of a hard beat. For instance, a boat may plane or she may not, and if she does plane then it may be either a refined Stage One plane, or a screaming, sit-on-the-transom-and-hang-on, Stage Two plane. There is also the difficulty that any point of sailing may obtain, from just off the wind on either tack to a dead run.

To cut down this infinitude of possibilities to a manageable few, let us take the following cases:

    (i) Off the wind with comparative freedom of course, but with the true wind forward of the beam.

    (ii) Running before the wind.

The good advice which is offered by those who know about sailing off the wind is: "Bear away in the gusts, and make up in the lulls."

This is usually the fastest course to sail, but it is interesting to see why. First we need some data:

    (i) a standard wind situation, and Fig. 3.16 is a simplified gust and lull sequence, lasting 4 minutes, to which a dinghy can be assumed to react. It is based on an actual anemogram.

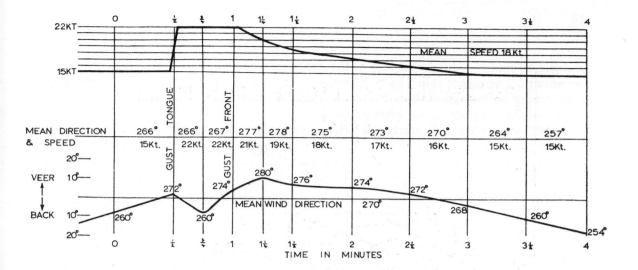

3.16: *A smoothed gust-lull sequence.*

(ii) a standard performance chart for the dinghy in question, so that we know something about the speed on different points of sailing.

Using a certain amount of guess-timation, and some runs over measured distances in known mean wind speeds, I produced the performance chart for my own Firefly which is Fig. 3.17. While I do not pretend that it is very accurate, it does fit certain of the observed facts, particularly with regard to the speed bulge when the boat is some 70° off the true wind direction. This bulge, which does not appear on similar charts for deep-keel yachts, is due to the planing ability. The curve specifying the speed on the various points of sailing, when the wind speed is 5 kt follows very closely the shape of the performance charts of displacement sailing craft but as V_T increases to 10 kt then the shape grows in the direction of the fastest point of sailing. This follows because the stronger puffs will yield short planes in this direction even though the craft is not long enough to plane all the time in a wind of this mean speed. Then with the wind at 15 kt or more true planing occurs and the craft speed increases relatively quickly.

As a rough guide, planing 14-footers of normal hull shape will have similar performance charts to this one but with the craft speed increased in the rough ratio of 1:1·5 and 18 footers in the ratio of 1:2.

In any case the performances shown in Fig. 3.17 will be sufficiently exact for the purposes of illustration.

One obvious conclusion from the performance chart is that the planing dinghy will go fastest when the true wind is roughly at 70° to the craft course. Thus, bearing away in a gust is advantageous if, and only if, it puts the true wind closer to the 70° direction. This is difficult to assess with any certainty, for to do the vector sum in one's head to find the true wind from the apparent at such a time, would require the phlegmatic qualities of a computer and not those of a highly stressed dinghy sailor. I do not believe that there

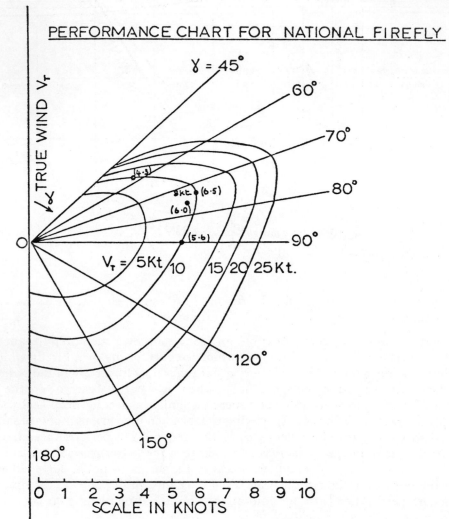

PERFORMANCE CHART FOR NATIONAL FIREFLY

TRUE WIND V_T

$\gamma = 45°$

60°

70°

80°

90°

120°

150°

180°

(4·3)

5kt. (6·5)

(6·0)

(5·6)

$V_T = 5Kt.$ 10   15 20 25 Kt.

0 1 2 3 4 5 6 7 8 9 10
SCALE IN KNOTS

Bracketted Figures Are Spot Speeds Obtained Over
Measured Course.

γ = Angle Between V_T & Craft Course.

EXAMPLE   The Figure (5·6) Is The Craft Speed When
Sailing At 90° To A True Wind Of 10Kt Measured From
Point 'O' On The Scale.

3.17

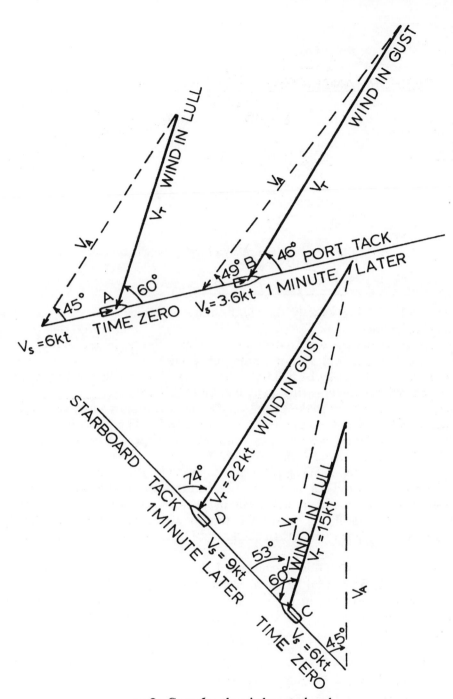

3.18: *Gusts free the wind on starboard.*

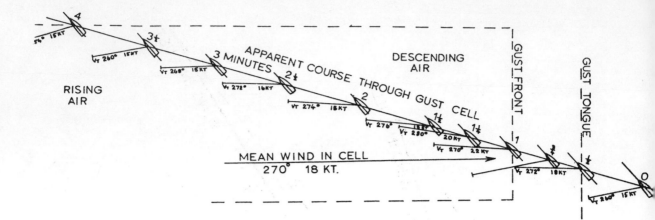

3.19: *Close reaching through a gust cell of normal dimensions.*

is any easy road to doing exactly the right things in a gust—one can only put down some general principles.

They are these: as the wind normally veers as it gusts, it is essential, when close reaching on port tack, to bear away to maintain speed.

On starboard tack it may be helpful to bear away, but not so vital as on port. If the veer is sufficiently large then bearing away can be a disadvantage.

A couple of illustrations make this clear. Consider a dinghy close-reaching at 60° to the true wind and on port tack (Time Zero in Fig. 3.16). The performance chart shows that on this point of sailing, with a 15 kt wind, the craft speed V_S is 6 kt, as she can just plane. This situation appears at A in Fig. 3.18.

During the next minute (Fig. 3.16) a gust tongue veers the wind by 12° and its speed increases to 22 kt. The wind backs temporarily, but this is only the herald of the true gust and the wind speed does not fall, so at the end of the next minute the wind is veered through 14° and its speed is 22 kt (B, Fig. 3.18). The dinghy which was previously planing is now beating, and its speed falls to 3·6 kt. In such a case bearing away is essential if speed is to be maintained.

The exactly similar situation on starboard (C and D) produces a wind freed by 14°, and the craft leaps up on to a full plane near her maximum speed of 9 kt.

Thus the advice always to bear away in the gusts may not be universally good. When the wind really veers between a lull and the following gust, and the reach is close enough to produce an apparent wind at less than 45° to the centreline, then bearing away is essential on port tack, but it need not be on starboard. In fact it is easily verified from the performance chart that bearing away on starboard would have meant a loss of speed, as the sum of veering gust and bearing away would have taken the course right through the maximum of the reaching sector.

Before we go any further some proof must be given that it is reasonable to assume that a gust–lull sequence, as recorded by a static anemometer, would have a similar effect on a moving dinghy which is close reaching. To do this on a static diagram we must again

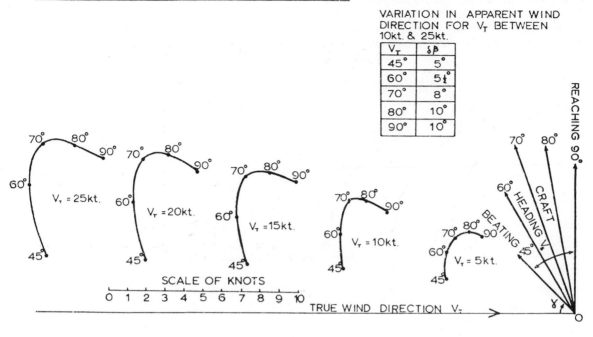

VARIATION IN APPARENT WIND
DIRECTION FOR V_T BETWEEN
10kt. & 25kt.

V_T	$\delta\beta$
45°	5°
60°	5½°
70°	8°
80°	10°
90°	10°

3.20

use the concept of an apparent course, because at the same time as the dinghy is moving through the gust cell the cell is moving across the dinghy at the mean wind speed. Such a course is shown in Fig. 3.19, and the assumptions made are that the dinghy has the performance chart Fig. 3.17 and sails through the smoothed gust-lull sequence (Fig. 3.16) playing sheets to maintain a heading at 50° to the mean wind. For simplicity the cell has been made oblong, but this does not affect the argument if the 3:1 ratio of length to width is accepted.

The diagram serves to prove that even with the true wind nearer to the beam than in the chosen case much of a gust cell may cross a reaching craft. Therefore the gust-lull sequence of Fig. 3.16 will be taken as a basis for arguments about points of sailing near and within the reaching sector.

THE APPARENT WIND DIAGRAM   The apparent course is easily defined in direction from the craft herself, as it is a line to windward through the pennant, but where is the true wind? Dinghy sailors have no time to draw anything but rapid mental vector diagrams, so it is revealing to construct apparent wind diagrams based on the performance chart (Figs. 3.20 and 3.21). Every point of a performance chart represents:

(i) a craft heading to the true wind,
(ii) a speed through the water, and
(iii) a true wind velocity.

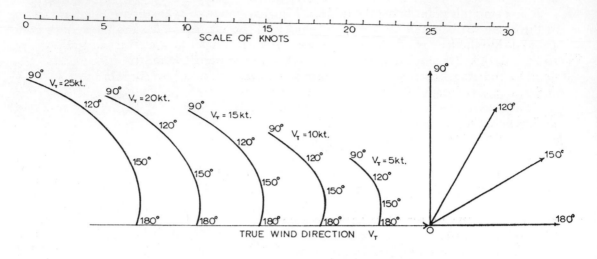

3.21

For instance, the spot marked (5·6) in Fig. 3.17 represents a dinghy making 5·6 kt at 90° to the true wind of 10 kt. This is enough information to enable one to construct the apparent wind and mark the point (90°, V_T = 10 kt) in Fig. 3.20. The end of the apparent wind vector for craft headings to the true wind (γ) between 45° and 90° can then be marked and the locus of the end of the apparent wind vector drawn for any heading. For clarity, the similar diagram, for headings between 90° and 180° to the true wind, has been put on a separate figure, Fig. 3.21.

In either diagram the apparent wind is found for any heading by laying a rule from the appropriate point on a locus to the origin O and measuring it off along the scale. Any helmsman interested enough to do some measured runs, and record some mean wind speeds at the same time, can produce performance charts for his own craft and draw apparent wind diagrams such as these.

Other craft with different performances from that of the 12-ft Firefly can modify the chart given, for the only variable is the craft speed. Thus the curves specifying the apparent wind will be displaced perpendicularly away from the true wind vector. The amounts, however, cannot be great. With planing 14-footers speeds can be increased in the ratio of 1:1·5, and for planing 18-footers they may be doubled. These are, however, rough figures and only by measurement can the correct results be produced.

The effect in 15 kt winds is to bring the apparent wind some 10° or less nearer the centreline in Fourteens and 20° or less with Eighteens. These figures refer to reaching whether it be close or broad. When beating, the angles may be halved. The apparent wind comes 5° closer to the centreline in Fourteens and 10° closer in Eighteens. It will be generally agreed that a change of 10° in the direction of a pennant is difficult to assess, so for practical purposes there is little variation in the direction of the apparent wind when beating, whatever conventional craft may be sailed.

To bring this point home the table in Fig. 3.20 shows the variation ($\delta\beta$) which occurs in the angle (β) between the apparent wind and the centreline for craft headings from 45° to 90° to the true wind. At speeds below 10 kt the angles become bigger, but between 10 kt and 25 kt (true wind speeds) the variation in apparent wind direction is really too small to be noticed even when one is broad reaching, being 5° on the wind and only 10° on a reach at right angles to the true wind. The angles refer to Fig. A.1 (page 218).

For example, when one is sailing perpendicularly across a wind of 10 kt the apparent wind is at 62° to the centreline. It is still 72° to the centreline when the wind has increased to 25 kt. The variation in the apparent wind direction is quite minor.

Some rough rules can therefore be given for finding the true wind in planing 12-footers when this is 10 kt or more, and anyone can deduce his own values which will not differ much from these.

When beating—add 10° (or less in increasing wind) to the apparent wind to find the true wind.

When close reaching—add 20° or less.

When broad reaching—add 30° or less.

A further yardstick is that the true wind is about 60° off the stern when the apparent wind is abeam (Fig. 3.21).

THE REACHING SECTOR To return to the question of reaching through the gust cells, the dinghy in Fig. 3.19, which maintains its heading and plays sheets to meet the wind changes, does so, one imagines, because dead ahead he can see the mark, and he goes straight for it fondly believing that the shortest distance between two points is a straight line. It may be, but not always in racing, for the shortest time is the criterion. A dinghy may sail a longer course, but providing it does so at a fast enough speed it can make up the extra distance and more.

The performance chart (Fig. 3.17) shows that while 70° to the true wind is the most advantageous course we might well define a "reaching sector" between 60° and 80° in which to wander and yet maintain a high speed (V_A between 45° and 55° to centreline in a wind of 15 kt from Fig. 3.20). With this in mind consider a dinghy (A) on port tack which bears away in the first couple of minutes of the gust (Fig. 3.16) and then makes up to regain distance to windward (Fig. 3.22).

Using the times as reference points, A planes away as the wind veers. The gust tongue arrives ($\frac{1}{2}$ min), after which the wind then backs strongly but does not fall in speed. A could have made up in this freeing wind but suspects it may be only temporary so maintains course playing sheets. This still keeps him within the reaching sector, and good progress is made. The true gust arrives at 1 minute, and the wind veers again, this time solidly, and then begins to back. As soon as he has recognised the back as a true one (*i.e.* it has persisted for a minute or more) A decides he has had his spree and continues to use the backing wind to keep his planing reach going but still make some way back towards the mark.

Helmsman B, who is steaming straight for the mark, is headed by the veering wind and even has to bear away (1–1$\frac{1}{2}$ min.) as the wind comes ahead. He is forced to beat by the veering gust and so makes very slow progress compared to A. The mark may be

F

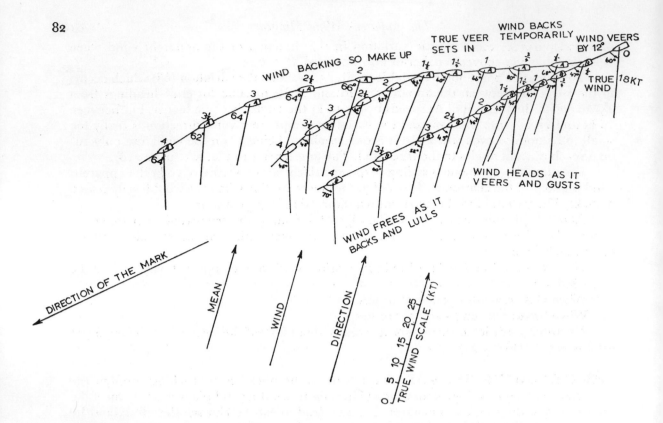

3.22: *Sailing through the gust-lull sequence on port tack.*

upwind of A but his position (assuming there are no other craft who may hamper him) is better than that of B who will again be headed by the next veer of wind. Even if A now decides to close-haul towards the mark he should still be well ahead of B, who will also be forced to beat by the next gust.

The difficulty in practice is to make the right decision. In this armchair sailing the right tactics can be worked out in the light of fore-knowledge of the wind which is to come. Not so in the race where only the merest of clues and intuition must be mustered if boobs are not to be made. Thus suppose that A, planing away from the direction to the next mark, loses his nerve after the gust begins to slacken and comes back on to the wind ($1\frac{1}{2}$). By so doing he forfeits most of his advantage because B is then gaining speed in a freeing wind while A is travelling slowest. In spite of the loss of windward distance, it pays in general to sail boldly away from the wind when it gusts, and not be too easily panicked into beating back unless, of course, it is essential to make the buoy. It is as well to remember that on port tack the gust will head in most cases and the succeeding lull will free the wind. Thus if the mark is close, and one suspects that one is in the lull before the next gust, then on port tack it is as well to make windward way in the backed wind while the going is good, in anticipation of having to bear away as the wind gusts, and so risk being forced the wrong side of the buoy.

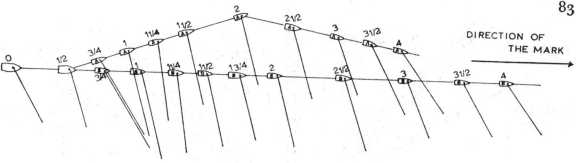

3.23: *Sailing through the gust-lull sequence on starboard tack. Winds and times as in Fig. 3.22.*

Now consider the same pair of dinghies on the starboard tack and let the initial conditions be the same, *i.e.* true wind as at time zero in Fig. 3.16, and craft heading at 60° to this wind (Fig. 3.23).

Helmsman B is now the gaining member of the pair as he heads straight for the mark for he starts off on the edge of the reaching sector and knows that a veering wind can only be helpful even if it veers by 20°. His progress is almost the fastest that he could make, and only in the relative quietude of the last of the lull does he find the wind coming so far ahead as to force him into displacement sailing.

Helmsman A who bears away in the gusts regardless, while he gained handsomely on port tack, now finds himself the loser. He bears away by 20° as the gust strikes, but at the same time the wind veers and brings the true wind farther and farther aft, so that he has left the reaching sector. After a while (2 min), as the wind begins to falter, he realises his mistake and tries to rectify his loss by making a bold 30° alteration back towards the direct course, but the wind is backing against him, so from being outside the reaching sector on the leeward side he changes to being outside it on the windward side and completely misses the high performance bracket.

Thus by this manoeuvre A defeats his own purpose, and it is evident that the advice to bear away in the gusts and make up in the lulls is not universally applicable. It needs some qualification.

The technique of bearing away in the gusts applies to either tack when one is close reaching (*i.e.* outside the reaching sector on the windward side). Then the alteration of course will bring one into the reaching sector and one can begin to plane, but if one is close-reaching on starboard in a lull one can expect some sort of veer as the wind gusts, and the alteration away from the direct course need not be as great as in a similar situation on port.

When one is inside the reaching sector alterations of course, or wind, which keep one within it will be advantageous. If one is reaching on port on the windward side veers will carry the wind out of the sector, with consequent sharp loss of performance. On starboard a veering wind will bring the course into the sector and bearing away may not be necessary, or if it seems necessary then the alterations can be relatively modest. On port one will have to bear away as the wind veers.

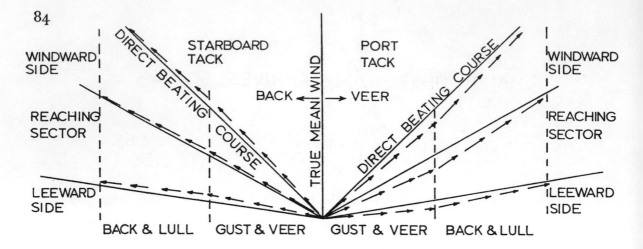

3.24: *Tendencies for the fastest courses on either tack when beating or reaching in normal gust-lull sequences.*

Broader reaching on the leeward side of the sector will entail the same sort of procedure. On port tack the veering wind in a gust will bring the wind from within the sector, and thus bearing away is not so necessary. But one must not forget that every veer has its back to come, and in anticipation of this it is also useful to bear away a little. On starboard tack, when broad reaching on the leeward side of the reaching sector, it may be helpful to make up a little in the gusts in anticipation of having to bear away in sympathy with the succeeding lull.

The tendencies away from the direct courses which will normally lead to the highest speed and the shortest times are summed up in Fig. 3.24.

RUNNING IN GUSTS When one is running before the wind there is a choice of tacks, but in gusty winds this choice is not arbitrary. The normal wind pattern is for a veered wind to accompany a gust, and so the strong wind impulses come more from the port quarter, assuming that one has been running dead before the wind in the preceding lull. Therefore, unless other considerations are more pressing, it pays to be on port tack, for then the wind's change of direction does not run the craft by the lee. If one is dead before the wind in the lull, and on starboard, then the strong impulse of the gust might just run the craft by the lee and result in a catastrophic gybe.

Port is tactically shunned, especially since the introduction of the new rules, for starboard confers right of way over port tack craft, but here is a case where port tack can enjoy some advantage.

In practice a gust tongue from a veered direction may well be followed by a temporary back, as in Fig. 3.16, page 75, but the wind rarely backs farther than its direction in the preceding lull, so it may be advisable to hold on to the course for 20–30 seconds before reacting to the main heavy wind of the true gust.

Holding on may sometimes prove helpful, especially when one is pressed into the mark and it is impossible or undesirable to gybe from port on to starboard. Then a glance over the stern for a handy gust which will temporarily free the wind may enable one to

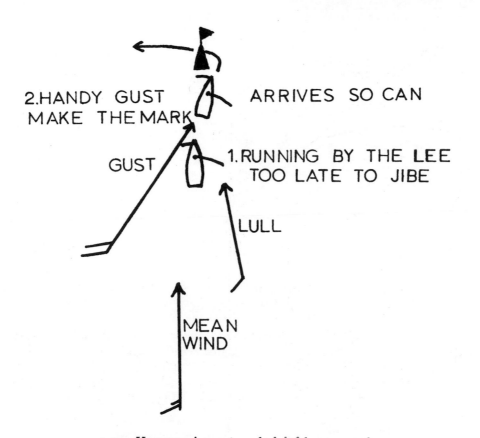

2.HANDY GUST MAKE THE MARK

ARRIVES SO CAN

GUST

1.RUNNING BY THE LEE TOO LATE TO JIBE

LULL

MEAN WIND

3.25: How a veering gust can be helpful near a mark.

bear away to starboard and make the mark which previously appeared certain to travel down the wrong side (Fig. 3.25).

THE RUNNING SECTOR As is well known, the fastest course before the wind is not a dead run but is achieved by tacking down wind. Referring again to the performance chart a "running sector" can be defined such that within it the craft is travelling faster than on a dead run. How this sector is found is evident from Fig. 3.26, and for the Firefly, which does not carry a spinnaker, it is about 36° either side of the dead run course. With craft which carry spinnakers the reaching sector is wider by perhaps 10° either side of the dead run course, for on the latter point of sailing the mainsail blankets the spinnaker.

There will be one course which is faster than any other, and again Fig. 3.26 shows how to find it. It is about 20° either side of the dead run course for the Firefly, but John C. Sainsbury in his book *Sailing Yacht Performance*[10] gives typical performance curves for a displacement sailing deep-keel yacht which shows little advantage in any other course than a dead run—until the spinnaker is hoisted. Typical performance curves for

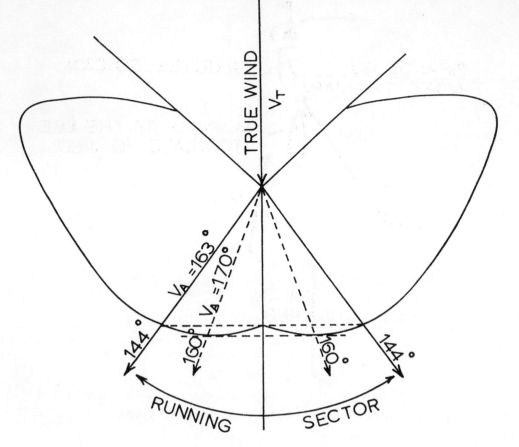

3.26: *Defining the running sector.*

different types of sailing boat are compared in Fig. 3.27. Craft which habitually set spinnakers are bound to gain proportionately more by angling their downwind courses within the running sector than those craft which cannot or do not.

It would obviously be an advantage to be able to gauge the correct angle for the fastest running course. This will, however, vary as the wind direction varies and the course would have to change to follow the wind changes. Keeping the apparent wind 10° over either quarter produces the fastest run in the Firefly and the performance chart for any other craft will yield (via an apparent wind diagram) the corresponding value of apparent wind direction for the highest speed.

Thus the technique of tacking downwind is governed by the necessity for keeping within the running sector and as close as possible to the fastest running course.

In this connection a useful diagram appeared in *Yachting World* for July 1956[16] to illustrate an article by M. Lindstrom. He concluded that there are only two variables:

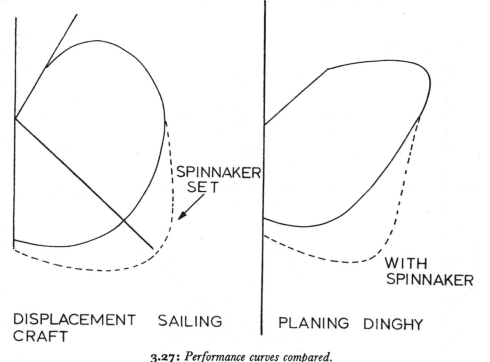

SPINNAKER
SET

WITH
SPINNAKER

DISPLACEMENT SAILING   PLANING DINGHY
CRAFT

3.27: Performance curves compared.

(i) the extra distance sailed by altering course,
(ii) the extra speed acquired by so doing.

He deduced that for deep-keel yachts when running near the maximum speed there was little to gain from tacking downwind, but in lighter airs the technique could pay handsome dividends. Lindstrom's diagram is reproduced as Fig. 3.28. Enter it with an intended deviation from the dead run course and the percentage increase in speed which will accrue (and comes from the appropriate performance chart) and hence find if the manoeuvre will yield a gain or a loss.

Thus imagine a dinghy which is dead before the wind in the lull before the smoothed gust sequence depicted in Fig. 3.16. Let it be on port tack, and achieving the speeds on the various points of sailing in Fig. 3.17.

In the first instance use as a reference a dinghy M which sails a direct course (Fig. 3.29). As M is on port when the wind veers the strongest wind is brought in over the port quarter and thus M can sail his desired course. It is not the fastest course, but at least it is possible. If he had been on starboard at the time marked O the veering gust would have run him dangerously by the lee and he would have been forced to bear away to starboard to avoid a gybe in the worst of the wind.

Now consider the port tack dinghy P who sails a genius's course to keep the true wind 20° over the port quarter. We know from Fig. 3.26 that this is the wind orientation which

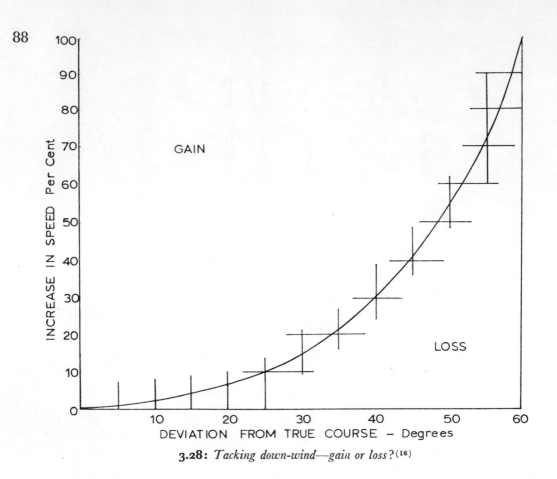

3.28: *Tacking down-wind—gain or loss?*[16]

will give the highest speed. The angle of bearing away to port is small as the necessary 20° is nearly provided by the veering gust. This excellent fellow is not upset by the back which sets in immediately after the veer and sharp rise of wind. He plays it cool, for the wind has not gone back very far and he expects the true veer to set in after this gust tongue has passed, which of course it does in most cases. The diagram shows that because of this gentle wander from the straight path a dinghy on port in a normal gust–lull sequence can hold the tack until the wind has really fallen with all the attendant advantages of quiet gybing that that confers. An added consolation is that the starboard course, with the wind from the fastest quarter, is strongly angled back towards the direct course. We find that in a four-minute manoeuvre he can gain 6 seconds over the man who sails the direct course.

But, should he try to do the same thing on starboard then trouble ensues, for a veering wind will angle his fastest course right away from the direct course, and he will soon be forced to gybe back on to port as he sees himself falling behind those who are sailing the ostensibly slower direct course. The course depicted for starboard tack craft S after 1

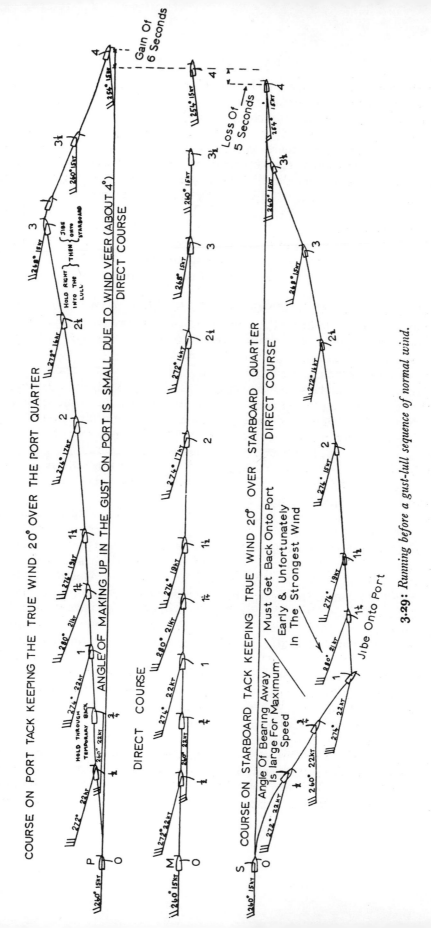

3·29: *Running before a gust-lull sequence of normal wind.*

minute is the same as for the port tack craft after 1 minute, but S is always behind in spite of his maximum speed being greater than that of M. He ends up in this armchair race some 5 seconds behind M and 11 seconds behind P.

Even though no one could be expected to achieve the optimum performance as depicted here, the lessons are there. Port is the best when running before gusts; and one need only bear away through relatively small angles if one is dead before the wind in the preceding lull. One can hold the slightly angled course for longer than would appear beneficial, and only when the wind has really gone down to a lull need one attempt to gybe on to starboard. This starboard course is then angled sharply back towards the mean course for maximum speed.

Starboard tack—so useful in close tactical work—comes out worst in this technique, and tacking downwind can well pay better in the wide open spaces away from competitors if this does not take one too far away from the direct course.

SAILING IN THE RUNNING SECTOR

Here, as with any other point of sailing, the mark is unlikely to lie on the dead course. When discussing reaching we were able to simplify the vast number of possibilities by using the notion of the reaching sector. Here, again, we can use the concept of the running sector.

In the example which showed that the fastest course was on the port tack the reference wind direction was assumed to be that in the lull. This has certain advantages, as it is in the lulls that any thinking (as opposed to instinctive reaction) is usually done and there is time to collect one's thoughts and perhaps even note the wind direction.

The difference in direction between gust and lull is rarely more than 20° in gust-lull sequences of normal wind, so if the next mark lies within the running sector (*i.e.* within the angle obtained from a polar diagram similar to Fig. 3.26 for the craft in question on either side of the mean wind direction) then the fastest course is one which maintains the apparent wind from somewhere within the sector.

However, Fig. 3.30 gives a little more information, for a craft at O on port who manages to select the fastest running course to the gust (taken to be a mean of 20 kt from the direction shown) and is making for the mark in the port half of the running sector, gets there before one who sails a direct course. There is not much in it, but only one such manoeuvre has been depicted (OAP) while the actual run would usually encompass several gust-lull sequences. However, all the idealised courses to the gust could be summed and depicted as OA and likewise all the alterations as the wind backed and lulled could be added into AP. Once again the speeds are for the Firefly in 20 kt and 15 kt winds but the results will be applicable to other similar dinghies, and presumably also to keel-boats.

We shall find, however, that when the mark lies in the starboard half of the running sector, the direct course can be fastest, for backed wind in the lull comes from so far out on the quarter that the speed from D to S is greater than from C to S and amply makes up for the slight loss in running dead before the gust.

Thus, in normal gust-lull-gust-lull sequences with accompanying veers and backs and the mark downwind but to port of the mean wind direction, a legged course may be fastest. When the mark is to starboard of the mean wind direction then a dead run for the mark may well be faster than a legged course. In either case no gybing is entailed.

When the mark M is directly down the mean wind then the angled course OAM is

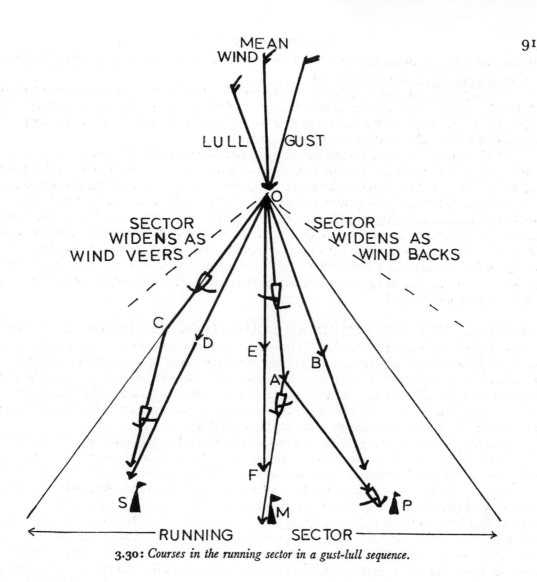

3.30: *Courses in the running sector in a gust-lull sequence.*

undoubtedly faster than the direct run OEF. They also both entail a gybe from port to starboard as the wind backs.

TIME SPENT IN THE GUSTS When beating, a faster craft will spend a shorter time in a gust than a slower one, for the relative speed of passing is roughly the addition of gust-cell speed and craft speed.

Before the wind, on the other hand, a faster craft can hold the strong impulse of the gust for longer than the slower. At the upper end of the possibilities is a craft which could run at the speed of the gust. Such an ideal mount would only come off a plane before the wind when the gust died a natural death.

Such sailing craft cannot exist, but the idea is right. A Dutchman which planes off before the wind at twice the speed of a Firefly will stay in the stronger wind for nearly twice as long as its shorter competitor.

Taking the ideal gust (Fig. 3.16) we find half a minute of 22 kt wind at a static point. A Firefly would do about 6 kt before this gust and the relative wind speed is thus 16 kt. The Dutchman might well make more than 12 kt, but we will assume the latter figure for argument's sake. The relative wind speed is then 10 kt.

Half a minute of strong wind timed by a stationary observer is extended to a little more than 40 seconds if one is running before the wind at 6 kt and to 66 seconds if running at 12 kt. This confers a tremendous advantage on long fast craft racing against shorter slower craft on handicap in gusty weather. Not only do they plane earlier and hold their planes in lighter wind than their shorter competitors, but they also stay in the strong wind for a proportionately longer time. The balance is not truly restored on the windward legs, as the shorter craft are not planing at any time, while the long ones may well plane to windward in the heavier wind. Other factors are the ability to slice through waves which slow shorter craft and the great advantage both actual and psychological of standing out clear away from the ruck.

FINDING THE REACHING AND RUNNING SECTORS It is notoriously difficult to judge the actual angle between pennant direction and the heading of the craft if it is less than 10°. The line of sight is usually so close to the vertical that one can have only a vague idea of the apparent wind direction. It would help one to maintain the fastest reaching and running speeds if one could recognise the centres of the sectors easily. They would be a yardstick by which to gauge whether the apparent wind was in fact being maintained in roughly the correct place as the wind shifted back and forth.

The simplest device is to fit stiff wire arms to the shaft of the racing flag in the appropriate directions (Fig. 3.31). These must be obtained by a helmsman from his own performance diagram as indicated earlier. The arms should lie as close under the balancing device of the flag as possible or parallax will induce a false reading. Also remember that if the mast rotates with the boom the shaft of the racing flag will do so too. The only way round this for the reaching sector is to locate the approximate angle of the boom to the centre-line when on the fastest point of reaching and then subtract this from the angle obtained from the apparent wind diagram. Because of the variation of the angle with wind speed, etc. only an approximate direction can be obtained (say correct for 15 kt) but it has already been shown that the variation in the apparent wind direction with craft and wind speeds is not great for conventional craft.

On rotating masts the shrouds will normally indicate the boom angle fairly clearly when running, and the necessary corrections can be made.

I think this device would be quite seamanlike, but that curious thing called, with big-ship grandeur, "flag-etiquette" may rule it out. It seems odd that on retirement and perhaps after a cold capsize one should be asked to lower the means by which the wind direction is obtained, thus making it more difficult to reach home safely in the shortest time. The usual fittings for racing flags in dinghies provide no directional stiffness, and one cannot give it to them without making the flag hard to strike. If the racing flag cannot be carried in a directionally-stiff seating then this device is out of the question.

It might however be adapted for larger craft with sufficient rigging to carry both a wind-direction indicator (be it flag or vane) and a racing flag which is capable of being

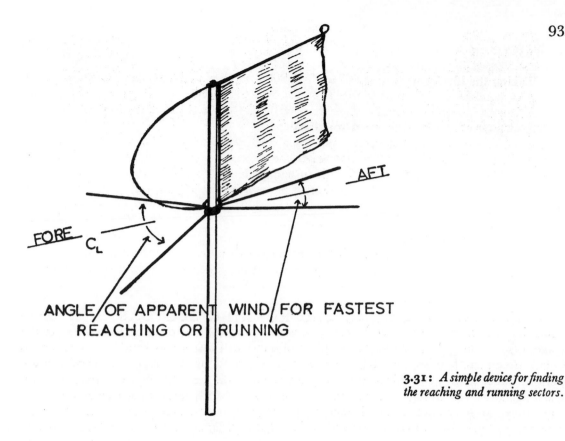

FORE C_L

AFT

ANGLE OF APPARENT WIND FOR FASTEST
REACHING OR RUNNING

3.31: *A simple device for finding the reaching and running sectors.*

struck, and it should materially aid the helmsman in selecting the fastest courses on those difficult points of sailing—reaching and running.

GUSTS AND THE RIVER If one is sailing in normal winds on narrow rivers there is a new factor to consider. It concerns the time of the wind features and the time of decision. To give a clear example: let the day be gusty with the mean wind at about 45° to the river. Let there be medium dense obstacles on the windward side. In the gaps the wind is fairly true but it cuts in strongly around the obstacles. Only the lee side of the river is out of the strongest part of the wind-shadow, and even then the surface wind is well below the true mean speed and angled by the trees and the banks. Into this quiet come the strongest gusts. Such puffs may leap up to 25 kt from a previous lull of 5–10 kt with a caprice that is well known to river sailors.

The gusts have only a very short distance beyond the tree-tops in which to reach the water, and so they need an express lift to bring them down. Thus only the air which is descending fastest reaches the surface of the river while the rest of the more slowly descending air finds itself on the lee bank and beyond. These fast parts of the gusts are very short-lived.

Let us take the upper anemogram of Fig. 3.3, page 55, as typical and imagine these

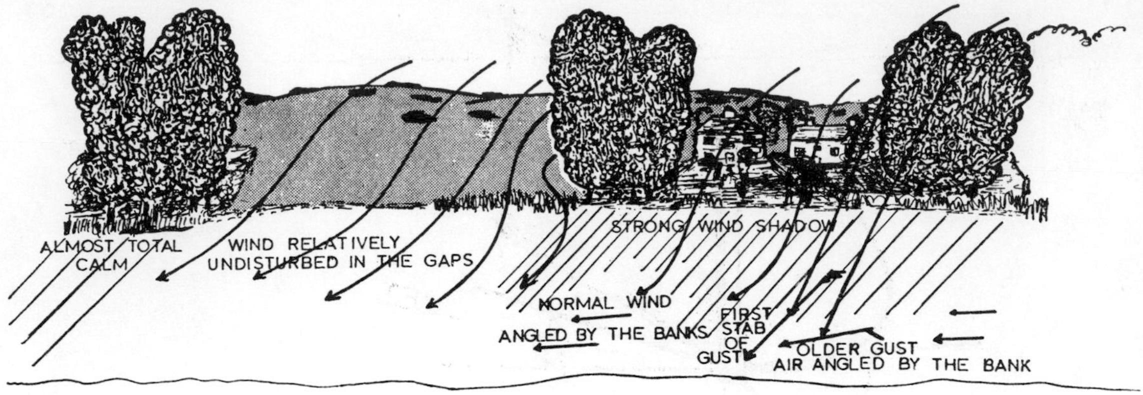

Labels in figure:
ALMOST TOTAL CALM | WIND RELATIVELY UNDISTURBED IN THE GAPS | STRONG WIND SHADOW | NORMAL WIND ANGLED BY THE BANKS | FIRST STAB OF GUST | OLDER GUST AIR ANGLED BY THE BANK

3.32: *To illustrate gusts on the river.*

conditions on the river depicted in Fig. 3.32 where the strongest puffs on the water are the spikes of the trace above 20 kt. Such spikes of wind will last for as little as 5–10 seconds before they pass, leaving the surface wind to be moulded by the river for a much longer period. Tacking to such shifts as these is really a matter of luck. Often they arrive without warning, and even though the waving and sighing tree-tops tell that something is on its way, they rarely say what. Crash tacking as the gust arrives occupies the time that the increase and veer is with you, after which the wind rapidly reverts to "river" wind again. Without a doubt gusts on the river are the shortest-lived and most frustrating of all gusts. One can at least say that as they are chunks of undisturbed wind from way above the sheltering trees they will have the direction of the wind aloft; so once a couple of gusts or the lower clouds have told you this direction then it is fair to expect the rest to come from the same direction. But if a meeting lasts for a whole day the passage of a front or a crop of thunderstorms may alter the whole wind situation. For instance a wind angled across the river in the morning can veer along it by the afternoon, in which case the gust–lull sequences will. be more normal as most of the gusts will be able to reach the water.

If we apply this argument to the general case of sailing in the direct lee of trees or other impediments, a 20 kt gust descending at 10 ft/sec arrives on the water in a distance of about $3h$ where h is the height of the trees (Fig. 3.33). The upper reaches of few British rivers are much more than 100 yds wide, and the tallest trees approach 100 ft, so only the most rapidly descending air at the head of the gust actually reaches the water. This is why the gusts are so sharp and short and why tacking to them, as one might in more open water, is likely to be frustrating and lose places. If the wind is angled strongly across very narrow waters with upwind barriers, true gusts can only be found on the lee side and be short-lived. As the angle of the wind to the river decreases so more of each gust will find its way on to the water. Then tacking to the veered wind is practicable.

When the general wind aloft is angled across the river, the surface wind will tend to be canalised along the river, and one will obviously have to make against it by short tacking on the lee side to stay in what wind there is. This will constantly bring the craft towards the

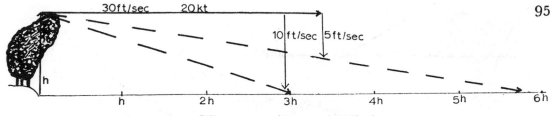

3.33: *Why gusts on rivers are short-lived.*

lee shallows and force one about. However it is not wise to go too soon—better even to lift the plate somewhat and pinch as long as possible, for a handy freeing gust is somewhere on its way if only you can hang on long enough. Sometimes it is possible to slide along the bank for a long way while more hasty competitors have tacked into the gust, into the stream, and by so doing have given you the gift of several places.

GUSTS AND SEA BREEZES Everything that has been said up to now about gustiness depends on the winds being the normal large-scale ones blowing at the behest of pressure systems like depressions and anticyclones. But in Chapter Five it will be shown that the sea breeze is a very prevalent local wind which can replace the normal wind on as many as half the days of summer. When the sea breeze is in action the normal sequence of gust and lull associated with veer and back will not always occur.

The wind features will then be quite different depending on the direction of the wind before the sea breeze set in. If it is offshore, cool sea air (which occupies only the lower 1000 ft or less) will flow in under warm land air. This situation of warm air over cold is stable, and one would not expect the two winds to mix. But the cool sea air is flowing over warm land, and this *is* unstable, so that convection currents can occur in the sea breeze current. They can be warm enough to penetrate the stable division between sea breeze and overlying offshore wind and thus bring it down to the surface. Now, since the offshore wind is flowing out above an onshore sea breeze, somewhere between the two opposed currents the wind must be zero or nearly so. It follows that the descending convection currents will bring down, not faster wind from aloft, but slower wind.

Thus what would normally be a gust is a lull while what would be a lull (where the air is rising) is stronger sea breeze.

The main points are illustrated in Fig. 3.34 where a hypothetical coastal sailing area has been split into two sectors. A red sector to "port" of the normal sea breeze direction and a green sector to starboard. Let the wind above the sea breeze be from the green sector. The surface wind will then be a mixture of the true sea breeze from seaward and puffs of green sector wind brought down by convection currents. The mean wind is not really very helpful here, for the mean rarely occurs. The wind is either sea breeze off the sea or it is a puff from above which having spent itself is replaced by the sea breeze again. The anemograms of such winds show strong direction changes, even though the wind speed is not much different between one direction and another.

The classic case is when the wind off the land is opposing a sea breeze and neither is really winning the battle. Then the wind is sometimes offshore and then goes onshore

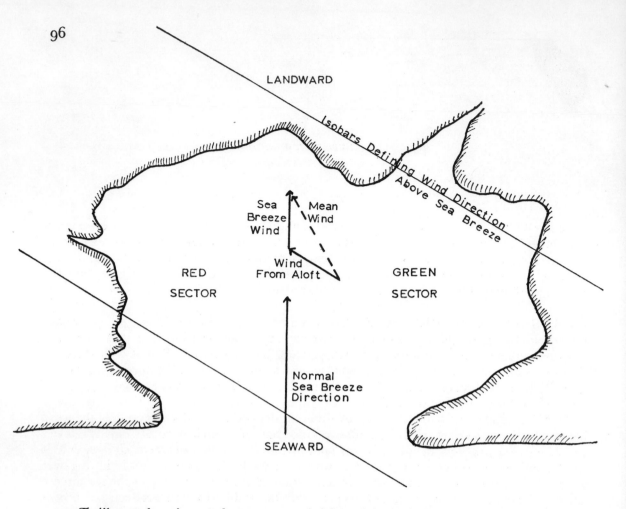

3.34: *To illustrate how, in a sea breeze current, wind from aloft may be backed to the surface wind rather than veered to it.*

only to revert a little later to offshore again. These violent and perplexing swings are relatively rare but they do occur. Figs. 5.2*f* (page 133) and 3.35*b*.

If the isobars had been orientated so that the wind above the sea breeze was from the red sector then the wind at the surface is again capable of being a mixture of wind and breeze.

Wind brought down from aloft is now veered to the normal sea breeze direction. If the wind above the breeze is light, "holes" of such wind turn up in the stronger onshore sea breeze. Here is one of the situations where veered wind is brought down from aloft. It is, however, lighter than the chunk of backed sea breeze which follows it. So lull and veer, gust and back form the sequence in direct opposition to the normal gust and veer, lull and back of a classic gusty airstream.

However, while such winds are "abnormal", they differ from the abnormal winds described in the next section by virtue of their more rapid time of repeat. This is of the order of 2–3 minutes rather than 5–7 minutes.

When the wind before the sea breeze is from the sea, all the sea breeze does is to reinforce it and perhaps shift its mean direction more nearly perpendicular to the coast, or whatever the sea breeze direction normally is. Now cool sea air arrives over heated land and convection is strong and deep. Gusty winds approaching gale force can be the result of the addition of an onshore wind and a strong sea breeze. But, as cloud usually results from strong convection currents, the sea breeze force tends to die as the cloud increases, so the process is often self-regulating. Even so, dry winds from the Continent can blow ashore on the south and east coasts in which no clouds develop, and these may get very strong and gusty in the afternoon.

AN ABNORMAL WIND SITUATION As a rule the wind veers as it gusts and backs as it lulls. But there are times when this pattern is reversed and then the wind will seem very curious. Under what sort of conditions will this anomalous situation occur?

An example is the three hours of wind from 0900 to 1200 G.M.T. 6 July 1959 recorded at Thorney Island (Fig. 3.35*a*). The wind was northerly and gusting to 15 kt, but during the three hours it gradually backed to a mean of about 300°. Not that means meant much, for it was one of those curiously variable mornings when the wind swings back and forth through 90° or more and the speed rises to as much as 10–15 kt and as rapidly sinks to practically nothing, sometimes for minutes on end. It seems from other similar anemograms which have been studied, that this "spikiness" in the wind is the characteristic feature of the inverted wind pattern.

By carefully assessing the major gusts and lulls for speed and direction it was possible to expand the first three hours of Fig. 3.35*a* and see what the wind direction did when the wind gusted and lulled (Fig. 3.36). If the wind is acting normally it will veer as it gusts and back as it lulls. If the lines connecting the gusts and lulls and the backs and veers slope in opposite directions the wind is abnormal, and the 27 instances out of the 35 wind shifts where veer accompanied lull and back accompanied gust are shown at the bottom of the diagram. Thus on 77 per cent of the occasions in this three hours the wind did the opposite to what it would do under normal circumstances.

Now that we have seen that, in one case at least, the wind can behave abnormally, and now that we know what to look for in anemograms, that is to say, corresponding speed and direction traces converging or diverging will indicate abnormal wind, while if they rise or fall together, the wind is normal, we can go on to look for further cases.

By taking three summer months from three succeeding years (June 1958, July 1959, August 1960) we can show that when the sea breeze is trying to come in (whether it actually does or not) periods of abnormal wind are the rule during the time that the forces that generate the sea breeze are at their strongest—that is during the hours 0900–1600 G.M.T. Similar local times would apply near other coasts overseas. The wind shifts backwards and forwards over periods measured in tens of minutes with back attending the strengthening wind and veer accompanying the wind as it slackens. The wind before the sea breeze of 14 July 1959 illustrates the point nicely (Fig. 3.35*b*). If we scan the speed and direction traces and find the periods of abnormal wind by noting when they converge to, or diverge from, one another, we shall find that this is what is happening in the two hours before the sea breeze eventually managed to get in (for an erratic half-hour). Abnormal

G

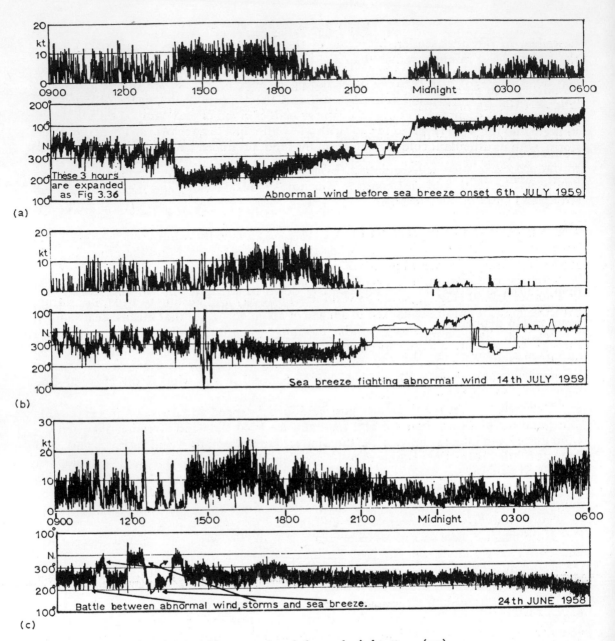

3.35: *Some examples of abnormal wind patterns* (MO).

wind which backs as it gusts and veers as it lulls is thus an indication that the sea breeze is coming, and this state of affairs is at its most obvious when the sea breeze is fighting the wind off the land for supremacy. If they are pretty evenly matched "swing in—swing out" is the order of the day.

Abnormal wind before a sea breeze will be mixed with normal wind when a battle ensues between the effects of local thunderstorms, the gradient wind and the sea breeze trying to press inshore. Such a fight is illustrated in Fig. 3.35c for 24 June 1958. The gradient wind was 250° 7 kt between 0900 and 0940, after which the sea breeze generating force tried to shift the wind towards south and the abnormal divergence of speed and direction traces occurred, but probably the growth of cloud inland damped the sea breeze strength and the wind reverted to 250° with a few attempts to go seaward. Then a thunderstorm, with its attendant cold rush of air off the land, produced a normal veer and increase for half an hour or so. When the storm drifted away the west-south-westerly wind came back. Then, just before midday, came another storm in whose calm rear the sea breeze managed to drift the wind to south, but not for long. The influence of the storm passed, and the south-westerly came back only to be bent to the will of yet another storm just before 1400, after which the fight between the normal south-westerly and the sea breeze force commenced and the way the speed and direction traces diverge and converge over the same periods of time (notably 1500–1700 diverging and 1700–1800 converging) is quite marked. After 1800 the sea breeze generating force has failed, and so the wind then returns to normal for the night, going down in strength and backing ahead of a depression. The previous thunderstorms were probably there in association with a front from an old depression.

Thus the abnormality of the wind over the coast on summer days is demonstrated and must be allowed for. If it is found that backing accompanies the wind increases then it is reasonable to expect this to be the main pattern of wind changes when the other conditions make it likely. These conditions are those which make for a strong sea breeze generating potential, *i.e.* clear skies and some instability.

TACKING TO THE ABNORMAL WIND The correct reaction to such a wind is to try to be on port as the wind increases and on starboard as it decreases, which is the exact opposite of the advice given earlier for the normal wind with its gust and veer, back and lull.

By using the data of Fig. 3.36 the technique can be illustrated. The average period between gust and lull over the first 30 minutes is 6 minutes and this seems to be usual for this sort of abnormal wind situation. The changes are on the whole relatively gentle compared to the normal gust which rises rapidly in a period measured in seconds. These abnormal rises and falls occupy minutes, the wind advancing and retreating towards the new direction and speed in a series of swings which eventually result in increase and back or decrease and veer.

Fig. 3.37 shows a dinghy on port tack beating towards a mark M which is in the direction of the mean wind—in this case north. The wind at time zero is (Fig. 3.36) from 320°, *i.e.* backed some 40° from the mean direction. The wind begins to decrease and veer, so a port tack yacht will be forced to bear away towards its position 5 minutes later when the wind has fully veered to 020° and dropped to virtually nothing. Two courses have been shown and these are smoothed for convenience, as the end result is not greatly affected by this simplification.

Course A shows what happens to a yacht which sails for the first 12 minutes to the wind as it comes and makes no effort to tack.

Helmsman B employs the technique of tacking whenever his course shows signs of

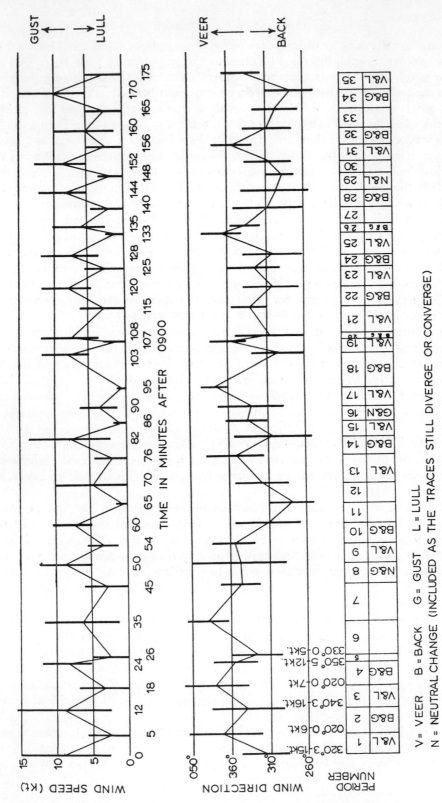

3·36: *The first three hours of Fig. 3.35a expanded to illustrate the pattern of abnormal wind. The blanks in the table are periods when the wind was normal.*

V = VEER B = BACK G = GUST L = LULL

N = NEUTRAL CHANGE (INCLUDED AS THE TRACES STILL DIVERGE OR CONVERGE)

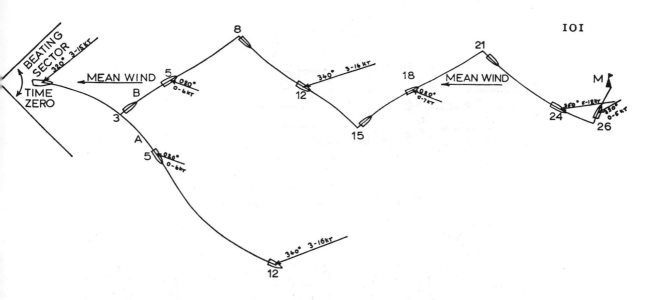

3.37: *To illustrate tacking to an abnormal wind pattern.*

wandering from the "beating sector". This is the sector spanning 45° on either side of the mean wind direction. To simplify matters the mark has been placed in that direction also. After 3 minutes on port tack B sees his course moving out of the beating sector, and, with the wind showing every sign of continuing to veer, he tacks and thus takes advantage of the second half of the veer to make to windward. After 5 minutes he is on the mean course again with the wind at its lowest ebb, even going to zero at times, which happens in this sort of anomalous situation. This very low wind speed tells of a probable increase and back, but the starboard tack course is still well within the beating sector, so he continues sailing on this tack for a further 3 minutes. Then he tacks and the diagram shows how this technique must provide the greatest way to windward as one is never outside the beating sector and for most of the time well within it. A course within the beating sector is bound to be advantageous. The rest of the diagram can be followed with the aid of Fig. 3.36.

Note that the technique of tacking to be on the advantageous tack within the beating sector is a more leisurely one than when tacking to gust cells. In the latter case crash-tacking on to starboard for the gust is imperative if the maximum advantage is to be gained. The simple difference is the rate of rise of a true gust compared to these slower changes.

TACTICS IN A VARIABLE WIND WHEN THE NEXT MARK IS NOT IN THE EYE OF THE WIND

It is obviously very rare for the next mark to lie dead to windward, except perhaps on the first leg of a course which has been properly prepared from a careful assessment of the wind field. Thus some thought must be given to the veering-backing pattern whether this be due to an abnormal or normal gust and lull sequence. If one always sails at the maximum speed the wind will allow

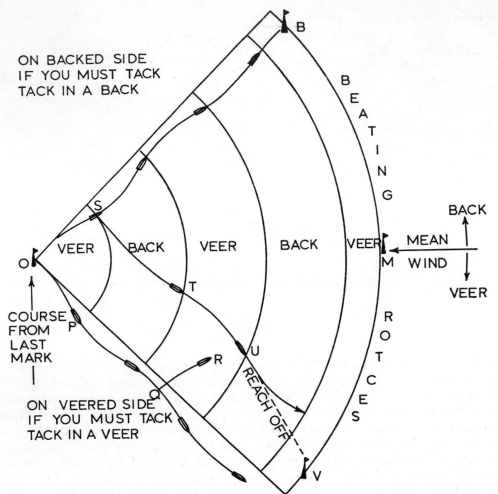

3.38a: *Some rules for gaining maximum advantage in an abnormal wind situation when the mark is not in the eye of the mean wind.*

then only direction changes are important, and it does not matter much whether they are accompanied by an increase or decrease of wind strength.

The mark must be within the beating sector, or no true windward work is entailed, so let us assume in Fig. 3.38a that the mark is at B on the side backed from the mean wind direction but still within the beating sector.

First one must decide whether the wind is veering or backing when the mark O is rounded. If the wind-pattern is repeating at intervals of 5 minutes, as often occurs in such wind situations, one can forecast the wind pattern in the latter part of the reaching leg, and the likely situation at the mark. Even if the stress of the race makes this impossible, one can often assess the wind change which is in progress at the mark and act accordingly.

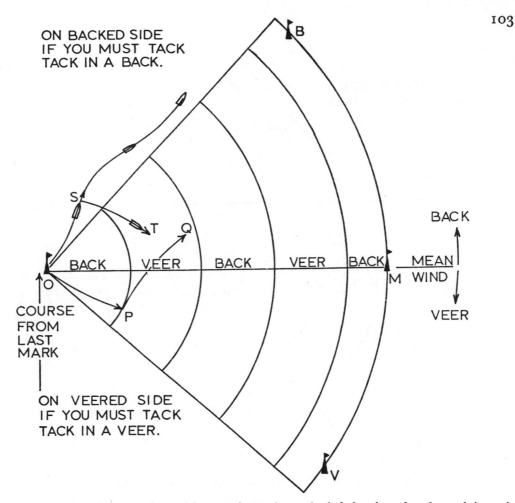

ON BACKED SIDE
IF YOU MUST TACK
TACK IN A BACK.

COURSE
FROM
LAST
MARK

ON VEERED SIDE
IF YOU MUST TACK
TACK IN A VEER.

BACK   VEER   BACK   VEER   BACK   MEAN
WIND

BACK

VEER

3.38b: *Some rules for gaining maximum advantage in an abnormal wind situation when the mark is not in the eye of the mean wind.*

If the mark is at B on the backed side of the beating sector and the wind is veering, then in Fig. 3.38a OS shows that it is advantageous to hold on.

If the mark is on the veered side it is also advantageous to hold on and then tack, preferably when the wind begins to back again (OST).

This is in deference to a rule which can be formulated for tacking in a variable wind.

In the *backed* octant of the beating sector if you must tack then tack in a *back*.

If on the *veered* side then tack in a *veer*.

Examples are OST and OPQR in Fig. 3.38a and OPQ in Fig. 3.38b. With the course from the last mark as shown, then coming about round the mark O in a veering wind hauls a craft out of the beating sector (OP Fig. 3.38a) and away from the intended mark. But if it was imperative to come about at O then follow the dictum to tack in a suitable veer (QR) as you are on the veered side of the beating sector. Holding on along OS on the backed side tells of not tacking until the wind begins to back.

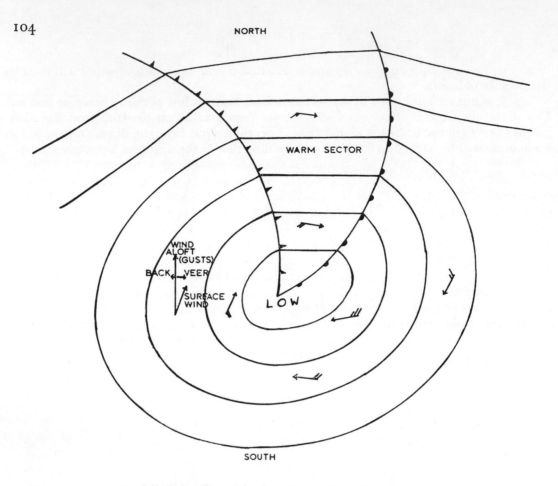

3.39: *Winds and fronts of a depression in the southern hemisphere.*

Similarly when the wind is backing when one rounds the mark O (Fig. 3.38*b*) a tack about the mark is good, as tacking in a back is allowed when the mark is at B.

The course OST in Fig. 3.38*b* is obviously quite out of phase with the wind shifts.

It must be pointed out that although the wide direction changes which accompany abnormal gust–lull sequences have been used to introduce these rules they are applicable in any wind situation. They are just more likely to be effective in the more leisurely back–veer sequences of abnormal wind.

GUSTS DOWN-UNDER   It must be explained why the wind in gusts will be backed from the mean direction in the southern hemisphere in direct opposition to gusts being veered to the mean in the northern.

Winds rotate about lows and highs in the exactly opposite sense in the southern hemisphere. That is, Buys Ballot's Law must be re-written as:

"Stand **facing** the wind in the southern hemisphere and Low pressure is on your Left."

Thus the winds and fronts of a southern hemisphere depression will be somewhat as in Fig. 3.39. The warm air is on the north side nearest the equator and winds will back on the passage of fronts.

The winds will still blow in across the isobars towards low pressure however and will flow along the isobars above the friction layer (again taken as around 2000 feet aloft) just as they do in the northern hemisphere. Therefore wind brought down from 2000 feet up in gusts will be backed to its mean surface direction in the southern hemisphere.

Therefore a helmsman who has learned the correct reaction to gusts in one hemisphere must anticipate an intrinsically odd feel to his mount under similar conditions in the other hemisphere. Helmsmen of equal calibre bred in opposite hemispheres and competing under identical conditions may well lose the edge in a beat to windward if the sailing site lies in the unfamiliar half of the world. While the reactions of years cannot normally be overcome in a few sorties at least the knowledge that the strongest wind will come from the opposite side of the mean wind to normal could go some way towards redressing the imbalance which is inherent in the fine structure of wind.

It follows that anywhere in these pages where an obvious back or veer favours one tack or the other then that advantage will be gained on the other tack in the southern hemisphere. Interested readers must perforce work out the correct reactions for themselves should they be contemplating sailing in the opposite hemisphere to the one in whose wind cradle they have been reared.

CHAPTER FOUR

Things in the Wind

AT various points in the previous chapters the effect of surface friction and obstacles in the wind's path has had to be taken into account. For instance in Chapter Two we saw how the wind varied in strength and direction with height in the friction layer of the atmosphere (the deck below about 2000 feet). It was said that as a rough rule the wind will be twice as strong over the sea as over the land while the wind at 2000 feet will be three times as strong as that over the land.

Taking the very lowest layer of the atmosphere—what can be called the sailing layer the wind near the surface varies with the size of objects in its path and with the degree of stability of the atmosphere. But only relatively small objects can be taken into account when considering the way the wind increases with height in the sailing layer.

It is evident that larger obstacles to the wind are going to upset any smooth flow over the land and the shoreside objects are going to have a supreme influence on the wind in any land-locked or shoreside locality.

While small objects produce small-scale turbulence, which will generally be smaller in size than a sailing craft, bigger objects such as trees and buildings will induce eddies in the wind whose size is somewhat bigger than the objects.

The following table gives some representative heights of shoreside objects:

		Fully grown trees	
Bungalow	15–20 feet	Lombardy poplars	100 feet
2-storey house	23–30 feet	Ash and elm	100–150 feet
3-storey house	35–40 feet	Larch and oak	80–100 feet
Boat sheds	25–40 feet	Birch and Scots pine	60–80 feet
		White willow (unpollarded)	70–80 feet
		Alder	30–40 feet

Fully grown trees can produce eddies which are perhaps 200 feet in diameter but, of course, there must be enough of them to impede the wind on a broad front or else the wind which goes through the gaps breaks up the eddies which have been formed by the wind going over the top.

There is very little practical value in knowing the sizes of eddies except to infer that in a stable airstream they may be the only way in which the air layers can be mixed. This fact is brought out in the following table which shows the heights in feet to which turbulence usually extends under normal (day sailing) and stable (night-time) conditions. It is well to remember that the stability of the airstream over the open sea depends on the relative temperature of air and sea. If the air is cooler than the sea surface the airstream is unstable, while if a warm wind flows over a cooler sea the airstream is stable—and liable to fog and low cloud.

TABLE 4.A: *Height in feet to which turbulence extends*

Wind Force	Normal conditions Land	Sea	Wind Force	Stable conditions Land	Sea
1	500	300	1	220	100
2	1200	700	2	700	350
3	2000	1300	3	1300	800
4	3000	2000	4	1700	1200
5	4000	3000	5	2200	1700
6	5000	4000	6	2700	2000

The table shows that the depth of 2000 ft usually assumed for the friction layer is only very approximate. It is true over the land under normal conditions but not over the sea unless the wind is Force 4 or more. When the airstream is stable the winds have to be Force 5 or 6 over land and sea respectively before the full 2000 ft is affected by turbulence.

This table does not take into account strong convection when cumulus and cumulo-nimbus clouds push up to thousands of feet higher than the figures quoted. Values cannot be given then, for the only criterion is how far aloft the convection can penetrate. Certainly wind speed has some effect, but it is largely indirect such as the ability of strong winds to shear off the tops of big cumulus clouds and prevent them growing into cumulo-nimbus.

When conditions are stable the table gives the size of the eddies produced, for they have to be forced against the natural inclination of stable air to sink rather than rise. The eddies can only occur due to the upward deflections the wind receives from objects in its path. The wind, for instance, slides up the backs of waves and is lifted, but in a Force 1–2 wind it is only pushed up by a couple of hundred feet, and after that the natural tendency takes over and it sinks back.

When conditions are normal the wind is forced up by an object, be it tree or building, and the tendency to sink is replaced by a tendency to rise. Thus the sizes of eddies are about twice as great.

The wind at the top of the layer that is mixed by turbulent eddies is the strongest wind that will find its way to the surface. But, as in general the wind increases with height, the deeper the mixing the stronger the mean wind and the stronger the gusts.

If the wind should decrease in strength with height the wind near the surface will be the stronger wind and the eddies will bring down slower wind from above. This has been described in "Abnormal Winds" on page 96.

BARRIERS TO THE WIND   Those who have studied shelter-belts for crops have unwittingly given sailing people some very useful information about the wind in the lee of large objects.

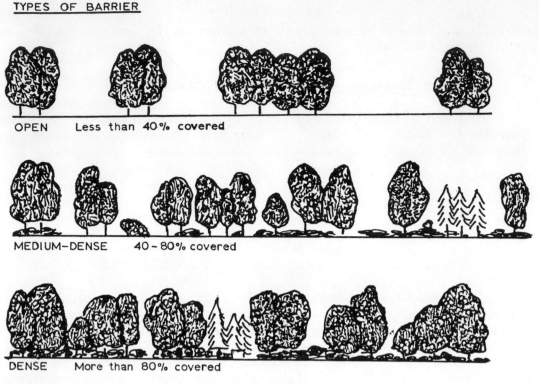

OPEN   Less than 40% covered

MEDIUM-DENSE   40 - 80% covered

DENSE   More than 80% covered

4.1: *Types of barrier.*

Agriculturalists are interested in the sort of arrangement of trees that will keep the strongest wind from damaging vulnerable crops in its lee. For this purpose three sorts of barrier have been defined[13].

(1) An open barrier = less than 40 per cent of the frontal area covered.

(2) A medium-dense barrier = between 40 and 80 per cent covered.

(3) A dense barrier = more than 80 per cent covered.

Examples of these barriers in the form of trees are given in Fig. 4.1. Such barriers are encountered most by river and lake sailors. An open barrier might be a line of willows or osiers stretching along a river bank. A medium-dense barrier might consist of a closer, deeper, grove of trees at the foot of a long terraced garden ending on the bank. A dense barrier could be a really large and deep thicket of trees, bushes and general undergrowth stretching into the water. Dense barriers must be impenetrable to the wind and therefore woods and copses must be wide in the wind direction to qualify. Dense barriers can also be a line of buildings sitting close together with the spaces between them filled up with garages, etc.

In general, to qualify as a barrier there must be a uniform distribution of the objects which are interfering with the wind. Detached houses with spaces between them which are greater than the house widths themselves would perhaps qualify as open barriers, but the wind in their lee would normally not be quite what we find for an open barrier of trees.

The practical way to measure the effects downwind of a barrier is to record it in terms

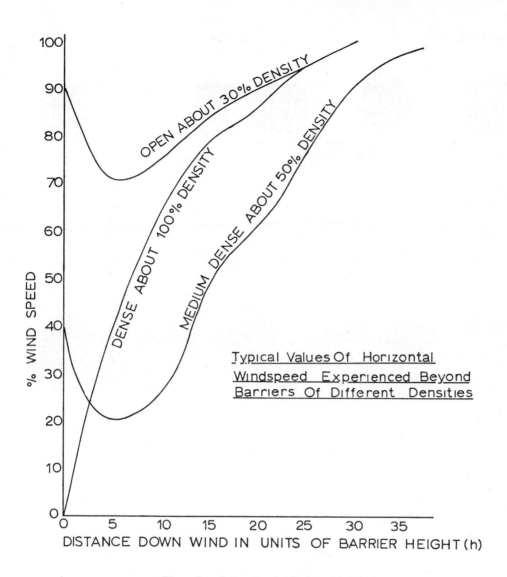

4.2: *How the wind varies in the lee of barriers.*[13]

of the height *h* of the barrier. Then at the outset we can say that 30–40*h* is the practical limit to the effects on the wind. Inside this range the wind is slowed by having to flow over the barrier. It regains its full strength beyond the 30*h* limit. Thus if the average height of a copse proves to be 100 feet then the wind in its lee does not become normal again for a full 3000 feet, *i.e.* 1000 yards, or a sixth of a nautical mile.

In Fig. 4.2 the rather surprising results of wind speed measurements downwind of the three types of barriers are shown. Only with the dense barrier does the wind do what one might expect: it increases from zero at the lee edge to its full strength at 30*h*. With both the open barrier and the medium-dense one the wind is stronger close under the lee edges than it is a little further out. This odd result accounts for the often uncanny way in which

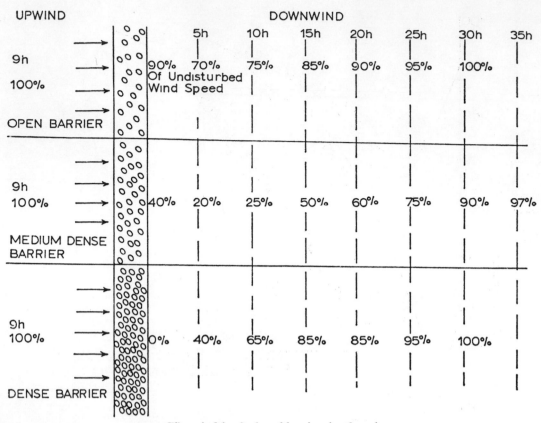

4.3: *The wind in the lee of barriers in plan view.*

certain river helmsmen manage to creep along the very edge of the stream and into the lead while their deeper water opponents struggle vainly with next to no wind.

The effect is to reduce the wind in lee of an open barrier from 90 per cent of the full wind speed, when the racing flag is brushing the branches, to 70 per cent at $5h$ from the barrier, after which the wind climbs up to 90 per cent again at about $20h$ (Fig. 4.3).

The width of British rivers is not normally vast, and with a 100 foot barrier the mini-mum wind speed is to be found at 500 feet from the shore, so this may well be on the lee bank of the river or beyond it. Thus with an open barrier it may happen that, quite contrary to what one would think, the chap on the windward "blanketed" shore will have more wind than those who have chosen the more obvious leeward shore.

The same goes for the medium-dense barrier, only more so. Close under the trees one may find 40 per cent of full wind speed; this drops to 20 per cent at $5h$, climbs back to 30 per cent at $15h$ and then gently increases to full wind speed at $40h$. The medium-dense barrier is without a doubt the biggest disturber of the wind in its lee. The wind beyond a blank wall of height h is stronger at $5h$ than it is at the same distance downwind of a medium-dense barrier of the same height. Moreover the medium-dense barrier prevents

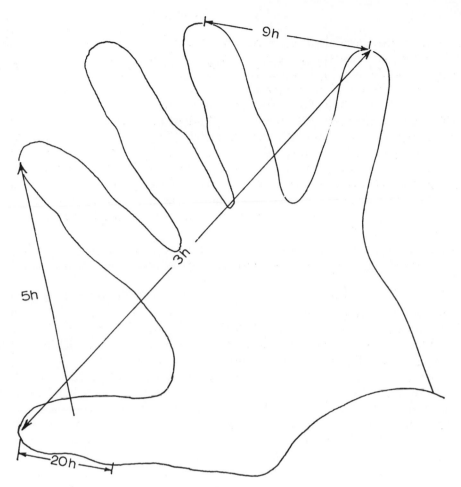

4.4: *The hand as a yardstick of distance-off.*

the wind from regaining its full strength for a full 10*h* further than the other two barriers.

For the helmsman who wishes to take advantage of these facts some simple yardsticks must be provided. Assuming that there is normally 25 inches between the eye and the outstretched fingers of an outstretched arm the following are useful natural yardsticks (Fig. 4.4):

For 5*h*: the distance thumb to tip of forefinger (5 inches)
For 20*h*: the distance knuckle to tip of thumb   (1¼ inches)
For 30*h*: the thumbnail   (5/6 inch)

Obviously people's personal dimensions will differ, but the above general criteria are useful.

The distance 20*h* is the practical limit within which the wind speed is much reduced. With open and dense barriers the wind is back to 90 per cent at this distance. Only the medium-dense barrier will keep the wind speed down to 60 per cent at this distance. A barrier which is 50 per cent covered is the most effective of all.

The reason the wind behaves as it does in the lee of these barriers is this. The dense barrier forms a pocket of still air directly to leeward and the wind coming over the top flows down the back of this close little pocket and rapidly recovers.

The medium-dense barrier, however, allows some wind to trickle through and this extends the region of near stagnation much farther. The wind above this has to come down over the low-speed cushion and only regains its strength at a correspondingly greater distance from the barrier. The minimum speed at $5h$ is due to a war between opposing winds. That which is filtering through the trees meets the strongest reverse wind in the roller eddy, which forms in the lee of the barrier as the wind comes over the top. The filtering wind wins, but its initial 40 per cent speed is reduced to a mere 20 per cent by having to fight the roller.

A similar explanation applies to the open barrier, but, of course, here the wind which flows through the gaps is strong enough to counteract the effect of the rolling eddy very quickly.

If there is a succession of barriers and the distance between them is $40h$ or more the effects are not cumulative. For instance an upwind wood of height 80 feet will have no effect on another which is 1000 yards or half a mile downwind of it. But it is often difficult to assess what lies to windward of a shoreside barrier, and therefore the distances, etc., that have been given are likely to be the maximum one can expect.

Strong convection will also affect the wind speeds and distances. When there is instability the gusts brought down from levels far above the barrier height will precipitate into the regions of low wind speed. Occasionally, as these descending gusts miss the immediate shoreside zone, the craft farther out from an open or medium-dense barrier will have more wind. When one is obliged to sail in a "canyon" between trees, the wind brought down in gusts is often all the wind there is; thus a puff will appear and then there will be a flat calm until the next puff comes along. If there are no gusts, tree-lined confines of this sort will be quite devoid of wind unless it happens to be blowing along them, and even then the wind will be fitful.

The shape of the area affected in lee is a blunt triangle of reduced wind, so that the distance through which one has to sail is less the farther one goes from the barriers. This may sometimes make it advantageous to sail farther from a barrier even though the results in Fig. 4.3 would not make it appear so.

Another interesting question is how far to *windward* of a barrier the wind begins to be affected. The wind reduction starts at about $9h$ to windward of the barrier. Thus it is better to be outside this limit if other considerations are not more pressing. A yardstick for this distance will also be found in Fig. 4.4.

A barrier 80-100 feet high will affect the wind for some 300 yards to windward. Admittedly the wind will not be affected greatly at this distance, but the speed will fall very rapidly as a stagnant cushion builds up and the rest of the wind rides over the top. The cushion will, of course, only be stagnant with a dense barrier where the wind speed must fall from full strength to zero in a short $9h$. While there are no actual figures for the percentage wind speeds upwind of a barrier one can infer that with a dense barrier they will be as given in Fig. 4.5. With the other types of barrier it is more difficult to judge, for in the case of a medium dense barrier, covering about 50 per cent of the frontal area,

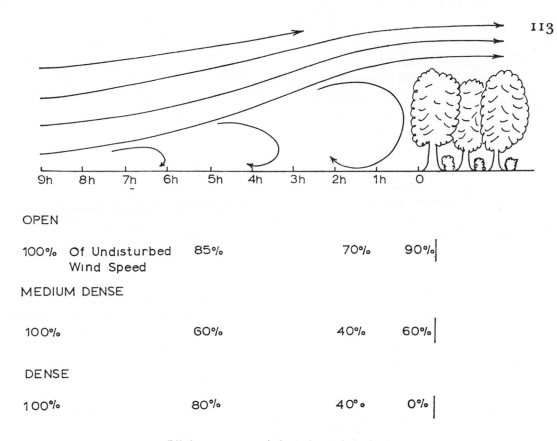

9h	8h	7h	6h	5h	4h	3h	2h	1h	0

OPEN

100% Of Undisturbed Wind Speed	85%		70%	90%

MEDIUM DENSE

100%	60%		40%	60%

DENSE

100%	80%		40°°	0%

4.5: *Likely percentage wind speeds upwind of a barrier.*

some 40 per cent of the wind speed survives the passage through it. This means that the wind as it enters the barrier must be stronger than 40 per cent. I have therefore assumed, though this is open to doubt, that the wind is 60 per cent of its undisturbed speed right up to the trees, and again it must occur that the wind speed a little farther from the shore is less than this, say 40 per cent. The open barrier will hardly affect the windward side at all, but all the same one would be wise to avoid that minimum at about $2h$. Though there is no $2h$ yardstick on a normal hand, there is one for $3h$ which will enable one to avoid the area of minimum wind area.

While the height of the barrier is the primary property which affects the wind around it, the shape and size in the direction of the wind also have a bearing. Of course, a dinghy sailor may well be unable to assess the shape and size of the barrier, but Fig. 4.6 gives the facts[22]. A barrier which is wedge-shaped with the thick end towards you slows up the wind more than one with the thin end of the wedge stooping down to the water. Moreover a relatively narrow belt of trees, etc., will slow up the wind more than a wide one. At first sight this may seem odd, but one must remember that anything which smooths out the wind's passage over it will contribute to orderly flow in its lee. A flat plate held perpendicular to a wind provides far more drag than an aerofoil section of the same depth, and

H

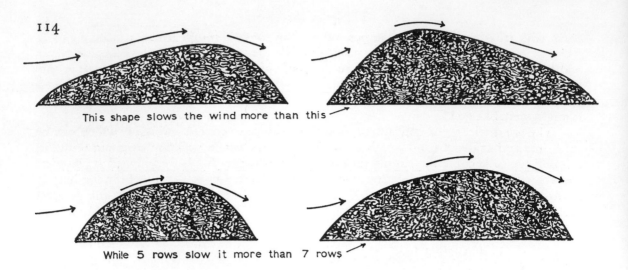

This shape slows the wind more than this

While 5 rows slow it more than 7 rows

4.6: *How the shapes of barriers affect the wind in their lee.*[23]

these extremes embrace all the possible conformations of shape in between. Thus the longer and smoother the top of a barrier is, and the more its shoreside trees drop away, the quicker will the wind return to normal in lee. This shoreside dipping of the trees must be taken into account when looking at Figs. 4.2 and 4.3. The wind speed will generally be greater than the given percentages when a great tangle of trees spreads back from the water's edge because the tree-tops will usually follow the contours of the bank on which they grow.

I had occasion once to regret not having this knowledge. You may know Frensham Pond in the heathy commonlands of Surrey. It is a good-sized and delightful lake with a sandy shore on its north side and an almost continuous line of woods and copses on the southern side. It was their annual open meeting for Fireflies, and late in the season, but the wind was kind, and on a pond without waves we had done well enough to hope for a place if we could pull something out of the bag in the last race of the series. The wind was southerly right over those trees and we were inexperienced in the ways of wind barriers. It seemed good tactics to start as far upwind as possible for the starting line was along the wind direction. The locals knew better, and, starting in our lee they and their gaggle just left us standing—an ignominious start from which we never recovered. Today I should hold up the $9h$ yardstick of my thumb and make sure that whatever other tactical advantage I sacrificed I should at least be outside that zone of frustration.

On lakes such as Frensham and on rivers like the Thames long wooded shores may be your happy lot, but there are also the gaps. Woods give way to meadow, and tree-lined banks are cut short for the habitations of humans and boats. Lower Thames clubs sail under the capricious hand of winds dropping and stabbing willy-nilly from every crack and crevice in the environs of the embankment. Gravel-pit sailors will have to contend with the contours left by the unheeding arm of drag-lines. Always there are holes, and they can be very upsetting in every sense of the word.

It is well known that the wind seeks the gaps in the shoreside barriers. It cuts through them with increased force, and in general we can make a rough rule that size of gap × increase in speed it produces is a constant. This is the same as saying that a gap of a certain width will produce twice the increase in speed of one which is twice that width. It is only the *increase* in speed that is referred to here, not the actual speed. One does not expect a gap to produce a 30 kt wind from a 15 kt one, although when that wind suddenly hits you it might seem like 30 kt.

The wind tries to be continuous, and this is another general principle which can be used time and again. A wind which is thwarted by an obstacle will flow over and round it, but will try to become the simple uncomplicated thing it was before it met the barrier. Thus it will cut round the edges to try to fill the stagnation in lee. Its flow from the barrier edges to where it resumes its normal flight will be a converging one with the greatest tendency to converge just beyond the barrier. Obviously the dense barriers and buildings near the edge will produce the starkest effects with the wind going from nothing to tens of knots without warning. It is the unstable day with shower clouds about which will upset the most boats in these conditions, for the wind will be channelled by the surface objects and in any local spot this would seem to be the wind direction. The gusts, however, coming down on their eddy escalators do not know what the surface wind is doing. They arrive literally out of the blue with increased speed and a direction bequeathed them by the isobaric tramlines. There is something therefore to be gained on a gusty day in restricted inland waters from observing the direction of the cloud movement. This will usually be the gust direction. To this one must add a mental picture of the wind flowing about and around the shoreside obstacles. For instance if the clouds are from the north-west this will be the direction which virgin gusts will assume. If the river happens at some point to be orientated east-west, and rather densely cluttered with buildings and trees, the surface wind will be channelled east-west, too. The lightest wind will therefore tend to come from the west, while the gusts (clear of the clutter) will be from the north-west. However any gaps will take a gust and try to turn it parallel to themselves. It may bluster out of a hole in the shore barrier at right angles to the gentler wind which it replaced, or it may just become channelled along the river itself. Either way the basic rules are that the lighter wind will tend to flow along the river while the gusts will tend to come from the direction that the lower clouds are taking (Fig.3.32).

The previous remarks on wind barriers tended to assume the wind was perpendicular to the line of the barrier, and this is, of course, a special case. What happens to this pattern when the wind strikes at an angle to the barrier? The Royal Aircraft Establishment did some work in 1938 on this problem in connection with barriers to protect aircraft at dispersal. What they found out is interesting. Fig. 4.7 illustrates what happens beyond a medium-dense barrier when the wind is at 90°, 75° and 45° to the barrier. The main point is that the greater the angle of the wind from the perpendicular to the barrier the closer in will the wind resume its normal strength. But the effects on the wind tends to stretch beyond the end of the barrier farthest from the wind. It also appears that at fairly acute angles (75° case) the wind beyond a barrier develops gustiness off the end farthest from the wind. As the angle increases so this gustiness tends to be ironed out. The reason seems to lie in the rapid way the wind speed increases and flows parallel to the barrier. Any given wind speed will be found at about half the distance from the barrier when the wind strikes at 45° rather than perpendicularly.

To illustrate this with some practical experience anyone who has used Bosham

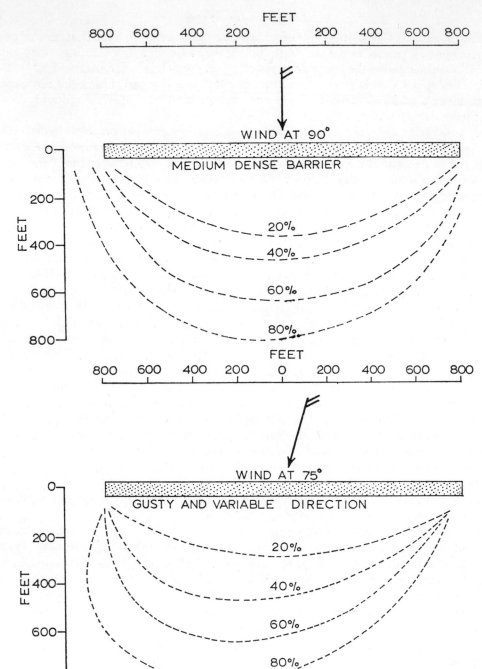

4·7 *a and b: The results of tests on a medium-dense barrier with the wind at 90°, and 75° to the barrier* [8].

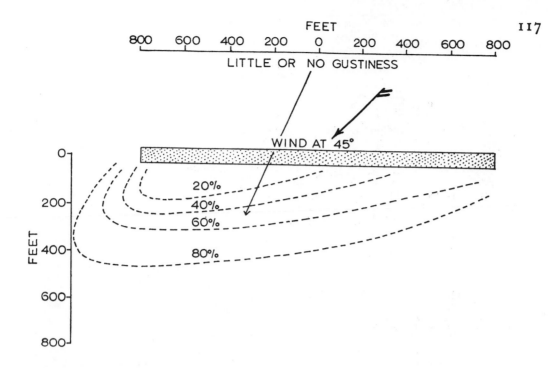

4.7c: *The results of tests on a medium dense barrier with the wind at 45° to the barrier.*[8]

Channel, or has raced from Cobnor Hard, or perhaps used Cobnor buoy as a turning mark, will know the considerable effect that the copse to the immediate north of the Hard has on the wind over the water there. If the reader has not, he can obtain a picture of this locality from Fig. 4.8, and there will undoubtedly be places he knows which are akin to it.

The overall height above low water of the shore, bank and copse itself is perhaps around 50 feet and the barrier is not very wide and can probably be considered to be medium-dense. At low water when getting away from the Hard there is a very noticeable lack of wind when it is from somewhere around west, but as soon as you push off the wind climbs in strength very quickly. This is good evidence for the general correctness of the rule that the minimum wind speed occurs at around $5h$, for the plan shows that this 5×50 = 250 ft line comes right along the water's edge at low water. Moreover $15h$ lies over the mud on the far side of the channel and the wind is not much more than half of its undisturbed speed over the whole of the available water. Thus sometimes with a westerly of some strength a quiet start off the Hard develops into a screaming plane and a barging match at the not-far-distant Deep End buoy, for Cobnor Point is largely unencumbered and the wind gathers almost its full force before one is clear of the land fetch.

Even so it is surprising the degree of shelter afforded by the barrier of the sea wall, for its top is some 20 feet above low water. The $20h$ practical limit to the shelter of a dense barrier such as a sea wall (found from Fig. 4.2) comes near the middle of the channel at low water and shows just how far the sheltering effects of quite modest shoreside barriers can extend.

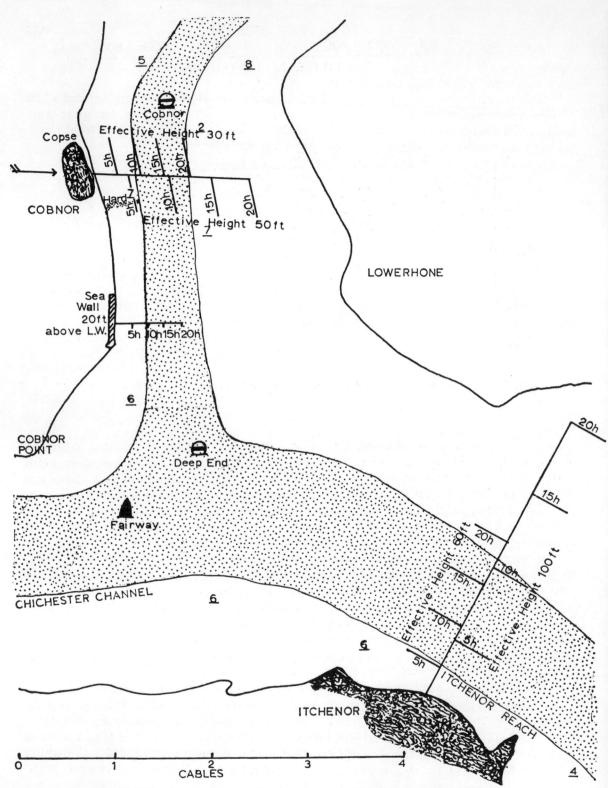

4.8: *Part of Chichester Harbour to illustrate the extensive influence of shoreside barriers.*

Of course, when one beats out into Chichester Channel one finds the wind has developed a force not far removed from twice its mean overland speed, and this again is very noticeable when the wind is strong.

This example illustrates amongst other things the advisability of a prudent reef when leaving a sheltered anchorage. It can always be shaken out if not required, but quite open land-locked anchorages afford a great deal of shelter. It will not hurt to do a wind check with the anemometer on the sea wall if possible, or somewhere reasonably open, and then be prepared for twice this wind speed if you are going clear of the land.

A racing helmsman will generally, of course, carry that amount of sail with which to outsail his competitors, but how often in a blow have the leaders been those with rather more reef than the others or those who have lowered their jibs.

Take one more example illustrated in Fig. 4.8, the village of Itchenor, with its small medium-dense mass of buildings, nestling amongst trees. An effective height of 60 feet might not be too far out as a barrier height and then $5h$ is again along the low-water edge as shown. With southerly winds this is confirmed by the almost total lack of wind which is found along this shore when one is trying to make Itchenor Hard, or the sailing club's jetty. Again $20h$ is as wide as Itchenor Reach itself at low water and at any time the wind is not normal again before the opposite mud banks are reached.

The gaps, however, will cause some spectacular planes suddenly to occur amongst the mass of moored craft, and many a capsize results. A village like Itchenor will shelter its own private waters, but the wind will try to get its own back by being stronger than normal through the gaps which must inevitably surround a small creek-side village.

The effective heights given above are those which are considered to be representative. They may in fact be underestimates, but, whether they are or not, Fig. 4.8 is only an illustration, and so, as well as the 50 ft copse, a 30 ft copse has also been included. Even so at low water the wind is still reduced across the whole channel.

Again Itchenor might well be a barrier of effective height 100 ft, in which case the $5h$ minimum is out on the water and the practical limit of $20h$ is on the farther shore.

The moral is: never underestimate the effect of a barrier, and the only effective action is to use the yardsticks and sail outside the worst of the blanketing.

CLIFFS, HILLS AND PROMONTORIES

One afternoon I walked out on the Naze—that elevated promontory which projects from Walton-on-Naze towards Harwich. The wind was a very normal offshore afternoon wind, about Force 4–5, as far as could be judged, and moderately gusty. The Naze is not sheer anywhere, but it is steep-to enough not to interfere with the flow of air leaving the edge for the water beyond. With wind that was not exceptionally gusty, this was a chance to observe the gusts going down on to the water and chasing one another out to sea. The main point of my close observation of these gusts was to see just how far from the cliff-edge the gusts got down on to the water.

The distance was about 200 yards, and as the Naze is about 70 feet at this point above mean sea level the distance proved to be about $10h$. Thus if we take the mean wind speed as 15 kt the gusts were sinking at a tenth of that rate, *i.e.* at about 1·5 kt.

This value ties in rather well with other people's estimates of the sinking speeds of gusts and enables us to make a rough rule that under normal gusty conditions the gust-edge will be $10h$ from the cliff or whatever the wind rides over. This is for days where some

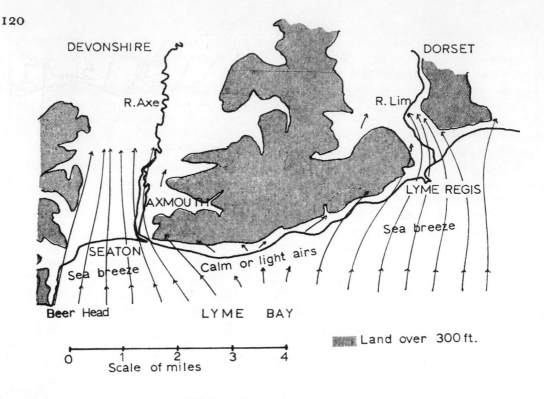

4.9: *Likely sea breeze flow from Lyme Bay.*

scattered cumulus can be seen, or the cloud may be banks of stratocumulus, but there must be some breaks in the cloud masses to show that the air is sinking fast enough to dry out the cloud in the gaps. When there are big showers about, or when thunderstorms threaten, then the sinking speeds will be greater and the gusts will be found closer to the cliff-edge. On more stable days, say with a low, amorphous cloud-sheet or a layer of lumpy turbulence cloud, or, in summer, a largely cloudless sky following a cloudy morning, then the gusts that there are will find their way on to the sea surface more slowly and appear farther from the shore.

This gives some idea of where the edge of strengthened wind due to gusts can be found. When one is sailing off a cliffy coast the $9h$ yardstick will suggest the limit of the zone of very much reduced wind. If there are no other more pressing considerations it will considerably help one's progress to be outside the $9h$–$10h$ limit. However, if the wind is almost as strong as the craft and crew can stand, being in the gust-shadow of the cliffs or other high ground may well help by allowing a more relaxed and therefore more careful progress through the easier wind. When, as assumed in this section, the wind is offshore, its fetch is small and the question of wave-making need not enter into the calculation.

SURFACE HUGGING WINDS In lesser offshore winds, over a terrain of cliff and combe, with the coastal towns and villages sheltering in and around the estuaries and the

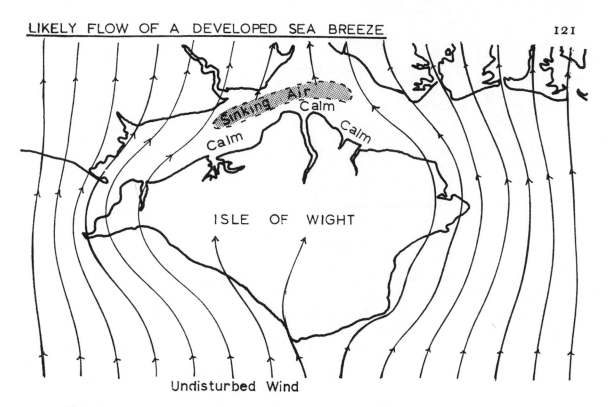

4.10: *Likely flow pattern of the lower levels of the sea breeze, or other surface wind, in the Solent and environs. Unless the air rises as much must flow ashore beyond the barrier of the Isle of Wight as flows from seaward.*

sun beating a shimmer out of the beaches, the sea breeze effects will usually predominate during the day. The cliffs will shelter the embryonic sea breeze at the start of its shoreward progress, thus leaving the coastal waters with very little wind at all. That which there is will be angled towards the gaps—steered there by the land-mass which the breeze cannot top. Thus the valleys which run back from the sea will be channels for the sea breeze where it will develop very strongly. Examples will be found along any high coast, and mention may be made of the valley of the River Axe with Axmouth and Seaton at its mouth and land rising to 400 feet on either side. An even more likely place for a channelled sea breeze is Lyme Regis where the little River Lim sinks down a 100-foot valley between 500-foot hills. The coast between these two places is almost entirely 300-foot cliffs, and the land then rises in places to over 550 feet. Such a barrier will effectively shelter a coastal strip half a mile or more wide and promote coastwise sea breeze drift which gathers strength and funnels inland where it can—this at both ends. Fig. 4.9.

It must also be remembered that a cliff is a completely dense barrier, and so we must expect its effects to be felt some $9h$ to seaward when the wind is onshore and deeper than the land height, which it normally will be. Thus in general it can be said that with winds both offshore and onshore the effective zone which is sheltered is one of $9h–10h$.

If the wind is at an angle and onshore then the high ground will channel it as shown

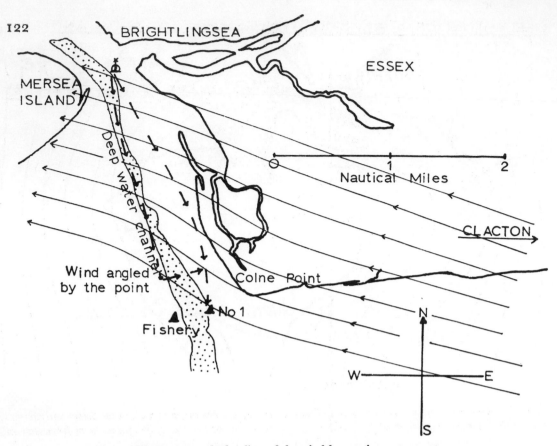

4.11: *To illustrate the bending of the wind by a point or promontory.*

in Fig. 4.10, which is for the Isle of Wight. Winds along the shore will be increased and canalised parallel to the cliffs where they cannot get away, and then when a gap appears they will push off inland. Thus using the Seaton–Lyme Regis coast again as an example a south-west wind will be given a tendency to flow east and increase in strength, but will rapidly develop an inland tendency in any of the bays.

Easterlies will find themselves with a south-west-going aspect where the coast dictates, and the example of the Royal Sovereign light vessel given on page 145 shows just how far from the coast this steering effect can extend.

The land does not need to be high for light winds in stable conditions to be canalised by the land. I recall a particular example while sailing from Brightlingsea (Fig. 4.11). It was a long-haul course out to No. 1 and Fishery buoys off Colne Point and back. The wind was one of those warm, unpretentious south-easterlies. In fact it was a little east of south-east at first, so it came over the flatlands from Clacton. The tide was just on the ebb, and it was a question of a direct inshore course or taking the main channel where the tide would provide the most help. As it was early in the flood this was not a critical decision. Thus there was a gaggle in the deep water channel and the rest of us along the shoreside, more or less far out as mood dictated. As we approached the Point it channelled the wind more

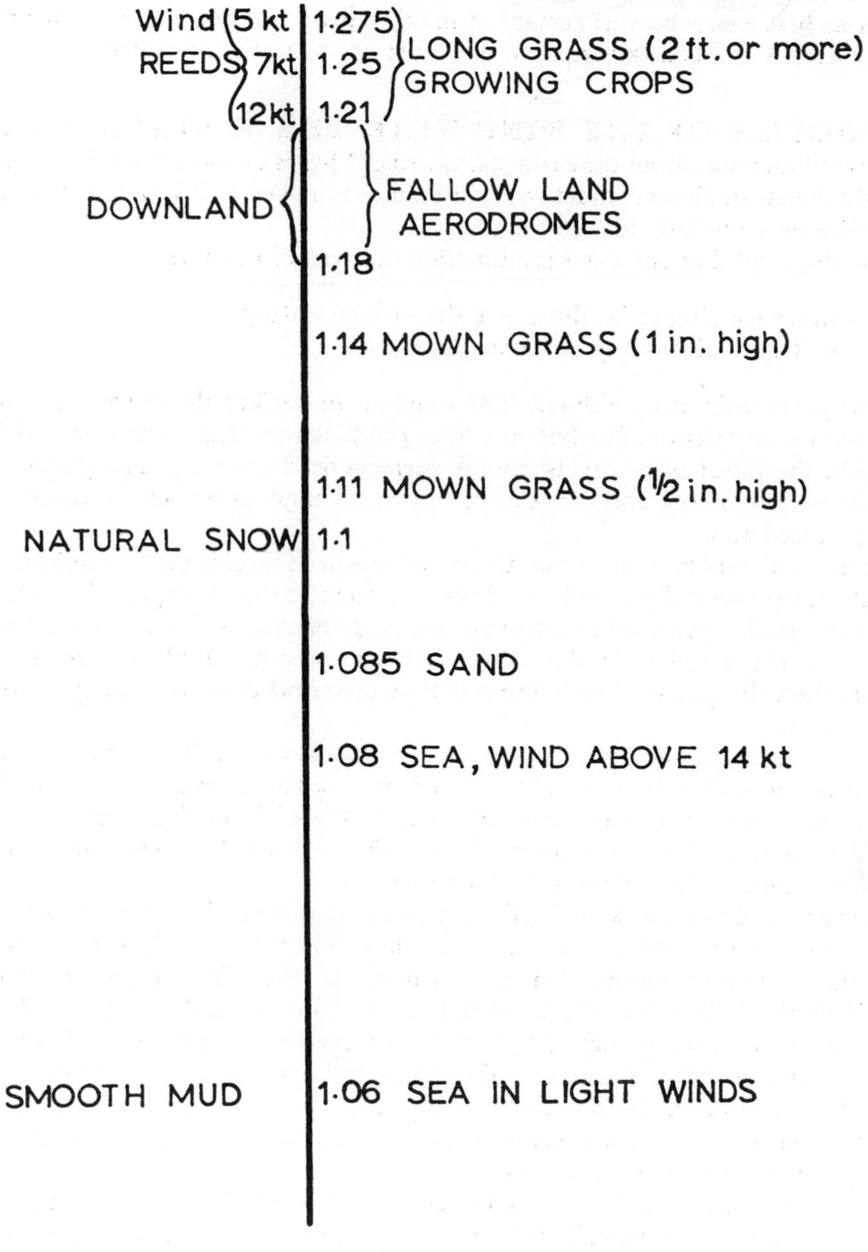

Wind (5 kt   1·275)

REEDS 7kt   1·25   LONG GRASS (2 ft. or more)
                   GROWING CROPS

(12kt   1·21)

DOWNLAND {   } FALLOW LAND
                  AERODROMES

1·18

1·14 MOWN GRASS (1 in. high)

1·11 MOWN GRASS ($\frac{1}{2}$ in. high)

NATURAL SNOW 1·1

1·085 SAND

1·08 SEA, WIND ABOVE 14 kt

SMOOTH MUD   1·06 SEA IN LIGHT WINDS

4.12: *Which terrains are smooth? None, but some are smoother than others.* [19]

parallel to itself, and the wind steadily became more south-easterly. We who were on the windward—and possibly sheltered side—were the only ones to make the buoy on one tack although at first everyone was certain of making it on the one leg. It seems that the influence of even a low coastal strip like this must not be underestimated.

THE PROFILE OF THE WIND NEAR THE SURFACE It is a platitude that the wind increases from the surface upwards. What is not so certain is how it increases. Obviously the air in direct contact with the surface is locked to it whether it be a stationary land surface or a moving tidal stream.

How the wind then increases is a function of two main factors:

(i) surface roughness, *i.e.* the size of the surface features.
(ii) the degree of stability of the atmosphere.

A few generalities can be stated. The rougher the surface the slower the wind and the greater the size and depth of turbulent eddies produced by that roughness. Without going into details, the effect of relatively smooth surfaces on the wind can be gauged by the use of a roughness parameter, and the relative roughness of possible shoreside surfaces is shown in Figs. 4.12 and 4.13.

It is immediately apparent from the way the wind increases with height in the sailing layer that aerodynamically smooth surfaces such as mud flats sweeping down to water will only produce (under normal day-time conditions) a very small change in wind speed in the vertical across the sail plan. In this case, and when some hundreds of yards separate craft and shore, then the practical conclusion is that the wind does not change with height in the sailing layer.

Now, however, sail along a reedy shore, and the situation is very different. The wind at the top of the sailing layer is twice what it is at 3 feet above the surface. Small scale turbulence will produce a variable wind speed as the eddies bring down wind which on the whole is twice as fast as the surface wind. Thus even light winds which are minutely gusty will produce rapid variations in wind direction.

How the wind changes with depth along a reedy shore, when the temperatures above and below the layer are taken into account, is shown in Fig. 4.14. In the evenings of quiet weather the air will be stable. That is, warm layers will exist over layers cooled by the surface. This stable layering of the air damps out any vertical motion, and the surface wind is not encouraged by mixing with more energetic air from above. So it is not surprising that wind at 3 feet is about $\frac{3}{10}$ of its value at 30 feet when real stability sets in.

On the other hand during the morning when turbulence is at its height it is not unexpected that the wind at 3 feet is 0·6 of its value at 30 feet, *i.e.* twice as great as in the stable case under the same conditions.

So if we call the change in wind with height the "wind shear" we can say that stability leads to a strong wind shear while instability leads to a small one. On a grander scale this variation of wind shear with stability leads to the days being gusty and the nights having steadier wind. Of course, strong stability can exist during the day, but this is not normal. Likewise a gusty night is not the sort normally to expect.

Another useful generalisation is that the wind shear (in the sailing layer at least) is proportional to the mean wind velocity in the layer. So that when the wind is strong the

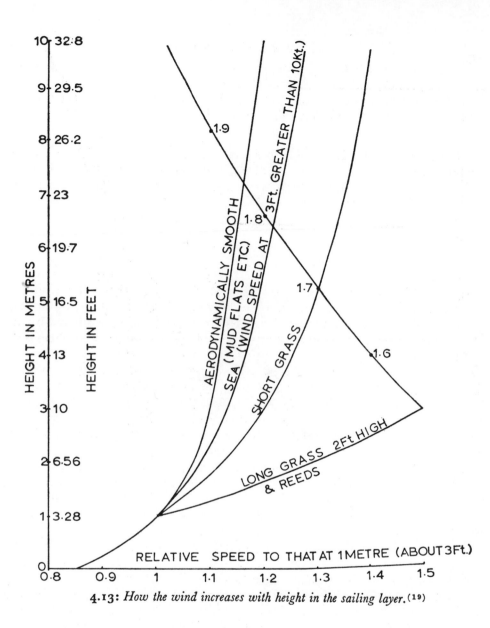

4.13: *How the wind increases with height in the sailing layer.* [19]

wind will increase with height much more rapidly than when it is moderate or light. Practical evidence for this is found in the lee of quite flat shores in strong winds. The strongest puffs are then of wind that is clear of the surface, while the lulls are characteristic of the wind slowed by surface friction and the variability of such lee winds is well known with Stage II planes alternating with Stage I planes for the shorter craft as the wind gusts and lulls about a strong mean wind.

The shape of surface elements has a direct bearing on the wind above that surface. Bluff projections lead to the drag of the surface increasing as the square of the wind speed.

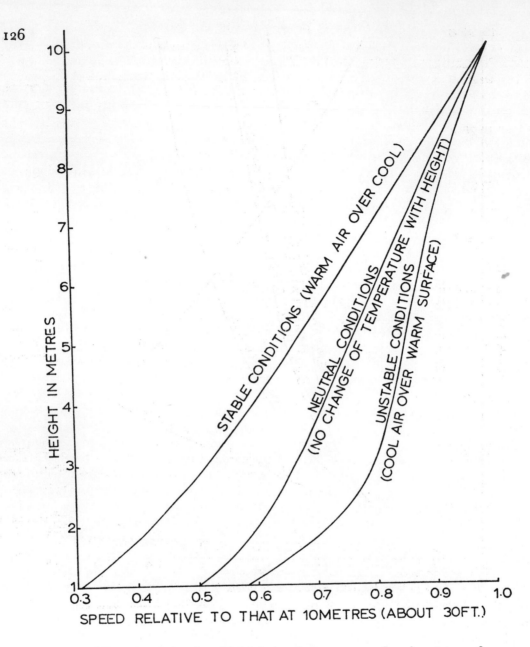

4.14: *How the wind varies with height over long grass or reeds under extremes of stability and instability.*[19]

This is, of course, for solid elements, and an example might be an expanse of rocks or a ploughed field.

Other surfaces, however, are different. Short grass is not bluff and presents a greater friction for its size than would be thought from just looking at it. With well advanced growing crops, however, the wind slides over the writhing backs of the supplicating grain, so producing a much lower frictional drag than would be expected. It is the same with the sea. It would be expected that if the waves were frozen then the roughness of the sea surface to the wind would increase immeasurably as the wind increased. Yet this is not so with dynamic waves, for they are moving ahead of the wind at perhaps 80 per cent of the wind speed, and their broad backs are turned to it. The friction does increase with wind speed, but not as much as one might think. After all, wind and sea are in equilibrium, on the average, and very strong discontinuities will tend to iron out as wave backs will broaden with wind increase. At the same time the wave velocity increases, so making the waves into smooth hummocks standing in the way of a relative wind some 20 per cent of the mean wind speed. Such a set of water hummocks will not impede the wind greatly.

Measurements of air-flow over the sea have led to the conclusion that with wind speeds less than 12–14 kt the flow is aerodynamically smooth, but conditions in which this is not likely to be so can be envisaged, such as over a wind against tide race.

Above these moderate speeds the flow is almost certainly rough, and the small-scale eddies will make it difficult to recognise the nature of the more useful larger-scale medium eddies. Such masking is a practical disadvantage of rough flow which will be almost universally present over vegetation.

Smooth flow is possible and by no means rare over the shores of muddy and sandy creeks, bays and estuaries, but, of course, the wind must have enough fetch over such surfaces for it to lose the rough eddies it has acquired. Even so it often happens that when sliding home in the evening, with the bows making the only disturbance of the mirrored sky, one experiences a curious physical union of craft and aerodynamically smooth wind. The feeling is of boat and gently undulating wind being one in a harmony which cannot be defined.

Such flow needs an inversion to be present so that the air near the surface should not be roughened by eddies from above. Strong inversions of temperature, however, are rare, and they do not persist in any one spot. Typically the inversion exists for half an hour and then breaks down for a while to re-form. When this happens a calm wind may increase to a few knots, and evidence of this is shown in the nocturnal wind trace between midnight and 4 a.m. in Fig. 3.35*b* (page 98), and in several of the examples of Fig. 5.2 (pages 132/3).

Taking the other extreme, the greatest instability occurs over grassland much earlier than one would expect. In fact the air near the surface is most unstable on clear summer days at about 0800 G.M.T. whatever the wind speed.

How the wind changes with the day is shown in Fig. 4.15. These curves show the average wind speed over open grassland on clear summer days, and they have been split into winds of less than and greater than 7 kt. They show that only when the wind is strong enough does the normally expected diurnal variation occur, that is a rapid increase after the sun rises with a maximum in the early afternoon; then, falling through the evening, to become the lowest value around midnight. The increases in the early hours are almost certainly nocturnal wind characteristic of downs and coastal plains and are local in origin.

When the wind speed is in the "light" bracket, however, the wind does not follow the normal diurnal variation, and this is an illustration of local effects, which even on the average are so prevalent as to distort the normal course of a day's wind. These graphs of average diurnal variation were obtained from 41 days with continuous sunshine and

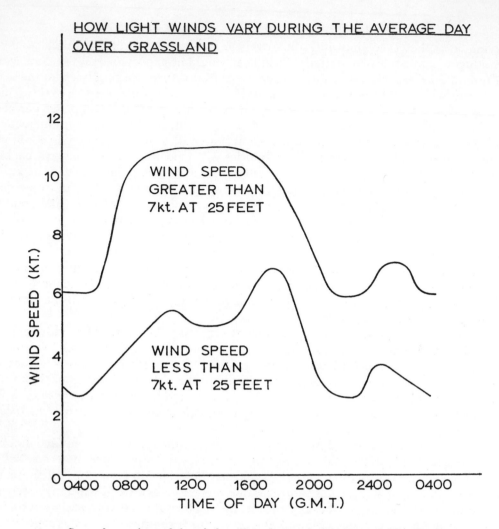

4.15: *Some observations of the wind on clear days and nights on Salisbury Plain.*[19]

starshine over a period of 6 consecutive years and are therefore representative of Salisbury Plain where they were taken and also of other similar places inland from the sea.

For instance this might well be the form of the average wind on clear days on natural and man-made stretches of inland water where people are wont to sail. What may seem strange is how late in the day the strongest wind is found at this inland site. It comes in the early evening and is probably due to the sea breeze which takes most of the daytime hours to reach the inland areas. More about this will be found in the next chapter under the heading of "Sea Breezes".

CHAPTER FIVE

Local Winds

A LOCAL wind is one whose extent may be measured in tens of miles rather than hundreds or thousands like the pressure systems of Chapter Two.

They are superimposed on the wind due to the adjacent pressure systems and profoundly modify them. Sometimes they may entirely replace the wind of the pressure system as can happen by day with sea breezes and by night with land breezes or other nocturnal winds.

In hilly districts, and where sailing is done at the watery foot of a valley which has run down from a mountainous interior, mountain and valley winds will replace the wind due to pressure systems in quiet weather.

Some local winds are far more permanent than this, and then they get special names. A well known one is the Chinook, which is a dry and warm west wind which flows over the lands to the east of the Rockies and is really a mountain wind of the *Föhn* type. Another is the Mistral, which is a mountain wind of great severity due to cold air sinking down the Rhone valley and becoming squeezed by the valley sides.

These are just two local winds of permanent recurrence which blow for days or weeks. When the words "local wind" are used here they will refer to less permanent features which can affect the course of a day's sailing.

As so much sailing is done in the immediate vicinity of coasts and in estuaries and land-locked harbours the sea breeze is perhaps the most important of the local winds and will be described first.

THE SEA BREEZE Most books on weather dismiss the sea breeze in a few words. This is a pity, because the sea breeze is of tremendous importance to sailing people, if for no other reason than it provides their motive power on quiet summer days, when otherwise they would sit below listless sails in attitudes of prayer for the wind that does not come.

The sea breeze is one of the most prevalent local winds, and it has rules which turn it from an unpredictable phenomenon into the useful friend of the informed racing, cruising, or just day-sailing, helmsman who wants to get from A to B in the shortest possible time.

In order to give an actual example, and present the reader with a place which he may know or can visualise, most of the sea breeze information to be given is for Thorney Island in Chichester Harbour.

The main points about the environs of Thorney which have a bearing on the behaviour of the sea breeze are:

(i) It is flat and part of a coastal plain.
(ii) It is backed by hills, as are many of the coastal plains in which land-locked sailing is done.
(iii) It is about 3 miles inland from the main coastline.

The flat lands of the East Coast are very akin to the South Coast from this point of view, and the sea breeze's behaviour in Norfolk, for example, can well be like that over the South Coast and its hinterland. As will be seen, the sea breeze exerts its influence over much of the country. The only terrain that it does not like are mountains and cliffy places. Even here it will occur when the conditions are right, but only local knowledge can be used to predict where it will assert itself. Over open coasts, with a fetch of some miles before meeting bluff obstacles, the sea breeze will behave itself in a manner akin to that which is to be described.

HOW THE SEA BREEZE STARTS Most people know the basic facts of sea breezes. They come in when the land warms up above the sea temperature. They are not very strong, amounting to 10–15 kt around our coasts, and only in the desert lands bordering the Mediterranean do they approach 25 kt.

The usual reason given for the advent of the sea breeze is that air over the land rises and allows the sea breeze to come in to take its place. This is not the whole story, although there is a strong element of truth in it.

When the sun rises on a clear morning and begins to warm up the land thermals will occur which will make the average temperature of the air column over the land higher than it was before. These thermals occur most where the land is warmest, and in the early morning are most likely over the sunward-facing hill slopes (Fig. 5.1).

First consider that it is totally calm over the whole of the coast and adjoining sea area and quite cloudless. These days do occur—mornings where the chug of a faraway engine mingles with the call of sandpipers and the tweetering of dunlin. On such mornings the sea breeze is almost certain to occur, but how?

Complete calm at the surface means that everywhere the surface pressure is uniform. That is over every equal area of land or sea there exists the same mass of air. For wind of any kind to occur mass has to flow out of one column into another. When a column is warmed from the surface the pressure at any given height, say 2000 feet up, becomes higher than it was before. So over the sun-warmed land the pressures in the upper air will rise by a small but significant amount, whereas over the sea, which is not warmed appreciably by the sun, they will remain the same. Air will flow directly from where the pressure at a given level is high to where it is lower. Thus a weak outflow of air begins to occur which is quite undetectable because a lot of air moves over a considerable depth measured in thousands of feet. This makes the mass of air in the warm column less and the surface pressure falls. The large air mass aloft eases out over the sea but the surface pressure there remains virtually the same (Fig. 5.1*b*).

Now, as the pressure at the surface over the land becomes lower than over the sea, the air will move from sea to land at the surface. Because the sea breeze current is shallow, being typically 1000–2000 feet deep at full development, the wind speed in it can be relatively large.

The sea breeze on quiet calm mornings starts because the air aloft gently drifts towards the sea, but this calmness is a comparatively rare occurrence. More often than not the wind will either have components onshore or offshore in the early morning, or what looks like a calm in the very early morning may be merely an illusion produced by the overnight inversion, and as soon as the thermals begin to mix up the surface air layers the true wind will appear.

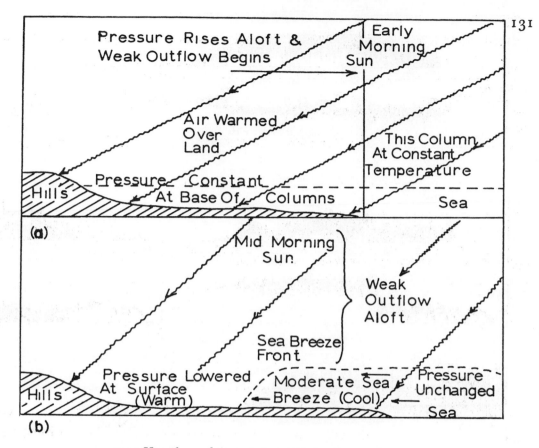

5.1: *How the sea breeze starts on utterly calm mornings.*

An example of the growth of the true wind in the early morning is to be found between 0600 and 0930 on 13 June 1959 (Fig. 5.2*b*). The wind before 0800 is so gentle as to move the wind vane only, and the speed pen does not even record. Then the wind begins to pick up in a puff or two for ten minutes just before 0800. The inversion which is keeping it damped down, however, reasserts itself, and the wind dies again for a quarter of an hour, crawling back towards north as it does so.

Eventually, like a sleeper who knows he must get up for the day's work, the wind comes. Puffs of up to 8 kt are brought down as the thermals mix up the quiescent air. These are a good indication of the strength of the wind to come. As is usual the wind then holds. Its mean speed in this case is about 4 kt from a mean direction of 070°. From Fig. 5.3 it seems most likely that the sea breeze will come in around midday.

It is difficult to be more explicit than this, but there is one other indication to be watched for. The wind trace shows that the sea breeze comes in with a bang at 1145, but just before this it can be seen that the offshore wind has lightened gradually for the previous half hour. This lightening of the wind before sea breeze onset is very typical, and the

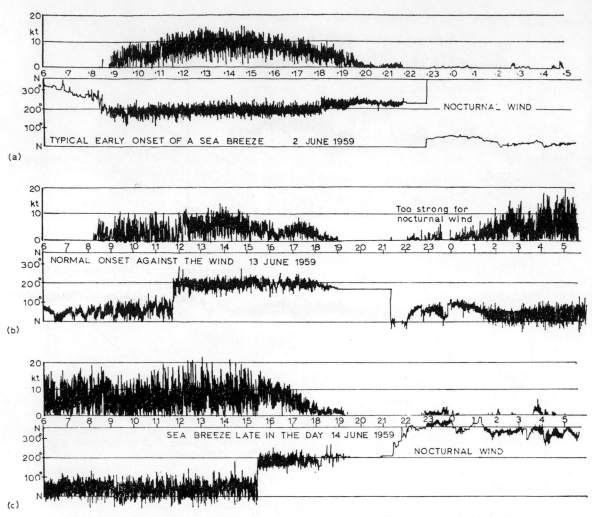

5.2 *a, b, c: Three characteristic ways for the sea breeze to arrive at a coastal site* (MO).

trace of Fig. 5.2*b* is the archetype of the most normal sea breeze onset on a warm and sunny summer's day with a light offshore wind.

Therefore people who are racing and want to take advantage of the sea breeze, should assess its likelihood, its likely time and then keep an eye on boats sailing nearer the main coastline to see if they have the sea breeze: at the same time they should suspect that any gradual lightening of the offshore wind is its precursor.

HOW THE SEA BREEZE WORKS WHEN THE WIND IS OFFSHORE

Regardless of what wind is blowing the sea breeze generating process described above will occur when the land becomes warmer than the sea as it will very often do. What happens after that, however, depends on whether the wind existing before the sea breeze sets

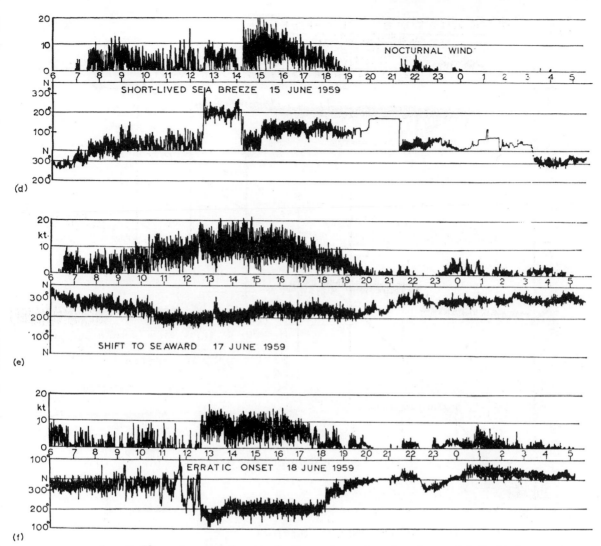

5.2 *d, e, f: Three characteristic ways for the sea breeze to arrive at a coastal site* (MO).

in is onshore or offshore. In what follows the "wind" is the wind which existed before the sea breeze set in to differentiate it from the sea breeze itself, *e.g.* in Fig. 5.2*b* the wind is 070° 4 knots and the sea breeze 200° 7 knots.

When the wind is onshore, or has components onshore, *e.g.* when over the South Coast it occupies the southern quadrants in the early morning and the day is not wholly cloudy, then the only worthwhile thing one can say about the sea breeze is that it will reinforce the existing wind and will turn it more perpendicular to the coastline. There is evidence that in some way which is not understood the sea breeze still arrives all at once, as it does when the wind is offshore, but there is no known way of predicting this arrival, so it is not of great use to small-craft sailing people. However, what can be said is that

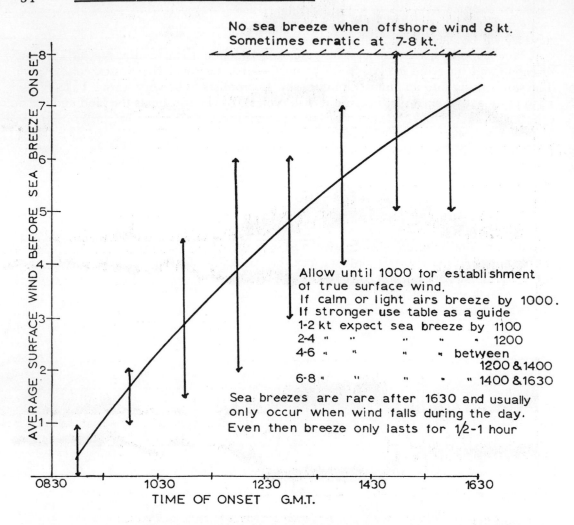

No sea breeze when offshore wind 8 kt.
Sometimes erratic at 7-8 kt.

Allow until 1000 for establishment
of true surface wind.
If calm or light airs breeze by 1000.
If stronger use table as a guide
1-2 kt expect sea breeze by 1100
2-4 "   "   "   " . 1200
4-6 "   "   "   " . between
                                   1200 & 1400
6-8 "   "   "   " . " 1400 & 1630

Sea breezes are rare after 1630 and usually
only occur when wind falls during the day.
Even then breeze only lasts for 1/2-1 hour

5.3: *A forecast graph for the sea breeze when the wind is offshore. The vertical lines show the range of wind speeds which have preceded actual onsets in the periods centred on the hour* (MO).

there are, on the average, some 15–20 days of the summer months when a wind which is east to south-east or west to south-west swings round to become a sea breeze at Thorney.

When, however, the wind is offshore, the sea breeze has to set in against it, and it becomes a much more predictable and law-abiding wind. The reason for this is that there must exist between the wind and the sea breeze a zone of convergence into which both winds flow and where the air must then ascend. The wind off the land is warm and that off the sea cool by comparison, and where they meet there must therefore be a sea breeze front. If we follow the convention for naming fronts, *i.e.* that the relative temperature of the air behind the front gives its name to the front, then the sea breeze front is a cold front, as the cool sea breeze reaches any particular locality behind the front when the latter moves inland. This front can be traced 50 or more miles inland on light summer days as will be shown later.

How does the sea breeze set in? Again, take Chichester Harbour as typical. It is early forenoon and the wind is light from the north-north-east over the Sussex coastal plain. The sun is rising into an almost cloudless sky. It promises to be very warm. Take 13 June 1959 as an actual example, because it is so typical. As the sun heats the land and the air over it, this warm wind flows out over the sea and finds itself over a cooler surface. Without going into unnecessary details, we can say that the cool sea air at the surface begins to develop components of velocity towards the land, because the pressure over it is lower than over the sea. The outflowing warm wind flows over this embryonic sea breeze. Thus in the example, for the daylight hours preceding, say, 1000, there will be little wind over the offshore coastal shallows. Coastwise passage-making at this time of day will be aided by staying say 5 miles or more off the coast (Fig. 5.4*a*).

As the embryonic breeze grows in the womb of the coastal sea area it deepens and the "front" develops between offshore wind and sea breeze (Fig. 5.4*b*). Over this front, where the air must perforce rise as its only means of escape, a line of cumulus clouds may develop. If the day is one with puffs of cotton-wool cumulus over most of the sky then that cumulus over the sea breeze front will often be darker than the rest. Such a cloud line is depicted in Photo 14 when a sea breeze set in over the Colne and Blackwater areas of Essex.

The rate at which the land heats will determine the sea breeze generating force, but the offshore wind will control when the breeze arrives. 13 June was a normal day and Thorney received the sea breeze front at 1145. It was quite definite, and the zone of convergence between the offshore wind and the onshore sea breeze did not take long to pass. It is this which accounts for the falling off of the wind before the sea breeze proper arrives.

When two opposing winds meet like this there must, of course, be some point where the wind is practically calm. One can imagine a strip of calm or fitful wind being generated over the coastal shallows in the early forenoon and advancing steadily inland. When there is cumulus about this calm zone advances inland quite rapidly—perhaps at several knots. The cumulus reveals convection, and convection aids the wind and breeze in rising up the "chimney" between them (Fig. 5.4*c*).

In the example of 21 May 1958 (see Fig. 5.5) the sea breeze front progressed inland from Thorney Island (at 1000) arriving over the Chertsey-Surbiton loop of the Thames some *two hours after sunset*. This gives an average speed of movement inland of 3 knots and the rate is typical for a "good" sea breeze day. By "good" is meant a day of prolonged sunshine with scattered cumulus to denote that convection currents are strong enough to aid the removal of the wind and sea breeze currents converging into the calm zone. Actually, on the day considered showers developed in the afternoon, which shows fairly marked instability, and this undoubtedly aided the sea breeze in running so far inland. What is interesting is that the sea breeze front does not run in parallel to all the coasts, but is greatly favoured over Sussex and Kent, even going so far as to emerge as a sea breeze *off the land* to fox early evening small-craft sailors along the north coast of Kent and over the lower reaches of the Thames.

There is some evidence that unstable winds from the north-west favour this more than normal incursion of the sea breeze. On the east coasts of the southern counties the wind would have been almost directly offshore and the sea breeze would have found difficulty

136

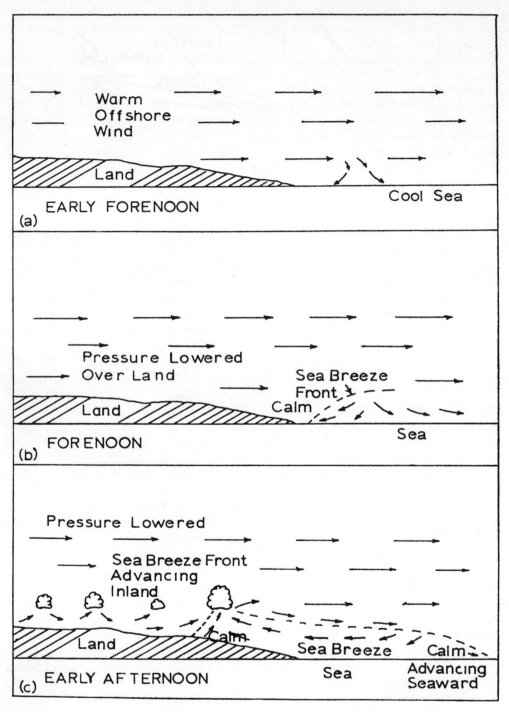

5.4: *How the sea breeze acts when the wind is offshore.*

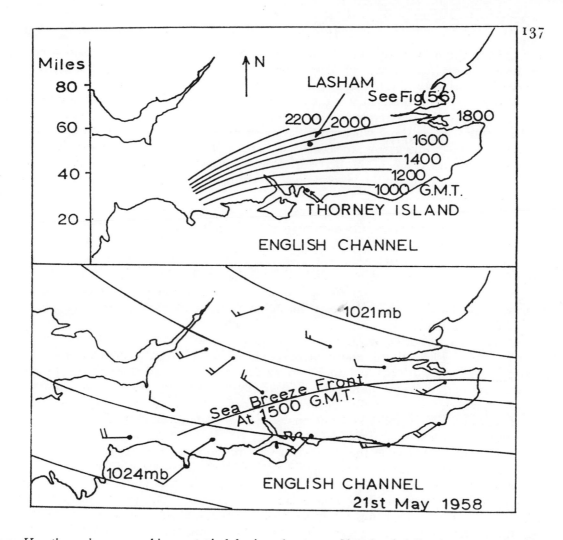

5.5: *How the sea breeze moved in on a typical day in early summer. Note the wind directions on opposite sides of the front in the lower diagram.*[14]

in reversing a wind component of 10–15 kt. The wind component perpendicular to the sea breeze front moving in over southern England, however, was much less than this, which may explain why the front moved as it did.

Much detailed observation of the way sea breeze fronts move in over the southern counties is being obtained by the glider pilots based at Lasham in Hampshire (see Fig. 5.5). On 11 June 1963 a front was tracked from Thorney at 1000 to beyond Reading at 2100[12]. It moved in at an average 3½ kt over Hampshire and Sussex and into Berkshire. Most of the stations in the area recorded the same sort of wind shifts from the north-to-east quadrant into the south-to-west quadrant. The average wind speed at the stations before the sea breeze front arrived was 2½ kt while after it had passed there was an average of 7 kt from the south-south-west. This effectively illustrates the point, made later, that wherever the sailing is done, whether it be in coastal harbour or inland lake, river or reservoir, the wind behind the sea breeze front is the stronger of the two.

While the speed of advance of the front was an average $3\frac{1}{2}$ kt it showed an initial reluctance to move in, making only a couple of knots over the coastal plain, but it speeded up to nearly 8 kt at times when 30 miles or so inland. This seems normal behaviour. However, 40 miles inland from the coast is the limit of penetration, and it loses itself in the evening on the backbone of the Berkshire Downs and the Chilterns. Thus it is not to be expected that more than a very occasional evening breeze will stir across the Thames above Reading.

This sort of sea breeze frontal movement is of relatively common occurrence when offshore winds are 10–15 knots. On days of lighter winds it can be expected that sea breezes will blow in over most of the coasts except in the west, where high ground will upset their development in any sort of ordered fashion. Sea breezes will occur, of course, but they will seek the combes and valleys which lead from the sea. It will be difficult to follow their progress, but in this connection Fig. 5.5 shows that neither the South Downs, Hindhead nor the North Downs can really upset the steady progress of a sea breeze over the southeast of England when the conditions are in its favour.

Some clues to the recognition of an approaching sea breeze front have been given already, but in Fig. 5.6 a cross-section through an actual front is shown. The way the converging air goes up the "chimney" above the calm zone and there forms a cumulus cloud bigger than the rest is quite evident in this figure. It has been noted that on dry days when no cumulus forms then the sea breeze front can sometimes be recognised inland by a curtain of haze. The visibility to the north of the front is good, while that in the moister sea air to the south is noticeably poorer.

The number of days in the year when sea breeze fronts can be traced inland as in Fig. 5.5 may perhaps be counted on the fingers, but the reasons are not far to seek.

One reason is shown in Fig. 5.2*c* and reinforced by Fig. 5.3. The wind over the South Coast during the day on 14 June 1959 was still the same direction (north-east) as the day before, but was stronger, being nearly 10 kt on the average, with gusts to twenty. Thus it took the sea breeze generating force all day to reverse this strong wind. When it did so it did it with a right royal bang, the direction going straight from north-east to south in one swing, but it did not happen until 1520 G.M.T. Obviously even at 3 kt the sea breeze front could not have been very far inland by nightfall—fifteen miles or so—which means it might have got to the foot of the South Downs and no farther. Anyway in Chichester Harbour it was calm by 1930. After days of sea breeze the evening is very often flat calm —a calm broken only by the soft meanderings of the night wind towards midnight.

Another reason for the slow advance of sea breeze fronts may be that the airstream is very stable. In this case warmer air exists not far above the surface and the convection currents are damped down. The state of affairs, where a warm deck of air exists above a relatively cooler one, is stable in that locally warmed air parcels push off to seek the upper air and find that there is air above them which is warmer than they are. They then tend to sink back. The warm layer is an inversion, and inversions inhibit sea breezes.

To understand this, think of the chimney up which the two converging winds must escape if the sea breeze front is to move inland. Prohibit this escape and the region between wind and breeze becomes wide and sprawls as a large zone of calm or fitful winds over the

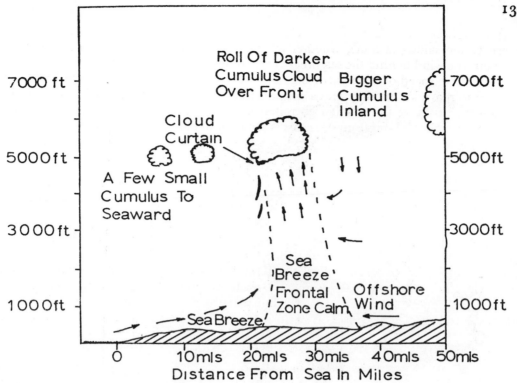

7000 ft

Roll Of Darker
Cumulus Cloud
Over Front

Bigger
Cumulus
Inland

7000ft

Cloud
Curtain

5000ft

5000ft

A Few Small
Cumulus To
Seaward

3000ft

3000ft

Sea
Breeze
Frontal
Zone Calm

Offshore
Wind

1000ft

1000ft

Sea Breeze

0   10mls   20mls   30mls   40mls   50mls
Distance From Sea In Miles

5.6: *Actual structure of a sea breeze front and its capping cloud over the gliding site of Lasham in Hampshire.* [14]

coastal land area. In this case the rate of advance of the sea breeze front is slow, being of the order of a knot or less.

On the most extreme occasions the rate of advance is as little as half a knot. I can quote a case from my experience which bears this out. The places mentioned are in Fig. 5.7.

It was 2 August 1953 and there was racing from East Head. We sailed down from Emsworth and it was a sultry, warm morning with a 5–10 kt offshore wind from the north-west. Over Stocker's Lake we ran into the sea breeze calm zone. At the same time we could see the craft lying close along the Winner Bank, some 700 yards to the south-wards, actively sailing in the southerly sea breeze while our pennant lay limp and listless as it waited for the breeze to come. It took us ten minutes to work through to the sea breeze, and the heat of the sand-dunes at lunch time was tempered by its coolness. The Fireflies started at 1440 and we had the sea breeze as far north as the village of West Thorney where we found the calm zone. Creeping through it, the fleet found itself once again in the north-west wind, which led to a scramble around the buoy at the head of Thorney Channel and then back, where sure enough a little farther north was the calm patch again with the sea breeze as a prize to be gained by him who worked through it the quickest. The southerly breeze was then with us all the way back to the line off East Head.

When Thorney Island's anemograph was consulted it was found that from a mean

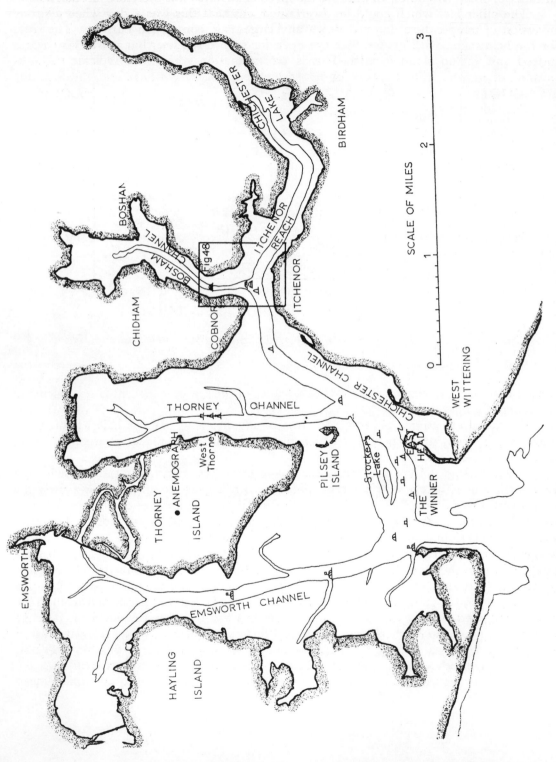

5·7: *Chichester Harbour—the environs of Thorney Island where much of the wind data was recorded.*

wind of 320° 5–12 kt the wind had abruptly swung 200° 5–12 kt at 1505. Thus it had taken the sea breeze front some four hours to crawl from the Winner to Thorney village—a distance of about two miles. In this case the speed of advance was therefore just half a knot.

The other fact which could be ascertained was that this was a day when a strong inversion of temperature damped down any large-scale convection currents. The clues for the helmsman, with his weather eye open for such days, are that it was very warm indeed and yet no cloud formed. This is a combination which will indicate the suppression of convection and a zone of calm which only edges slowly inland and does not get very far.

The rules therefore are:

(1) Big scattered cumulus with light wind—sea breeze comes in fast and goes a long way inland.
(2) Small puffs of cumulus over the hills—sea breeze not hindered but not greatly helped.
(3) Warmth and cloudlessness or a cloud layer which "burns off" in the morning—sea breeze comes in slowly and perhaps erratically.

Fig. 5.2*d* is typical of erratic sea breezes. The sea breeze came in with a bang at 1240 obeying all the rules. The calm zone which preceded it took some 20 or more minutes to pass across the anemometer. The sea breeze was light but dependable for about an hour. Then the tell-tale calming of the breeze began. It was a systematic fall which so often heralds either the onset or the death of the sea breeze, and sure enough at 1420 the sea breeze was blown back out to sea by the arrival of a wind from the direction it had that morning, but a lot stronger with gusts of up to 18–20 kt.

When thunderstorms build inland in summer then the wind can be amazingly erratic, even though the storms themselves are not over the coastal strip. The morning of 18 June 1959 (Fig. 5.2*f*) is typical of the sort of thing that can happen. The northerly wind was not at all strong, and the sea breeze came in for a few minutes at about 1100 and then was blown back out to sea. Half an hour later the breeze tried again but without much success, only managing to turn the wind direction towards west for less than a quarter of an hour. Soon after twelve it had rather more success pushing the wind through 160°. After that it swung back and forth violently until the sea breeze finally came in strongly, soon after half-past twelve. The relatively strong sea breeze in the afternoon is typical of days when there is a lot of convection inland. It is rising air in the hinterland of the coast that the sea breeze likes.

There are a few other useful points which are perhaps worth stating. When the wind is stronger than the upper limit of 8–10 knots which will allow a sea breeze to come in, the coastward wind shift (which often replaces the true sea breeze effect) occurs gently, taking an hour or more to swing slowly to its new direction. When it is flat calm in the hours after dawn then the sea breeze effect often just makes the wind wander slowly and fitfully off the land on to the sea. Such a day was 2 June 1959 depicted in Fig. 5.2*a*. The slow shift between 0600 and 0900 without enough strength to actuate the speed recorder is typical of calm summer mornings. As in this case when the sea breeze gets in first it is the wind of the day, but when the early morning wind picks up its strength from some other direction as in Fig. 5.2*b* then it is a question of waiting for the sea breeze to arrive—if it arrives at all.

Sometimes the sea breeze may set in in the early evening. This happens only on days when the offshore wind has just managed to keep the sea breeze out during the afternoon but the sun continues to shine. As always there is some slackening of wind-speed as the evening approaches, and this is sometimes just enough to give the sea breeze, which has been denied access to the land all day, a chance to assert itself, which it then does. These occasions, however, are rare, and a couple of evening breezes in any one year is all that could be expected.

THE SEA BREEZE AROUND THE BRITISH ISLES Sea breeze effects similar to those described for Chichester Harbour will occur in many coastal areas with environs of a similar nature.

Starting in the immediate neighbourhood of Chichester there are some useful things to be said about the sea breeze effects there. The Solent, for example, not only has a double high water effect it also has a "double" sea breeze effect in that the sea breeze current may grow up either the East or the West Solent depending on which is favoured by the prevailing wind at the time of the breeze's generation. (See Fig. 5.8.)

In its initial stages at least the embryonic sea breeze is a shallow area of light winds off the coast and therefore is going to find the Isle of Wight a barrier of formidable proportions. It will take the line of least resistance and flow up either of the flat floors between the land masses. (Fig. 4.10, page 121).

In its early stages, with offshore winds over say the New Forest shore, the sea breeze will generate itself in a strip of light or calm winds lying along the Solent, and although the north-west coast of the Isle of Wight will also develop some tendency for sea breeze the main effect is certain to be along the shore bounding the larger land mass.

An offshore (or onshore) wind in the western quadrants will tend to induce a south-westerly sea breeze as the wind already has westerly components. As the sea breeze effect grows the seaward extremity of the sea breeze zone moves into the Channel. Now the full sea breeze effect will become channelled up the West Solent finding the high land around Totland and the Needles a very real obstacle. It will become canalised over the water and can locally become compressed into a wind stronger than the normal 10–12 kt found at an open place like Thorney. It can in fact be as much as Force 6 when summer showers or thunderstorms are developing inland.

The seaward extension of a fully developed sea breeze is something of the ord   of 12–15 miles and its depth will often by then be more than the height of the Isle of Wight. Even so a sea breeze in the Solent is bound to have to flow around the Isle of Wight in its lower layers and this is where sailing is done. The sort of flow which might result is depicted in Fig. 4.10 (page 121), but it must be emphasised that this is necessarily a diagram produced from theory and not from observation. There are, however, observations which support it.

One feature which is worth noting is that when the sea breeze has become established from a wind with easterly components, and therefore blows up Spithead and Southampton Water it can, during the afternoon, change to flowing up the Solent. This is because the earth's rotation causes all sea breezes to veer with the day and so brings the breeze in the afternoon from a more westerly point. The tendency to flow over the smooth water of the Solent rather than over the rough land does the rest.

The breeze which flows about the Isle of Wight fans out over the flatter mainland and can produce some curious effects at Calshot. The sea breeze at places as near as Calshot and Lee-on-Solent can be very different.

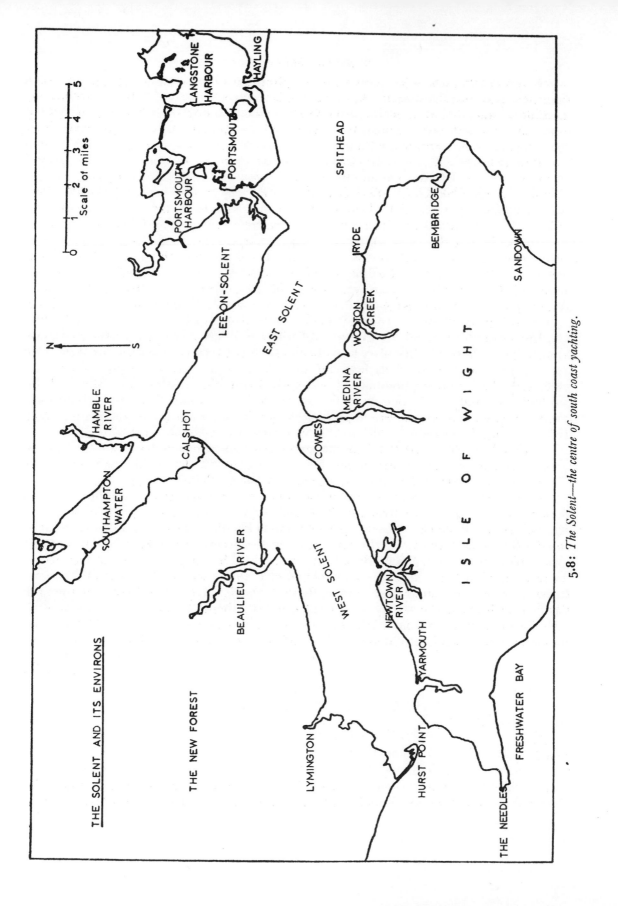

5.8: *The Solent—the centre of south coast yachting.*

It appears that when the breeze flows up Spithead it spreads its main energies over the Portsmouth and Southampton Water areas and is observed to be very light and shallow on the Calshot side of Southampton Water. On the other hand when it flows up the Solent it increases markedly on leaving the shelter of Calshot Spit. It may also exhibit considerable eddying to the north of the Castle itself.

If we cross the Solent to Cowes we may find that when the sea breeze is fully developed on to the mainland Cowes has an offshore "sea breeze", but this is usually rather weak even if it occurs at all. Observers at Calshot say that they have never seen smoke flowing onshore along the north coast of the Island and take this as an indication that there is little tendency for the Island to have its own sea breeze. This may be so, but my own observation is that the calm which often exists over Cowes Roads when sea breeze is blowing over the mainland shore, is due to there being just enough tendency for onshore breeze over Cowes and the Medina to nullify the stronger breeze blowing towards the mainland. The result is stalemate over quite a wide zone parallel to the Isle of Wight shore and the place to be for passage-making on sea breeze days is hugging the mainland shore as close as is prudent and practicable (see Fig. 4.10, page 121).

Incidentally it is worth recording that Calshot is a very abnormal place for onshore winds. For instance with winds which should have been from between south-east and south-south-west (that is winds from the most favourable direction of Spithead) and which have been blowing normally at places like Lymington and Lee (on either side of Calshot) the winds at Calshot are often backed some 2–3 points. This is such a strange result that strenuous efforts were made there to check that it was not a false reading, but without result. The wind-vane persisted in recording a much more easterly wind than at the surrounding places. As this happens sometimes with winds of Force 6–7 and in all sorts of circumstances it is worth noting. Fig. 4.10 may give a clue to this anomalous state of affairs when the streamlines are traced about the Isle of Wight.

Returning to sea breezes, and moving eastwards from the Solent, we find that the West Sussex coastal plain narrows until beyond Brighton the Downs are close along the sea. This area will have a sea breeze potential much like that at Chichester Harbour. It is only farther along towards Beachy Head that the sea breeze may depart from its normal coastal plain behaviour. Beachy Head—the end of the South Downs—is 340 feet above the sea and will present an insurmountable obstacle to the sea breeze in its initial stages. It can be shown to channel the wind at Royal Sovereign Light Vessel, some 7 miles off Eastbourne, into a southwesterly on many afternoons of the summer months. The following table for the months of June to August shows the number of occasions when the wind at Royal Sovereign was from different points, and the records were checked over five years.

TABLE 5.A

At Sunrise	N.	N.E.	E.	S.E.	S.	S.W.	W.	N.W.	Calm
Force 1–3	38	58	31	15	23	50	43	55	7
By 1600									
Force 1–3	9	21	63	16	19	112	48	9	3

Thus, while the winds around dawn distributed themselves pretty evenly about the various directions, by mid-afternoon in summer the chances of having a south-westerly at

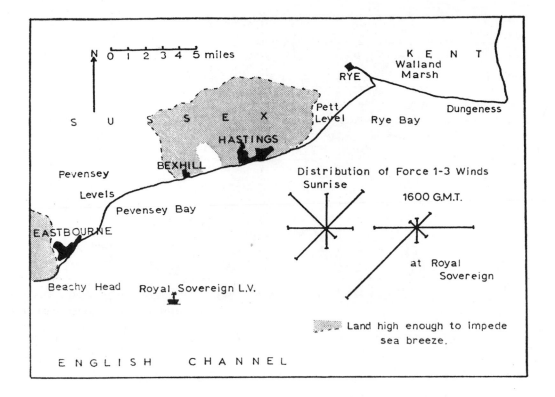

5.9: *Winds and rough topography at Royal Sovereign. The land not shaded is mainly low-lying (See Table 5.A.)*

Royal Sovereign (and by inference all along the coast from Beachy Head to Pevensey Levels) is very high. (See Fig. 5.9.)

If we take winds, which might not be sea breeze in origin, between Force 4 and 7 we find the records show that at both sunrise and in the afternoon the most prevalent wind at this light vessel is from the south-west or west and the only Force 8 gale recorded in the five years (1934–37 and 1939) was from the south-west.

The flatness of Pevensey Levels and the restrictions imposed by Beachy Head and Hastings make a "funnel" for the sea breeze and in Pevensey Bay it should be stronger than normal. These effects will provide only a local deviation in sea breeze behaviour, and in general the sea breeze front will organise itself all along the Sussex and South Kent coast and move in as depicted in Fig. 5.5 when the airstream is unstable.

Sea breezes on the east and north coasts of Kent will be difficult to predict, as the main sea breeze spreading in northwards will tend to override local effects. These, however, can make their presence felt early on days of light wind and become modified as the day progresses. Thus onshore sea breezes in the forenoon may well become *offshore* sea breezes by the afternoon along the North Kent coast.

When such a full-bodied sea breeze current arrives over the Thames Estuary (or any similar situation) it will kill itself and the sea breeze proper will reorganise farther north.

K

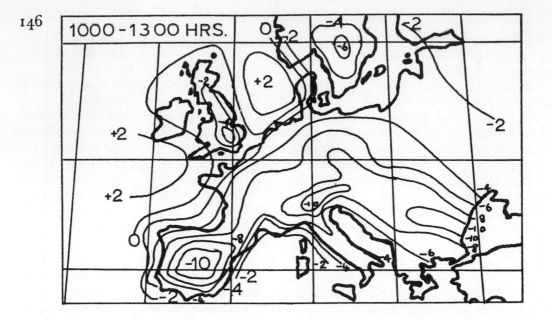

5.10: *Where the pressure is falling and rising over Europe during an average summer lunch-time.* [4]

Thus it does not seem likely that any effects of the sea breeze over Sussex and Kent will be felt over the coasts of north-east Essex even if they should manage to upset the Thames Estuary and south-east Essex. The main sea breeze driving force over the Colne and Blackwater is from south-east to north-west, and the cloud along the sea breeze front over Colchester which is Photo 14 bears this out, as it was orientated slightly south of west and the attendant sea breeze was from slightly east of south. This indicates that the sea breeze in the forenoon nearer the coast had been south-east as the sea breeze veers with the day and the photo was taken in mid-afternoon.

As one moves up the East Anglian coast the usual direction of sea breeze changes towards north-east at onset and veers east and eventually south as the day progresses. Along the whole of the east coast the sea breeze onset described for Thorney, when the wind is offshore, is the normal mode, because the prevailing wind is westerly and thus has components offshore more often than not. Also the flat-lands of the east have a high sea breeze generating potential and the breeze can well become 20 knots in high season. For instance at Gorleston (south of Great Yarmouth) on one typical occasion a west to south-west wind of 7–8 kt mean speed went abruptly to south-east soon after noon and increased to 20 kt between 1400 and 1500, before gradually reverting to its previous speed and direction in the late evening.

Before proceeding farther north it is interesting to look at Fig. 5.10. In this diagram the places where the barometer is falling or rising by equal amounts on the average during the summer months have been joined by lines. We find that in a small area centred on Bedfordshire and Huntingdonshire and running from the Thames Estuary to Nottinghamshire the barometer is more likely to have fallen by 4 or more millibars in the three hours 1000–1300 than not. Thus pressure is falling quite fast in this area during the average summer lunchtime and the situation has the makings of a small depression over the counties north of London.

Such a depression is called a "heat low" because in summer the area becomes one of the hottest parts and air must rise and flow out aloft so lowering the pressure.

If the directions for the sea breeze at Thorney, over the Colne-Blackwater estuaries and in Norfolk are drawn they will be seen to converge into this area. The low pressure centre is fed by sea breezes from around it with the east coast sea breeze providing the lion's share. Sea breeze air off the sea is comparatively cool, but its main attribute is that it is humid. When big thunderstorms grow over Herts and surrounding counties on summer afternoons the water vapour fuel for their immense slow explosions is furnished by the sea breezes. These are the days when the sea breeze really gets a hustle on over the east and south-east coasts of Britain. To a lesser degree the areas of falling pressure will be seen to provide a backbone moulded to the shape of Britain and indicating that sea breezes will be found on both east and west coasts and up into Southern Scotland. The direction which is most likely in any one locality can be roughly found by drawing an arrow from the coast into the area of falling pressure. The first inference is that sea breezes will usually be less strong on the coasts of the northern counties, but, of course, the channelling effects of high ground and cliffs can make the local picture very different from the simple one, obtained by just drawing a line as above.

And where does all this sea breeze air go to? The cells of rising pressure in the North Sea and South-west Approaches provide the answer. It flows out aloft and sinks back on to the sea to make up for what the sea breezes have taken away. The English Channel is such a narrow strip of water that while there is some sinking on to it the main areas are undoubtedly those mentioned above. From a weather point of view this will make the North Sea an area of diminishing cloudiness on summer days as the air sinks from aloft while the inland areas will be all set for crops of thunderstorms.

All along the French, Belgian, Dutch and German coastlines the tendency for sea breeze is also revealed as pressures tumble by more than 2 mb per hour in the heat of inland Europe.

Spain is a veritable cauldron of low pressure with the barometer tumbling by 3–4 mb per hour in its hot high interior. Such loss of pressure must be fed, and breezes off the sea must do it. The same applies to Italy and the coasts of the Adriatic. Everywhere the isallobars (as these lines of equal rate of change are called) run parallel to the coast. All Europe is tending to become one big depression on summer days and the sea breezes are the result.

Returning to England, however, at South Shields (the mouth of the Tyne) the sea breeze is generally east-south-east when it sets in, and the speed can climb up to 15 kt in the afternoon—not as much as over East Anglia, but a nice helpful sailing breeze all the same.

At the mouth of the Humber (Spurn Point) the sea breeze is usually from the south-east, and along this coast the breeze may get some 25 miles inland on good days, that is to the feet of the Pennines. At places some 15 miles inland from the coast and in the Tees Valley the sea breeze never arrives before 1100 but has usually arrived by 1500–1600. It disappears in the evening between 1700 and 2100 depending on how hot the day has been. Like sea breeze arrival at most inland places the wind changes slowly to the new direction and even more slowly reverts again at the end of the day. When industrial places lie to seaward of a sailing site one of the ways to detect the sea breeze is by the smoke wall which it brings with it. Expect the first **trem**ors of the breeze a little before the smoke arrives, but on sultry, stable days do not expect it at all. In the Tees Valley however, while the sea breeze front travels at as little as half a knot, it may travel at up to 10 knots. This express speed is probably typical of a coastal area with a massive hill range inland, especially when big cumulus can be seen growing over the sun-drenched slopes.

Going farther north into Scotland we find that at a place like Montrose in Angus, which is backed by a range of mountains the sea breeze is very prevalent. One reason is that the mountains impede the wind in the lowest 4000 feet and with it the offshore wind component. Thus when the wind is from the westerly quadrants it is less at the surface than it otherwise would be. Another reason is that the slopes of the Grampians face the early morning sun and are very prone to convection currents which promote the pressure fall over the land that brings in the sea breeze.

The observations at Montrose are interesting because they show some of the effects which high mountains within 20 miles may have on the sea breeze, and this will also apply to other places, particularly on the West Coast. Here, on unstable days, the sea breeze comes in and rises while air sinks over the sea some 10–15 miles off the coast. This has been checked by observations of sea breeze at Bell Rock some twelve miles off Arbroath. On more stable days the sea breeze flows in the confines of the coastal strip, being anticlockwise when the morning wind is westerly and clockwise when the wind is northerly. The sea breeze is normally from south-east by south, but may be anywhere between east and south. It is sometimes east-north-east when the flow is clockwise in the confines of the coastal plain. When the sea breeze is from this direction and the land-breeze takes over in the evening, it does so by backing the breeze through north to the north-west. Places like Montrose and its environs will have a very prevalent and relatively strong katabatic night wind as cool air off the mountain slopes sinks out over the coast to the sea. Such breezes may reach 10–12 kt and may be found as much as ten miles off the coast, but they are then very weak and perhaps just a ghosting 1–2 kt.

By contrast the sea breeze along the Angus coast is Force 4 in July. It starts about March or April when it approaches Force 3 and maintains this force into September, and October after which it hibernates.

Very sudden and quite spectacular changes of westerly to onshore winds may occur in the proximity of mountains such as the Grampians. Force 4 westerlies may, in high summer, suddenly become easterlies with speeds up to 35 kt in the early afternoon. However the inland temperatures need to be well into the seventies before such catastrophic changes occur.

Observations of the sea breeze on the west coast are sparse, but that is not surprising. It is difficult to divorce sea breeze effects from the prevailing wind which is in the same direction. On the whole the main effect of the sea breeze on the west coast is to increase the onshore wind in the afternoon, and what may not otherwise be a strong wind becomes one in the middle of the day. For instance at Valentia in South-west Ireland the mean wind for the year in the mid-afternoon is more than twice its mean value at midnight. In both cases the direction is south-west.

A similar sort of result appears for Tiree in the Inner Hebrides, but the speeds are about half of the values experienced at the exposed Valentia.

While the east coast of Scotland may experience sea breezes against offshore winds which seem very strong, the same is not true of the east coast of Ireland. Belfast has sea breezes which reverse westerly winds if they are less than Force 4. However, the effects of sea breeze can be felt with winds of Force 4 when a north-westerly wind can be veered into a north-easterly breeze by the afternoon.

In the West Country sea breezes will be modified by the topography. For instance around the Exe estuary north-west winds of Force 3–4 are enough to keep the sea breeze out. Offshore winds of less than 15 kt will often keep the sea breeze away from Plymouth Sound and coming back towards the Solent, Poole is only certain of a sea breeze if the wind is less than 10 kt, and 15 kt off the land precludes it altogether, while with offshore winds between 10 and 15 kt only backs or veers occur.

In this sea breeze tour around the British Isles enough principles will have been given for a better understanding of the sea breeze in any particular area. A talk with the local coastal met. office will often be fruitful, as forecasters make a full-time study of such effects in their local area.

THE FREQUENCY OF THE SEA BREEZE It may not be generally realised how prevalent the sea breeze is at coastal places, so the following table is revealing. It shows the days in the three years 1959–1961 when sea breeze activity was in evidence at Thorney Island. This includes three distinct types of sea breeze day. There are days with onshore winds when the sea breeze comes in to reinforce the existing wind. They can be recognised because the true wind is pushed nearer to directly onshore by the sea breeze effect. Those of the second type are very easy to recognise because they produce big changes of wind direction and occur when the general wind is offshore and generally 10 kt or less (Figs. 5.2*b*, *c* and *d*). Those of the third type are recognised when an offshore wind of greater than 10 kt mean speed is shifted towards the normal sea breeze direction by the sea breeze effect. At Thorney Island this latter direction is 200°, but, of course, the offshore wind is shifted towards that direction by only perhaps 20–40°. Figure 5.11 makes this clear. It shows a succession of days with wind increasing with time. On the first day the wind shifted to the roughly westerly point which it was to occupy for the next four days. On the second day it was not strong enough to prevent the sea breeze getting in for a while but the following day (7 June 1959) we see between 0900 and 1500 a 40° shift towards south. On the 8th the wind was stronger, but still between night and day there was a 30° coastward shift. The wind lightened again the following day and shifted 30° between 0900 and 1500. This behaviour is typical of summer weather with winds greater than 10 kt during the daylight hours. It is also worth noting that at night there is an equal tendency for the wind to go back towards north under the land-breeze effect.

The table gives the total of sea-breeze days, but the shifts had to be substantial before they were included in the table.

It is evident from the averages that June is the month when sea breeze activity is at its height and November and December the months when it is hibernating. This is not surprising when one remembers that sea breezes will not normally occur unless the air temperature over the land is higher than that over the sea.

The sea, of course, is a heat reservoir and acts like a storage heater, taking in its heat during the summer and giving it back throughout the autumn and early winter, to reach a minimum temperature during the freeze-up months of January and February. The land

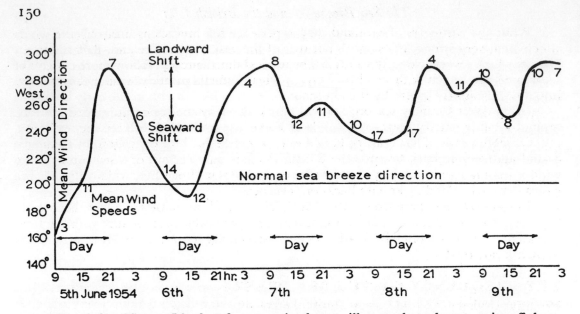

5.11: *The wind at Thorney Island on five consecutive days, to illustrate the tendency to swing off the sea during the day and off the land during the night. The numbers on the curve are the mean wind speeds at the given hours*

TABLE 5.B

The number of days of sea breeze activity at Thorney Island in three successive years

Month Year	J	F	M	A	M	J	J	A	S	O	N	D	Totals
1959	3	1	4	7	13	17	21	15	14	7	2	1	106
1960	2	1	3	7	16	13	4	12	9	5	0	2	74
1961	1	4	11	13	9	15	17	10	12	4	1	0	105
Average number of days	2	2	6	9	13	15	14	12	12	5	1	1	

however, while it has a certain storage heater effect from deep below the surface, accepts and rejects heat very readily at the surface. The curves of mean land temperature for the twelve months of the year will therefore largely follow the height of the sun above the horizon, being highest in June and July and lowest in December and January.

Near the coast the sea temperature tends to rule the temperatures over the land, especially on the south and west coasts where the wind is habitually onshore. However, any coastal strip will have cool wind on hot quiet days due to the sea breeze bringing it in off the sea.

In areas such as Chichester, Langstone, Portsmouth and the other harbours which indent our coasts, particularly on the south and east coasts, where the mud-flats and sandy strands abound at low tide, the sea temperatures about them will follow more closely the weather patterns. The mean temperatures quoted in official publications for the sea areas off our coasts cannot and do not take account of factors like an ebb in the early hours of a clear, cool night which leaves the exposed flats and banks cooling at the maximum rate. The succeeding flood is cooled by contact with the cold surfaces, which are very extensive, and its high-water temperature is very much reduced. The rapidity with which coastal land-locked harbours ice up in extreme winters like 1946 and 1963 is evidence of this. Likewise, turning to a warmer prospect, a morning's ebb on a fine summer's day will provide a lot of heated mud and sand to make an evening's swim seem warmer than one in high afternoon.

It is not surprising, therefore, to find that when temperatures were taken from a thermograph on a raft in the entrance to Emsworth Channel they proved to be 3–5°F above the mean coastal sea temperature quoted in M.O. 447 (Monthly Mean temperatures for Home Waters) in summer and 6–10°F below them in winter.

This pattern will be repeated wherever there are estuaries, creeks and harbours with extensive drying banks and must also make an important modification along the same lines around the offshore banks in the approaches to the Thames, so that the sea will be warmer in summer than farther off the coast and colder in winter.

The extra cold of coast water in the first months of the year, coupled to the increasing power of the sun, makes for the build-up of days of sea breeze earlier in the year than perhaps would be expected. I remember well a sea breeze on 20 January 1952 because I just couldn't at the time believe it. It brought a pall of smoke into Chichester Harbour which had apparently flowed offshore from Portsmouth and stagnated there during the morning. The fact was that when the sea breeze drift arrived the air temperature was 47°F, which was the same as that given for the coastal sea temperature for January. (See Fig. 5.12.) In actual fact the true sea temperature was 40°, which in the almost complete calm of a January anticyclone gave sufficient difference of temperature between land and sea to allow the sea breeze effect to work. On the whole when it is all but calm 3–4°F difference in temperature between land and sea will induce a sea breeze over the coastal strip and carry it a few miles inland. However, when the wind is a mean of 8–9 knots the difference may need to be 15° or more.

Thus sea breeze occasions in the bracket November to February inclusive are not only few and far between, but the opposing wind must also not be any more than a couple of knots or they are kept out. Even so Table 5.B shows that the Septembers of good summers such as 1961, have over a third of the days of the month showing sea breeze activity at work, and in phenomenal summers like 1959 nearly half the days of September may be blessed with some sort of sea breeze effect. The shading in Fig. 5.12b shows when there was a tendency for sea breeze in 1952 (and 1952 was a pretty typical year). The circles are the actual maximum temperatures recorded at Thorney on the 15th and 30th of each month respectively (28th February). The crosses are the sea temperatures actually recorded on a raft just within the Harbour in the entrance to Emsworth Channel on 15th and 30th of each month. This makes it clear why coastal places like Chichester Harbour get so many sea breezes. The curious result at the end of March was due to a cold snap.

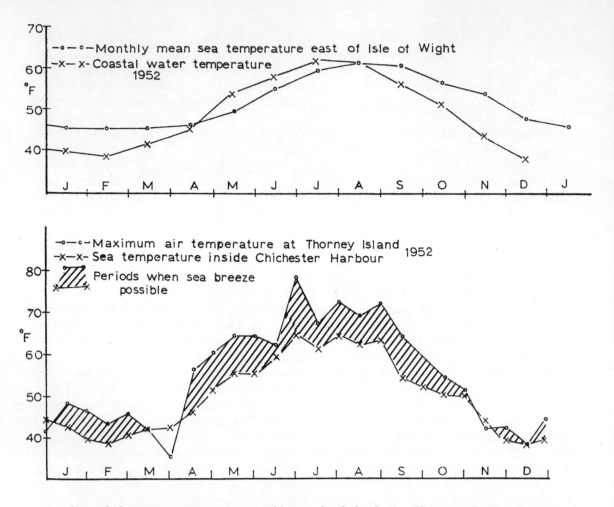

5.12: *Sea and air temperatures near a coast with extensive drying banks. The upper diagram shows that in Chichester Harbour the temperatures are higher than the mean in summer and lower in winter. The lower diagram shows that this tendency leads to sea breezes being possible for most of the year* (MO).

In general one can say that a sea breeze is the rule rather than the exception whenever the wind allows it.

THE NIGHT WIND On a coastal plain with a hinterland of hills the nocturnal wind is a common and helpful occurrence.

At Thorney Island in Chichester Harbour it usually comes from the north-north-east and can occur at any time of the year when the skies are clear and winds light. In a quiet way the night wind will ape its stronger day-time brother, the sea breeze, for when the wind in the evening is gently onshore the night wind will stop it and reverse it so that what was an onshore wind turns into an offshore one from about 030°. (See Fig. 5.2, pages 132/3.)

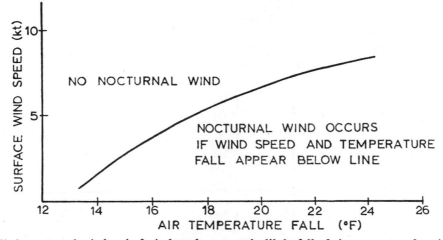

5.13: *Will the nocturnal wind arrive? A shrewd guess at the likely fall of air temperature from its day-time maximum, coupled to a wind forecast can sometimes provide the answer.*[6]

These night winds are not of one origin. They are mainly, though not entirely, katabatic. That is, they are air sinking off the hills and flowing out to sea under its own momentum. Just as the slopes of the hills will initiate thermals by day, with an attendant net ascent of air which helps the sea breeze to establish itself, so those same slopes will cool most readily at night and the dense air must sink across the coastal plain and out across the coastwise waters to aid the mariner who is making a passage in the early hours of the night. The katabatic effect is aided by the land breeze. This helps to strengthen the katabatic wind, but the katabatic effect will occur first just as by day the thermals will occur before the sea breeze comes in.

The katabatic effect will occur whenever the skies are clear and winds are light, but the land breeze needs the additional factor of the sea temperature being greater than the land temperature—which it usually is anyway when the night wind appears.

At Thorney the breeze arrives some 2–4 hours after sunset on 70 per cent of the nights when it occurs under clear skies, but when skies are partly cloudy 4 hours after sunset is the almost universal rule. Of course, complete cloud cover will blanket the cooling of the land, and neither katabatic wind nor land breeze will occur.

A certain amount of forecasting can be done with this wind when the topography is akin to that of the area surrounding Thorney, *i.e.* hills backing the coastal plain. It has been found there that 90 per cent of the night winds occur when the temperature has fallen by some 15°F from the day's maximum temperature. The wind will not occur when other winds are too strong, and Figure 5.13 shows how it can be assessed if a night wind can be expected.

In any case do not expect the breeze until 2–4 hours after sunset, and do not trust it later than a couple of hours before dawn. It is a cool, shallow wind, and it must circumnavigate any large buildings or groves of tall trees, but one can expect it to use creeks and estuaries as its open highway to the sea and be bent by them in the sailing layer if not farther up. Thus a nocturnal wind is one for running out on and later to be coveted by prudent coast-hugging. But it is not for tacking in against the tide, as shallow water

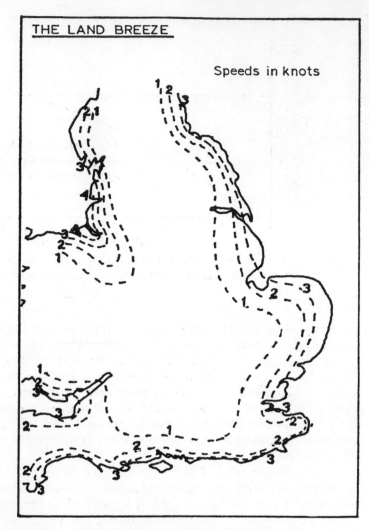

THE LAND BREEZE

Speeds in knots

5.14: *The speed of the land breeze around England and part of Wales. Offshore, reflect the lines of equal speed in the coastal water.* [1]

tacking is impractical after dark unless you know the waters like the back of your hand, and the night wind is just too light for significant way to be made.

The night wind can still be found ghosting out over the waters when a couple of miles offshore, but only near the coastline can it be relied on, and then any other kind of wind is bound to beat it out of existence.

This example, of a two-mile strip of very light airs, is for relatively low hills. On the east Scottish coast and similar hilly places, the night wind can be 10 kt and extend 15 miles out to sea. It can halt and reverse the sea breeze as soon as the east-facing slopes have lost the afternoon sun for an hour or two.

In general the night wind is weak, but a glance at the inland topography may reveal the possibility of a nice steady working breeze for quiet coastwise passages.

The land breeze to expect around the coastal areas of England and Wales has been neatly summed-up in a diagram due to E. N. Lawrence (Fig. 5.14). It shows that on the whole the land breeze is a maximum of 3 kt at most places on the coast, but that on the coast of Lancashire and Flint it picks up to 4 kt. Lawrence suggests that the land breeze

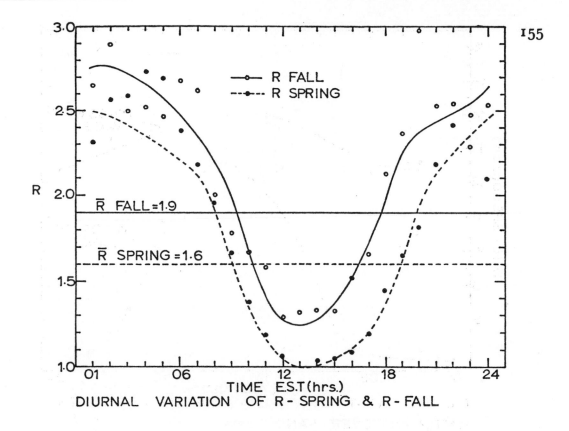

5.15: *Winds over the Great Lakes. R is the factor to multiply the wind recorded ashore in order to find the wind over the water. The difference between haven and open water is greatest at night and least at midday. It is greater in autumn than in spring. $\bar{R}$ are averages.*[21]

over the sea is the mirror of itself over the land. In other words, to take one example, a gentle knot might still be found 30 miles off the coast of East Anglia on a silent starry night([2]).

WINDS OVER BIG LAKES A big lake is one which is large enough for the wind which comes ashore on the leeward side to be independent of what it was when it left the windward shore. There are no such lakes in the British Isles and perhaps the most obvious examples of big lakes are the Great Lakes of North America.

There is nothing unique about North America's Great Lakes, and the arguments put forward about them in this book will apply to similar areas elsewhere. Winds which are variable will be variable for the same reasons, and suffer the same vagaries and constraints as winds in any other similar locality in the temperate latitudes. We might find substantial errors in the conclusions if they were applied to the equatorial belt or the polar caps, but so long as the weather is temperate latitude stuff it will obey the same laws of nature.

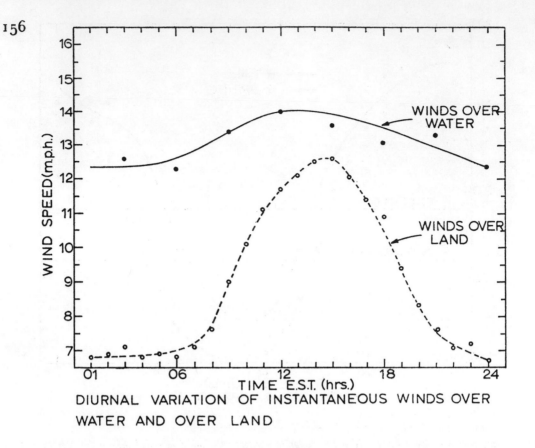

DIURNAL VARIATION OF INSTANTANEOUS WINDS OVER
WATER AND OVER LAND

5.16: *How the wind speed varies with the day over the Lakes and over the adjoining land.*[21]

Although I have never been to the Great Lakes, let alone raced a dinghy on them, I have confidence that what is written about winds over the Lakes is applicable to any similar widths of local water. What is important is that the wind should have an equal fetch.

In 1961 F. Lemire wrote a paper on "Winds on the Great Lakes"([21]). His conclusions are interesting and instructive. He took representative winds over the Lakes and over adjacent land areas, both throughout day and night and also from season to season. He divided the mean wind over the water by the corresponding mean wind over the land and called this ratio *R*. By dividing the year in half—spring half and fall half—he found that on leaving the land the wind speed picked up over the water by a factor of 1·6 in the spring and by a larger factor of 1·9 in the fall (Fig. 5.15).

He also showed that the difference between wind over water and the same wind over the land was greatest from midnight to 0500 E.S.T. and the two were nearest to one another at 1400 (Fig. 5.16). The wind over the water also showed some increase during the day, but not much. The conclusion is that when one leaves the shelter of a haven at night one should allow for the speed over the sea being twice that observed over the land,

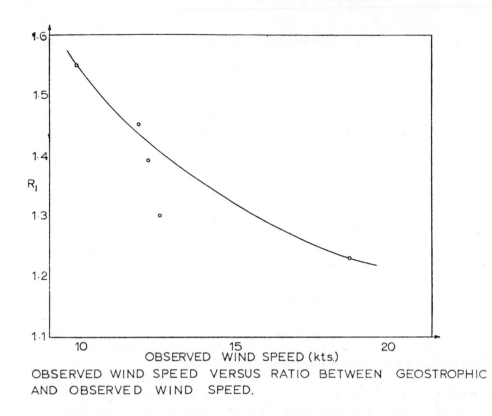

OBSERVED WIND SPEED VERSUS RATIO BETWEEN GEOSTROPHIC AND OBSERVED WIND SPEED.

5.17: *Wind speed aloft and alow. The ratio of the former to the latter becomes greater as the wind speed falls. This is more evidence for conclusions reached in Chapters Two and Three.*[21]

but in the middle of the day the wind over the water will not be vastly stronger than it is over the land.

He also shows clearly that as the wind speed increases so the winds at the surface tend to become as strong as those which would be measured from the isobar spacing on a weather map of the area (Fig. 5.17). Thus once again we see that lighter winds may be much more variable than stronger ones, because descending currents can bring very much stronger wind from above, and this will in its turn tend to keep the direction it had aloft and temporarily sweep the surface wind out of the way.

Another point which weighs heavily in favour of the conclusion that the gusts are normally veered to the mean surface wind direction, wherever you may sail in the temperate latitudes in the northern hemisphere, is the comparison of wind direction given by ships on the Great Lakes with the lie of the isobars, which is the same as that of the undisturbed wind above the friction layer. The results were as shown overleaf:

These results show that when one is sailing within the influence of land the wind over the water is still well modified by the land's proximity. The differences in direction quoted above (which are, after all, averages) are large, and over the truly open sea the wind at the surface would not differ from that aloft by as much as 30° let alone the 64° quoted for July.

TABLE 5.C

Month	Number of Examples	Average Veer of Isobars from Surface Wind	Average Observed Surface Speed
May	21	31°	14 kt
June	14	22°	12 kt
July	16	64°	12 kt
August	19	49°	10 kt
September	23	35°	12·6 kt
October	10	37°	19 kt
November	15	19°	19·4 kt
Average		37°	

This large difference during the hottest months, may be because the surface wind is often well modified by local lake-breeze effects.

LAKE BREEZES　　These are merely sea breezes which occur along the edges of large lakes such as Michigan. In summer time the lake breeze occurs almost daily, but it does not get very far inland—usually not much more than a mile. However, penetrations of eight or more miles do occur under favourable circumstances. There is usually a "lake high" over Lake Michigan during the day in summer, just as there is one over the North Sea, but the lake breeze does not seem to be quite as strong a character as the sea breeze. For instance, the offshore wind, which will prevent it, is less than along the south and east coasts of the British Isles—roughly 6–8 knots stop it altogether[25].

Similar results may be expected from other similar big lakes, and if one wants to read what has been written about the winds in these or any other local areas then the local weather office will put you in touch with the libraries. Meteorological libraries are a service which are not much used by the general public, but a little research off one's own bat can reap dividends when the racing is needle-pointed. This is particularly so if one is visiting foreign climes as a national representative. There is not time to find out by experience what the locals have spent years discovering, so reading the considered views of local met. men is the only way to redress the balance.

THUNDERSTORMS　　Because of their many unhappy effects thunderstorms have been held in awe throughout the ages, even being paid the supreme compliment of having a deity to control them. We cannot escape this ancient terror. One of the most naked feelings is to be in a small craft with the blackness of an approaching thundercloud arching over the leaden waters. There seems no way of escaping the monster, and the prudent will lower sail or shorten canvas because they know what torrents of wind can suddenly erupt with little warning out of one of Thor's chariots.

Due principally to the efforts of teams of meteorologists in the U.S.A. and this country the thunderstorm is better understood than it was, and thus something worthwhile can be said about the winds to be expected from thunderstorms. In order to understand the kinds and conditions of storms it is best to split them up as follows:

(i) Air-mass thunderstorms are the single cell variety which grow amongst other large cumulus and cumulonimbus in a very unstable airstream. Such streams are typified by the Polar maritime north-westerlies which blow for many days in the rear of depressions which are filling up over the North Sea and Scandinavia. They produce the showers of April or the scattered thunderstorms of summer and will sometimes give an odd clap of thunder in winter when the weather is unsettled.

(ii) Depression and trough thunderstorms are a very different affair, for here the tendency for strong ascent which builds a thunderstorm is ready made and the outbreaks are widespread, especially in the height of summer. One thunderstorm cell tends to build another on the back of the very cold air which cascades out of the parent storm and spreads about it. In this way groups of cells form, each one taking over from its dying parent and so keeping the chain-reaction going. These chains of cells may coalesce into areas of storms tens of miles across and can lead to "thunderstorm highs", of which more later. Occasionally a phenomenal thunderstorm area develops and can be labelled a "supercell". These deserve special mention.

(iii) Supercells are the most damaging and spectacular of the weather features of these islands, apart perhaps from tornadoes. They have been studied in some detail by F. H. Ludlam and R. S. Scorer of Imperial College amongst others. Thus we know that certain, luckily infrequent, thunderstorm areas of tropical intensity, which cut a swath across the country, are giant single features with a now fairly well-known structure. They produce hailstones the size of tennis balls, and when hail of this size is reported in temperate latitudes a supercell is almost certainly to blame, for no ordinary thunderstorm cell can support the updraughts in which such immense stones can grow.

It is helpful to have some idea of the stage in life to which a thunderstorm cell has grown. Strangely enough, contrary to popular conception, they are past their prime when they have pushed their cirrus anvils up against the tropopause. The hail stage of a growing cumulonimbus cloud is typified by a hard rounded top with perhaps an eyebrow-shaped veil of pileus spanning its upthrusting top. This latter cloud is a sure sign of very strong convection taking place and tells one to look out for subsequent thunderstorms (Photo 6).

During a summer's day, particularly after a long, hot, fine spell, the tendency for thunder grows with the day. The late afternoon and evening are the chief times for the thunder of sultry weather, and, while the storms may not be welcome, at least they serve to clear the oppressive air. What were quite modest cumulus clouds in the forenoon may erupt into thunderheads by the afternoon, as an inversion aloft can often be just broken in the early afternoon, and moist sea air will feed the growing storms. The hail stage of a growing cloud is when it is at its prime, and the hail lasts typically for 20 minutes or less from any individual cell, being accompanied and followed by rain. Photo 11 shows cumulonimbus in the hail stage. There is a high tendency for the hail to appear in the right rear of a storm, but this information may not be very useful when several cells are growing and dying over one area. Where it is useful is when a supercell threatens, for then something may be done to avoid the dangerous right rear. These scarce but dangerous features

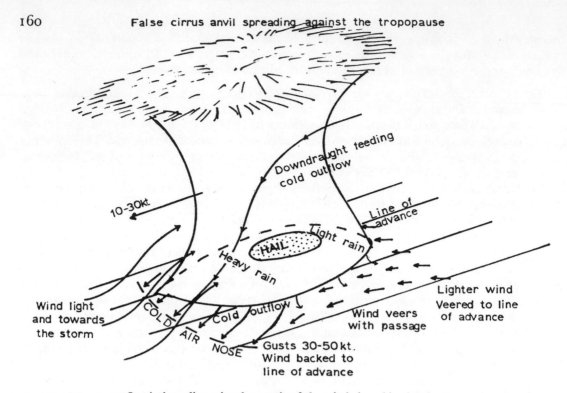

5.18: *A three-dimensional portrait of the winds in a big thunderstorm.*

can be recognised by their continuous cloud-to-cloud lightning of tropical intensity and rules for avoiding their worst effects will be given.

The next stage in the career of a single-cell thunderstorm is when the hail gives way to rain and then this also tails away. The recognisable feature of this stage is the false-cirrus anvil which is a visible sign of the ascending air meeting the inversion of the tropopause and being forced to spread sideways underneath it. The cell is then on its last legs, so cumulonimbus which display anvils is a dead duck. What makes the anvils good trademarks of thunderstorms is that an old cell will probably be growing a daughter alongside it. It does this because the cold air which flows out of its base must flow ahead and to the sides and will lift the warm air there into eruption on its own account (Photo 12).

This outflow is the carrier of the very strong gusts which accompany thunderstorms. Figure 5.18 is a three-dimensional sketch of the sort of winds which accompany big thunderstorms. Ahead of the storm the wind is gently towards it, being part of the wind it is drawing into its middle regions. Therefore the wind against which the thunderstorm has for ages been said to move is one of its own making. It is gentle and sultry—the calm before the storm.

As the black arch of the leading edge of the storm cloud approaches one must look out for the "cold nose", for here is the strongest gust (typically 30–50 knots) which strikes without any real warning other than a disturbed sea from the diametrically opposite

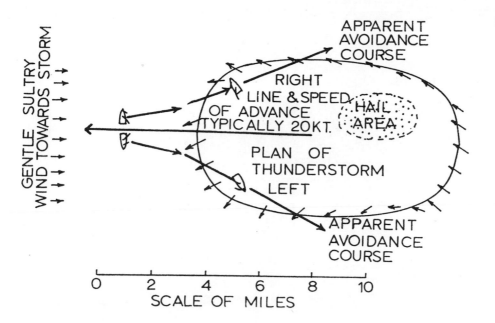

5.19: *Apparent avoidance courses to clear the worst of the storm.*

direction to the previously gentle wind. After this initial gust has been weathered, it is to be expected that the strong wind will continue with rain and a lot of gusting. It will be cold, dark and generally morale-killing, but there is nothing one can do but hang on. In the calm before the storm one should have taken in a reef, to allow for the worst that the wind can do, and made as accurate an assessment of the line of advance of the storm as possible. This can be gauged by the wind at medium cloud level, but if there is none then the lower cloud movement ahead of the storm may help, providing it is not being dragged in towards the storm on the back of the storm's own wind. Big storms cannot exist when there is a strong change of wind direction and speed with height, for such divergences would tear them apart and they would not have time to develop. So the wind assessed before the storm takes over is pretty certain to be the direction in which it is moving.

One can expect the initial gust to be somewhat backed from this direction and the wind to veer as the storm passes, being light and veered behind the storm. Winds observed in the rear of big cumulonimbus clouds which produced heavy showers have sometimes been almost from left to right of the line of advance gradually reverting to the normal direction.

Leaving aside the danger of being struck by lightning the danger area of any storm is likely to be its right rear, and it is as well to avoid that if you can.

If you decide that the approaching storm is likely to get you, the golden rule is to sail so that you leave the storm to port. Now this is easier said than done, for in the quiet of the pre-storm calm not many cables can be put under the keel. One may only make a knot or two, and if the storm looks threatening the motor might be justified. The distance of the storm can be assessed in the following way: we have said that the cirrus anvils press up

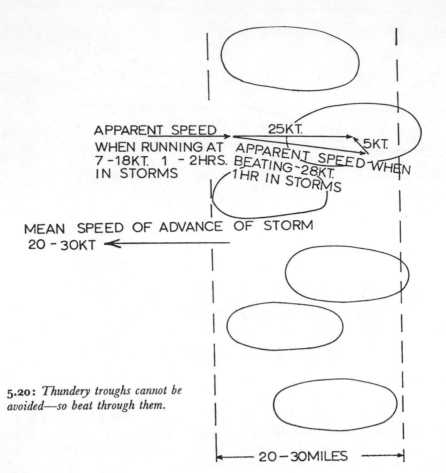

APPARENT SPEED 25KT.
WHEN RUNNING AT APPARENT SPEED WHEN
7-18KT. 1-2HRS. BEATING~28KT.
IN STORMS 1HR IN STORMS 5KT.

MEAN SPEED OF ADVANCE OF STORM
20-30KT

20-30MILES

5.20: *Thundery troughs cannot be avoided—so beat through them.*

against the tropopause and it is perhaps 6–7 miles high in summer over temperate latitudes. Therefore the 3h yardstick (Fig. 4.4, page 111) will indicate when such a storm is about 20 miles away. As 20 kt is a typical rate of advance of a thunderstorm, the storm will be with you in one hour. In that time all the distance you can achieve is a number of nautical miles equal to your maximum speed over the ground. If you are in the direct line of advance then perhaps 6 miles or so, using the motor across the storm's path (and leaving it to port) will help to keep the right rear on your port side.

A useful plan of action to avoid an individual storm is to sail to keep the true wind abeam. In the first instance as the storm approaches this may well be across the gentle wind which is towards the storm (Fig. 5.19). When the strong gusts from the opposite direction have been met and weathered, a broad reach across the wind will yield the apparent avoidance courses shown in the figure.

The storm overtakes you at perhaps 20 kt, so even if you run before it you cannot hope to run clear of it, and all that happens is that you are under its influence for an extended period (Fig. 5.20). The only thing to do is to hug a port-tack reach if you judge you are in

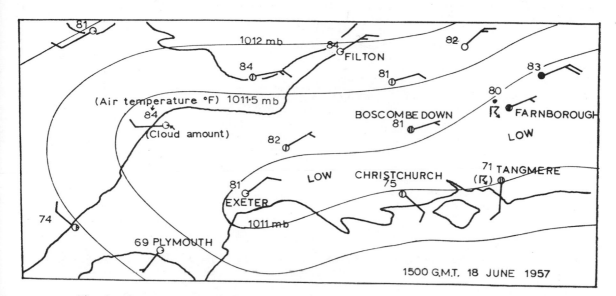

5.21: *The situation over south and south-west England on a hot summer's day with mainly easterly wind inland and sea breezes around the coasts.*

the storm's left area, and to reach off on starboard if in the right, thus getting through it as fast as practicable. This advice will of course, under the stress of racing, be largely ignored, but avoidance of the right rear is still often possible without jeopardising the chances, for at sea the choice of tack may well be yours, and even if you are going before the storm a broad reach on port tack out of the danger area is a very prudent move if only for the crew's morale.

THUNDERSTORM HIGHS AND OTHER THINGS The replacement of warm air by cold air will lead inevitably to a rise of surface pressure, so when a big thunderstorm area breaks out suddenly (as it may do when thunder-prone air gets pushed up over higher ground) then what was previously a "heat-low" fed by sea breezes may become a "thunderstorm high". Such sudden reversals of inland surface pressure patterns can occur, for instance, when potentially unstable air moves down from the hot Home Counties on to the rising ground of Salisbury Plain and the hills and moors of Somerset and Devon. A case where this happened is worth describing for there are lessons to be learned from it.

Let us set the scene. The afternoon of 18 June 1957 was very hot inland. The temperatures were well into the eighties and even where the sea breeze was blowing in over the coasts they were 75° or 76°F. Thus during the afternoon a heat low developed over Sussex and sprawled down into Devon. By 1500 G.M.T. thunderstorms were beginning to break out over Hampshire, and an hour later they were shown by radar to be developing over a wide area of Surrey, Sussex and Hampshire (see Fig. 5.21). However the winds

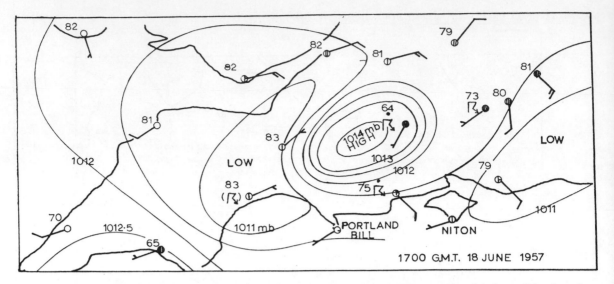

5.22: *The situation changes out of all recognition in two short hours. Thunderstorms break out inland, and coastwise mariners can expect onshore winds to go offshore soon.*

were not as yet being greatly affected. Storms could be seen growing inland by coastwise helmsmen, and inland-water sailors would have begun to feel threatened by them if they were not already getting wet.

However in one short hour the whole situation changed. The cold plunge of rain and hail-filled air out of the thunderstorms produced a thunderstorm high over Salisbury Plain and at places like Boscombe Down the wind swung from north-east to south-west while the temperature fell by nearly 20°F. This wind behaviour is typical. The wind must be expected to swing to a direction away from the storm centres which is what it did at Boscombe (Fig. 5.22) at 1700 G.M.T. But apart from there being thunderstorms at places like Christchurch, the south coast winds did not as yet know of the inland storm centre. The cold whaleback of air had not had time to get that far. However by 1900 G.M.T. the cold air had reached the coast (having warmed up somewhat on the way) and was flowing offshore, having killed and reversed the previous sea breezes at Christchurch (Poole) and Portland Bill. Ahead of the storm Exeter had had an easterly or north-easterly wind all the afternoon, but as the storm area approached so Exeter's wind swung round off the sea to help feed the advancing giant. By 2000 G.M.T. most of the sea breezes had been killed around the south and west coasts by winds flowing out of the thunderstorm high on to the sea.

The lessons of this example are:

(i) If thunderstorms erupt one can expect a cold river of air to flow out of them, and one should allow for it coming from the direction of the storms, reversing or modifying any other winds there may be.

(ii) Do not think that just because enough time has elapsed you are clear of the influence of these "precipitation downdraughts". In the same article in which the above

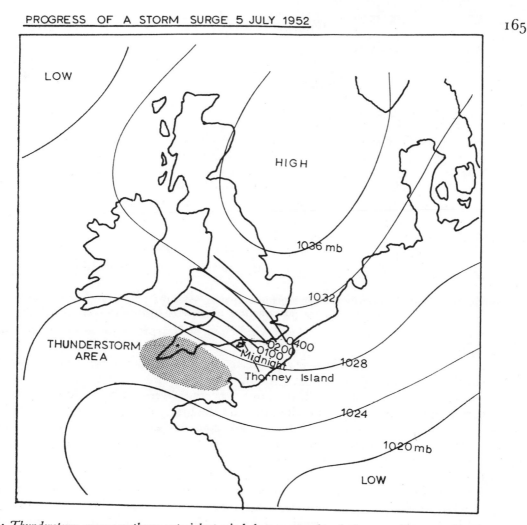

5.23: *Thunderstorm areas can throw out violent wind changes even though they are miles away. See Fig. 2.12 on page 39 for the anemogram.*

situation was described C. E. Wallington, who forecasts for gliding events, recalls how a fatal glider crash occurred due to a pilot entering such a draught which had flowed off the inland hills some 50 miles away. Admittedly this was in Spain but the lesson applies elsewhere.[7]

Another curious wind situation due to thunderstorms, this time over the sea, is also described by Wallington. The storm area in question was over the South-west Approaches and it was the sort of night when many a yacht might have been forgiven for imagining that all was right with the weather. This is a reason for carrying less canvas by night than by day. While a high dominated the British Isles this unseen thunderstorm area set up a pressure surge which moved as shown in Fig. 5.23. In most cases the surge tended to reduce the wind's strength, which was easterly 15 kt or thereabouts over the Channel, and rather more northerly 8–10 kt over the adjacent land areas, but the sharp and large direction changes could have been alarming as well as mystifying. Wind data for the inland stations serves to point to what may happen even when the thunderstorms are miles away. The wind at Farnborough went at 0120 G.M.T. from east-north-east through north to south and then back after which it fluctuated between north-east and north-west for the next hour or so. Other stations in the area show similar changes, along the Channel coast curious and violent gusts occurred from a few knots up to 20 or more knots.

The effect at Thorney Island and, by inference, in the Solent Area is illustrated in Fig. 2.12, page 39. The wind was all but normal and falling with the night. The direction was steady and due to the anticyclone over the North Sea as shown in Fig. 5.23. Then at half-past midnight a gentle 7 kt suddenly gusted to 27 kt while the direction backed abruptly through 180°. It was another hour before the wind returned to anything approaching normal. So if thunderstorms are forecast, even if none appear to be developing in the local area, consider the possible effects, especially at night when the range of vision is perforce restricted.

It is as well to remember that summer thunderstorms are mainly bred over land and may then drift over the sea, so an offshore general wind—that is one which is offshore above any sea breeze or other local wind effects—is a prerequisite for them coming coastwards.

However, coastal waters are very prone to the growth of big cumulus or thunderstorms in the early hours especially in autumn when the coastal waters are warm and the land breezes bring cool moist air off the land. The cold-over-warm situation is just right for cumulonimbus to develop, and when they do they may invade the land at first light. Such coastal storms can form only in practically stagnant air, so not much wind results, although the damping of morale, when a quiet night goes suddenly wet, may make those gusts that occur seem a lot stronger than they actually are.

One of the ways in which summer weather breaks down is by the encroachment of a thundery low pressure area from the direction of France. Winds do not become vastly strong under such thundery incursions, but there may be some nasty gusts from unpredictable directions. The electrical activity is mainly cloud-to-cloud lightning, which gives them a tropical appearance at night, but unless it is September such tropical-looking weather need not be very bad. In September the remains of old tropical cyclones may rejuvenate themselves over Britain or the Continent into the worst of all thunderstorms. However, such events are rare, although when they do occur (5 September 1958 and again the following year, to mention but two in which tennis-ball-sized hail fell in the Home Counties) they become remembered for their severity. Such storms are of the "supercell" variety and are in a class by themselves.

LIGHT AIRS The state of absolutely no wind is relatively rare, but when it does occur the man who knows where to find some motion of the air is the one who will creep ahead of his competitors.

Very much more erudite helmsmen than I have written reams on what to do in light airs, and as this is not principally a book on tactics I shall leave most of the tactical field to them. One cannot, however, describe the likely sources of wind without entering into some discussion of the way to steal a march on your competitors.

The prime rules in light airs are:

(i) Keep the boat moving, even in the wrong direction, for way engenders airflow over the sails and together with the breathing of the lightest of light winds this will move you to somewhere where more wind is to be found.

(ii) Do nothing which will upset the correct light airs trim. That is, maximum length in the water and craft gently canted to what you hope is leeward so as to induce flow into the sails. Also sit absolutely still like a cat waiting to catch a mouse—one false move and your little zephyr of a prey will escape.

(iii) Finally, concentrate absolutely and where possible forget your competitors. Look for and seek out every possible source of wind which may be about.

The wind-making forces always tend to remove calm when it is sunny, and overcast calms are usually only of a temporary nature.

The most prevalent times for calm are early morning and evening. During the day sea breezes will defeat calms near the coast, and land breezes will act against their continuance at night. Inland, calms will certainly be slower to change into conditions of some wind, but any inland water is surrounded by thermal sources in sunny weather, and again calm is most likely in the morning and evening when the sun is sleeping or only just up.

Before a calm can occur the isobaric set-up must be favourable. That is, the isobar spacing on a weather-map spanning the area must be very wide. Such wide spacings occur in the centres of anticyclones, sometimes in ridges of high pressure and in cols, although the latter are shorter-lived features compared to the former. Another temporary calm area, and one which is likely to cause a certain amount of embarrassment to a race committee who have sent a fleet on a long course, is to be found at the centre of slow-moving depressions. Such lows are very prevalent in the English Channel, and the rain or drizzle may soak luckless helmsmen attempting to punch tides to reach unattainable marks as the wind, which was so reasonable at the start, dies away to nothing. This, I think, is the most frustrating of situations one has to face when racing: the required mark receding on the tide while the moisture trickles off one's hair and round one's ears and down one's neck. When it blows a wetting helps the spirit of exhilaration—when it is calm a soaking puts morale at rock bottom. Such calms may last for half an hour, or perhaps for an hour or two, but it is rare for total calm to obtain even with slow-moving depressions of the kind which frequent the eastern end of the English Channel. The thing which lasts in these quiet downpours is the rain, which may go on sometimes for a day or even two without much respite.

Temporary calm periods sometimes set in ahead of advancing sea breezes when they are moving in to replace offshore winds. Offshore, on days when sea breezes are blowing over the coasts, the centres of limited waters such as the North Sea or Channel are regions of calm or very light winds, if the other meteorological conditions are right. On summer days the place to find wind is along the coasts, and the centres of waters which are feeding sea breezes should be avoided. When sea breezes are building against offshore winds in the morning or even early afternoon then calm can exist right over the coast. The normal thing, however, is for the calm zones to progress inland and out to sea, the sea breeze fetch being of the order of 10–15 miles to seaward on many occasions. For details see the Sea Breeze section on page 133.

There is a remarkable tendency for the sea breeze of summer days to be followed by an evening of the most complete calm we ever experience. For at this time there are no thermals to engender the weakest of airs. In fact the whole of the lower atmosphere is geared to produce air at rest. With the sinking of the sun, the air near the surface is cut off from that above by the evening inversion, and it loses its momentum in useless friction with the surface.

During the night near the coast, or where there are slopes down which the air may slip, katabatic winds occur. It follows that clearness and calm are enemies, and heating or cooling of the land above or below the water temperature (which remains to all intents and purposes constant) will lead to air drift.

The rules are:

If the land heats above the water temperature expect drift from water to land.

If the land cools below the water temperature expect drift off the land.

HOW DIFFERENCE IN TEMPERATURE LEADS TO AIR MOTION

When one portion of the earth's surface becomes heated above another the natural tendency is for air motion to equalise the discrepancy. On the smallest scale this is achieved by the "thermal" beloved of glider pilots and becalmed small-water sailors. When the sun is allowed to shine on the earth's surface thermals are inevitable. However, it is only when there is no other source of wind that they come into their own as a wind-generating source. The way in which the thermal acts is of importance for it helps in visualising the likely thermal sources and therefore in seeking their proximity. Often it is found in flat calm that one shore is slightly favoured over another. The best thermal sources are shores in the direct sunlight, that is on the side of the stream removed from the sun, which means westerly to northerly shores on summer mornings.

A surface which is inclined to receive the perpendicular rays of the sun would be the most likely thermal source. So hill slopes, and shores which stoop down to face the rising sun are thermal sources. It is also less likely that such faces will be shaded in any way. Water surfaces are anti-thermal areas because they absorb the sun's heat in depth or reflect it so they do not appreciably heat—neither do they appreciably cool—while the various solid surfaces of the earth will absorb the sun's rays, the greatest absorption being by those surfaces which are dull black, followed by shiny black or grey, and then through a succession of lightening colours to white, which will reflect much of the sun's radiation. Thus mud-flats will form a likely thermal source, especially those which have dried since the last tide and are on the side of the channel removed from the sun. If other things are equal some air motion due to thermals will be found here. It will only be odd puffs which will have an ephemerally short life, but still they will be there.

The thermals form due to an area becoming warmed above its surroundings. Such areas are thermal sources, and on a large scale towns are thermal sources of some magnitude. Black road surfaces are very efficient thermal sources, while concrete is also quite efficient. Therefore airfield runways and extensive slipways can form thermal sources especially if surrounded by grass. Those features which absorb the sun's rays in depth will be anti-thermal. Woods and thick vegetation are examples of these areas, while ploughed fields and areas of short grass can well be thermal sources. Areas of equal surface absorption may be split into thermal and anti-thermal areas by undulations: the undulating parts facing the sun being thermal, and those sloped away from the sun anti-thermal.

Thermals can form along mud-flats which are backed by sea walls for they are easily heated (if dry), while a sea wall will shelter an area behind it or in front of it from the sun.

In the early forenoon thermal sources are restricted to limited areas which face the sun, and they are few and far between. In general the rate at which thermals break away from any source region will increase as the sun climbs into the zenith.

It is during the first few hours of the sun that flat calm may exist and the thermals be the only initiators of air motion.

Assume that it is flat calm and that one is seeking airs along the side of a creek on which drying mud-banks are facing the sun. Thermals can be visualised as follows. A film of air becomes warmed by contact and sits domed over the heated surface as in Fig. 5.24a. When sufficiently warmed it lifts, and breaks away with a motion which is best visualised as the propulsion stroke of a jelly-fish (Fig. 5.24c). This leaves the thermal source deficient in air and slight flow occurs into it from all around. This breath is of short duration, but, if one can catch it, it can provide some way—perhaps enough to ghost on to where another bank has a handy thermal ready to lift off and provide a little transitory wraith of air motion.

Later when the sun begins to get to work on more areas of the surface the thermal sources multiply. By that time however they are usually so prevalent that they have started to mix up the lower levels of the atmosphere and real wind has been brought down from above on to the surface.

There are other conditions of partial cloudiness which will sort out thermal source areas. The cloud street is a well-known phenomenon where cumulus grows from a good thermal source area such as high ground to windward, and forms a line of cloud streaming downwind from the source. The area in the shadow of a street will be anti-thermal while in the surrounding clear lanes thermals will be prevalent. They will draw their air supply from the anti-thermal area. Thus there will be a tendency for airflow out of the shadows and into the sun.

Physically thermals are as big as large trees and the smaller ones require an excess of temperature above their surroundings of 3–4°F. in order to lift off. However, larger ones will sometimes require only a degree or two of heating to become airborne. In spite of this they get away as fast as the warmer smaller ones. The time between thermals over any one spot is of the order of ten minutes, but each tree-sized area can grow its own thermal, so local airs may come much more rapidly from the lifting off of different thermals. As soon as there is any wind to drift airborne thermals over others, with which they can combine, they reinforce and the advent of wind will be self-generating, so that the wind will tend to increase from nothing to several knots in a very short time. This shows that complete, or almost complete, calm quickly gives way to a reasonable wind on sunny mornings.

Thermal energy will continue to increase right up to, and a little after, the hottest hour. The visible signs are, of course, puffs of cumulus, and the trade mark of the fair day is a pleasant supply of fair-weather cumulus clouds sailing along in the light to moderate wind. Such cumulus first appears over the slopes and ridges of hill lines and is a sign that thermals are at work already over the best source areas and that they should appear on the lower-lying areas soon if they have not already done so (Photo 6).

Then as the sun's power wanes with the afternoon those same east-facing hill slopes will be the first to cool and the upward air motion will be reversed into a sinking current.

This sinking air will flow into the valleys and on to the inland stretches of water contained within the confines of the hills. There it will lift air over the valleys, and in the

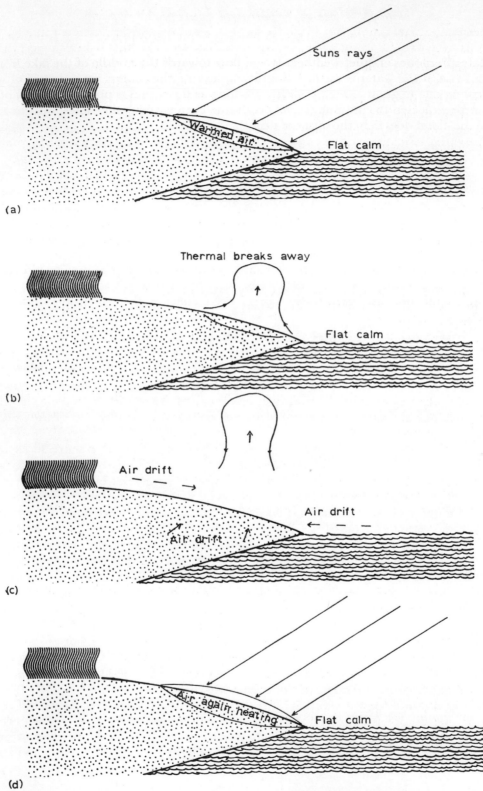

Suns rays

Warmed air

Flat calm

(a)

Thermal breaks away

↑

Flat calm

(b)

↑

Air drift – – →

Air drift ← – –

Air drift ↗ ↑

(c)

Air again heating

Flat calm

(d)

5.24: *How thermals produce intermittent air drift in flat calms.*

late afternoon cumulus lines can occur along the axes of valleys as illustrated in Fig. 5.27. Often this cool air settling on to a lake or reservoir between the hills is all the wind there is in the late afternoons of quiet weather. It will flow towards the middle of the lake from all sides and rise, if the water is warmer than itself, leaving the central areas devoid of wind, but allowing one to ghost along the shores. So long as the cumulus persists the drift off the hills can be expected to continue. It may continue even without the cloud, but the rising air into the cloud does help the offshore drift.

The valley effects described will work over a wide range of size from valleys some 20–30 miles across to mere clefts a few miles wide.

Thermals over the sea have no surface features to aid their formation, and they can only be formed by cool air flowing over progressively warmer water. Thus there is no such thing as an individual area over the sea. Thermals occur, and cumulus develops on top of their upward paths, but it is quite random, and as sunshine has no direct effect on deep sea temperature so they are just as prevalent at night as by day. It follows that over the sea an upper layer of cloud which blots out the sun does not prevent thermals forming, as it would over the land, and their own shadows do not inhibit them as would happen over the land. Thermal formation as described in the previous paragraphs is a restricted-water phenomenon, and deep-water sailors need concern themselves very little with thermals.

Within distances of the order of yards from shoreside thermals, air will be drawn to replace that which rises. At the same time air must also sink to feed this lifting. Herein may lie one of those ephemeral frustrations of light airs—the wind-patch which is never there when you work towards it. This may not be surprising, for it is my view that these little areas of darker catspaws are the visible signs of sinking jets of air from above, which are just ruffling the surface and spreading out. In support of this I remember once being utterly becalmed within sight of the French coast near Le Havre. The morning was very hot and quite lifeless. Then around lunchtime a curious set of catspaws formed all round us. They were widespread, being everywhere as far as we could see. Yet there was still no noticeable horizontal air motion. Soon the sea breeze arrived, moving out to sea, and we got under way. The most likely explanation is that the shell-like catspaws were due to the sinking air ahead of the edge of the sea breeze proper. It would seem, therefore, that local dark areas on otherwise calm water may just be vertically moving air and are not worth the effort of following. I think this must be so, for, if it were not, the dark patch would be a line or an area as the air moved across the surface, thus ruffling it. Horizontal air motion of very small magnitude produces very little effect on the water surface, and what it does produce is difficult to differentiate from other imperfections in the water surface such as clear lanes between oil films.

THE TIDE-WIND This is the wind which is entirely due to the tide, and here is an example of its possible use. Let it be flat calm ashore and the craft at A in Fig. 5.25 is becalmed inshore of the eddy on the corner while the full ebb is hurrying by out to sea through the narrow harbour constriction. Such an eddy must nearly always be there, for there exists a turning moment on the water due to the ebb outside and slack water inside.

As air motion is relative it does not matter whether a light wind blows over a boat or the boat is moved by some external agency across stationary air. Thus when a craft is locked in the tidal stream she moves with that stream and in flat calm will experience a

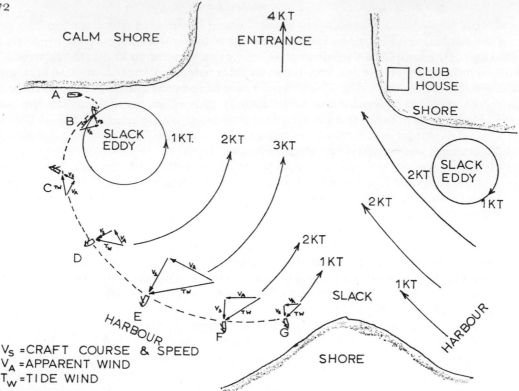

5.25: *An example of the use of the tide-wind.*

wind from the opposite direction to the stream's set of almost the same value as that of the stream itself. It will not be quite as much, for the sea surface is entraining the very surface air to move with it. However at the normal height of the centre of effort any wind with the tide will have a very low speed. For practical purposes let it be assumed that in a tidal stream of V kt a dinghy will feel blowing against it in flat calm a wind of V kt from the diametrically opposite direction to the stream.

Craft A desires to make the club-house on the opposite shore but he has no wind. Perhaps it is evening, and a flat calm has descended after a day of sea breeze. Obviously launching out across the 4 kt race is madness, so he uses the tide-wind. He purposefully seeks the outgoing limb of the inshore eddy and thus establishes for himself a slight shoreward wind (B). At the same time he endeavours to sail perpendicular to the resultant apparent wind (V_A). At first the motion is slight, but he orientates himself by the apparent wind direction to sail away and into the tide as at BCDEF, etc. All the time he is using the tide-wind to sail into the tide, and his trajectory is something like the one shown. As this is assumed to be a true story he cannot make the shore near G even if he wants to, but he has made way out into the stream which will enable him to reach the club shore even if he has eventually to dig out the paddle.

This is one example of obtaining wind from an external source of energy (the tide) in a flat calm, but there are aspects of the tide-wind which are worth noting when the wind is blowing. For example in the entrance (Fig. 5.25) a wind of 10 kt off the sea would become a wind of 14 kt off the sea, and in shorter craft, which will not plane in 10 kt, planing can ensue. In the converse case where the tide is setting in the same direction as the wind, and therefore is decreasing the true wind by 4 kt, this effect could lower the true wind speed below planing limits temporarily, and the fastest course might not be that which sought the full tidal stream but skirted its edges.

In offshore work the tide-wind will in the course of twelve hours experience a vector change of twice the maximum tidal velocity. A long haul down the English Channel, for example, will afford the experience of a vector tide-wind change approaching 5 knots, for the maximum speeds are of the order of 2·3 kt and more in the neighbourhood of the Cherbourg Peninsula and the Channel Islands. The method of computation of this effect can be judged from the vector triangles of Fig. 5.25, and drawing representative cases yields a total change in the sum of the true wind and the tide-wind over twelve hours approaching 30° or so. This wind is the wind one must use as the true wind in computations and therefore is not to be idly neglected in offshore racing[18].

SHORESIDE REFRACTION No book on wind could be complete without some mention of the refraction effect which can occur along shores off which or on to which a wind is blowing.

Refraction is a phenomenon which occurs when something which is flowing is suddenly forced to change its velocity. Lest the reader should be confused by casting back to school science days I should explain that the refraction of fluids, where higher speed appears over the surface of lower frictional drag, acts in the opposite manner to that of light waves. In the latter case the wave velocity as a whole slows down in a refracting medium such as glass. The laws of shoreside refraction are not the same as those of light.

To explain, let the wind over the land be V_L and blow at θ to the shoreline. On arriving over the water surface of lower friction the wind speeds up to V_W and in so doing makes a larger angle ϕ with the shoreline. But how much greater an angle? (Fig. 5.26*a*).

This depends on the ratio of $V_W : V_L$ which is the equivalent of the refractive index in light. We will call this ratio n, and if it were 1·5, for example, then the wind over the sea would have to pick up almost at once half as much speed again as it had over the land. This seems pretty unlikely except under conditions of almost streamline flow as can happen in the evening. For this reason no values of n greater than 1·5 have been considered.

The components of the two winds along the shore must be the same so

$$V_W \cos \phi = V_L \cos \theta$$

from which is found

$$n = \frac{V_L}{V_W} = \frac{\cos \theta}{\cos \phi}$$

To find the amount of refraction which occurs for various values of n less than 1·5, Fig. 5.26*b* has been plotted. Enter this with the angle of wind off the land θ, and read off the corresponding angle ϕ over the water.

For example a wind of 10 kt off the land at 45° to the shoreline which increases to 12 kt on leaving the shore will now make an angle of 54°—a refraction of nearly 10°.

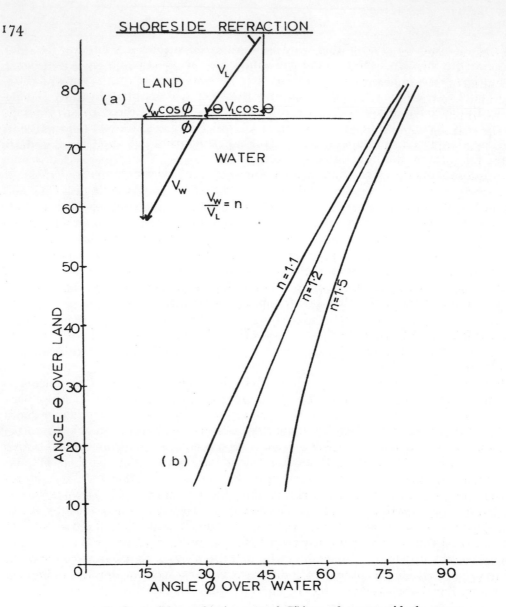

5.26: *Does offshore refraction matter? This graph may provide the answer.*

I contend that except under the most extreme conditions of stability, when winds will hug the surface very closely, 10° is the most likely angle through which a wind offshore will be bent. Even then sufficient space must be allowed for the wind near the surface to acquire the new enhanced speed. The refraction effect is not close inshore but perhaps tens of yards offshore.

It is a difficult thing to predict, for when the wind makes an angle θ which is small, *i.e.* blowing almost parallel to the shore, then there is often a tendency for the wind to hug the shore and be steered by it. This is, of course, especially true of rivers with significant barriers on the lee shore, even if quite open on the windward shore, for the barrier effect spreads back across the river and pilots the wind along the windward shore, that being the line of least resistance.

Refraction should be evident where there is only virgin water to leeward and the shore is rough, *i.e.* it is covered with vegetation or other protuberances of various kinds.

In the evening along a rough shore, which stoops down to the water's edge and does not allow the wind to slide over a shoreside zone of mud-flats or sand, etc., perhaps refraction may be such as to produce a 20° change of direction, but by day, and especially when the airstream is unstable, the effect must be negligible.

OTHER SHORE EFFECTS   That the shore-line is the seat of wind shifts which are permanent is undoubted, but they are more likely to be induced by local thermal effects or by katabatic or anabatic winds over steepish shores than by refraction. The two latter effects both contribute to winds tending to flow more directly offshore or on-shore.

When steep shores stand in the sun thermals occur, and the compensating flow must come off the water. This moist onshore flow can be the strongest form of thermal feed, for it is cool and dense. Thus the thermally induced onshore components may be relatively strong and light or even moderate winds can have the effect impressed on them. The air feeding the thermal "balloons" must slide up very steep-to shores and such upward motions are called anabatic as opposed to katabatics which flow down. In the evening or when the sun has left a steep shore a katabatic will occur, and this downflow will tend to be straight offshore. Lakes and lochs are the places for such katabatic effects to reach their greatest development. See Figs. 5.27 and 5.28.

MOUNTAIN AND VALLEY WINDS   Wherever there is enough water there will be boats, and so lakes in mountainous districts and at the foot of mountain valleys, as well as lochs and fiords, will have their complement of craft and their own special winds as well.

The simplest case to describe is the wind over a stretch of water between steeply ascending sides as in Fig. 5.27*a*. During the day the slopes and upper portions of the mountains enclosing the lake, etc., will be warmed, and upslope (anabatic) winds will occur with compensating down-currents in the lake centre. In the forenoon east to south-facing slopes will be the major seat of onshore wind due to anabatics while west-facing slopes will remain relatively cool. Air flow will tend to be from the shadowed side to the sunlit side. It has been found that the shading of a portion of a slope up which an ana-batic is ascending immediately affects it, weakening it and perhaps diverting the airflow towards the more strongly lit areas nearby.

The evening drawing (Fig. 5.27*b*) shows the tendency to stronger offshore flow on the shadowed side. That is off the east-facing slope which is shadowed early in the evening. The visual evidence of such motions is the appearance of cloud over the rising currents, *e.g.* cloud-streets over the ridges by day and cloud backbones along the valley axes by night. Lack of cloud also tells its tale. Wherever the air descends strongly there will be no cloud.

The upslope winds commence as soon as the sun is up and reach their maximum in the middle of the day. Their downslope counterparts get under way immediately after sunset.

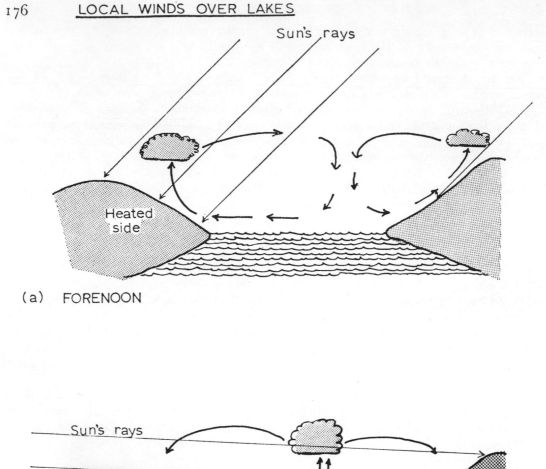

(a)   FORENOON

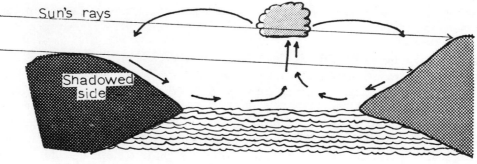

(b) EVENING

5.27: *Tendency for wind over lakes in light weather.*

This sideways flow is predominant on lakes closed by the mountains, but when the sailing area lies at the open end of a valley which rises in ridges to a mountainous interior axial flow along the valley floor is the more prevalent wind. In the Alps, for example, a

(After Defant)

(a) Sunrise

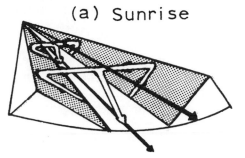

(b) Early Forenoon

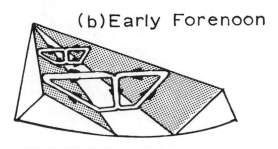

(c) Early Afternoon

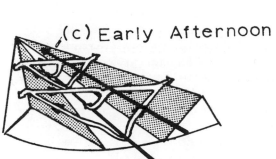

(d) Late Afternoon

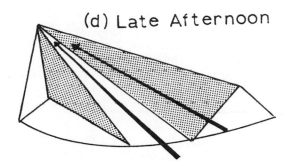

(e) Evening

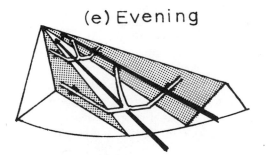

(f) Early Night

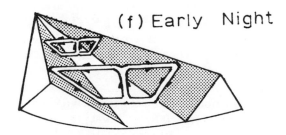

(g) Middle of the Night

(h) Early Hours

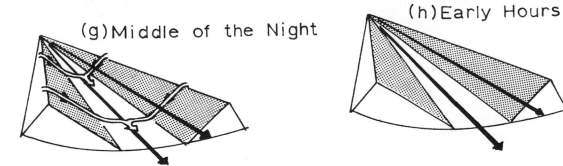

5.28: *In big valleys the winds will be a mixture of upslope-downslope and mountain or valley wind.*[23]

valley wind flows up the valleys from about 0900–1000 until sunset. By night the mountain wind reverses the direction and flows from the head of the valley.

There are thus two superimposed winds of thermal origin to be allowed for. As must be evident these will rarely be in phase. A morning wind in a valley with a north–south axil will have (if there is no strong opposing wind due to large-scale pressure patterns) a valley wind along its axis, and superimposed on this will be an upslope wind orientated towards the sunlit western slopes. The resultant wind will be skewed into having westerly components, but these will obviously vary with the nature of the terrain. This is such a difficult problem that the only thing to do is to reproduce more or less faithfully some drawings by a German oceanographer F. Defant which originally illustrated a study he made of these winds.

In Fig. 5.28*a* the mountain wind still blows down the valley while katabatic winds sink off the slopes. It is sunrise. By 0900 or thereabouts the mountain wind has fallen calm, while the upslope winds have commenced. The lake wind will be predominantly an onshore flow and weak at that (Fig. 5.28*b*). In the early afternoon (Fig. 5.28*c*) the valley wind has developed and the upslope wind has built to its maximum with compensating backbone downcurrents. In Fig. 5.28*d* it is late afternoon and the upslope winds have ceased, but the valley wind is still blowing at reduced strength. In the evening the downslope winds set in while the valley wind falls to nothing. The lake wind is now predominantly offshore and a cloud backbone may begin to appear over the rising currents in the middle (Fig. 5.28*e*).

Moonlit sailing in such enchanted surroundings will be aided by winds such as in Fig. 5.28*f* during the early night and reinforced in the middle of the night by the mountain wind which by the early hours (Fig. 5.28*h*) is left alone to sink coolly towards the plains.

FLOW IN THE LEE OF RIDGES   Mountain and valley winds are a phenomenon of settled weather, and they sink to nothing if the sky is overcast. What happens, however, when the moderate or strong winds blow obliquely over an upwind ridge and the sailing site is in the lee?

What *can* happen is illustrated in Fig. 5.29. With relatively light winds, whose speed does not change very much with height, laminar streaming may be the rule. This requires fairly gentle hills and a stable airstream. So an airstream of tropical origin flowing over downs, for instance, could produce this sort of flow. The whole airstream might well be cloudy.

Standing-eddy streaming is a big brother of the dense barrier flow discussed in Chapter Four. It likewise has a stationary roller in the lee, and under it surface winds can be towards the hills even when the forecast is for winds in the diametrically opposite direction. The situation, which is more easily recognised than either of the above, is when standing waves develop down-stream of the ridge. Such ridges do not need to be very high. A sharp set of craggy peaks are not as effective as more modest hills with relatively gentle upslopes stretched athwart the wind.

Roll clouds form some 2 to 20 miles downwind of the ridge, and the first of these is closer to the ridge than the second roller is to the first. Under these roll clouds the winds can be very variable and quite unpredictable. They can often be seen being shredded and torn by the rotating winds. Over them, at as much as 20,000 ft, lie the truly characteristic clouds of lee waves—altocumulus lenticularis to give them their full and explanatory

AIRFLOW IN THE LEE OF HILLS
(After Förchtgott)

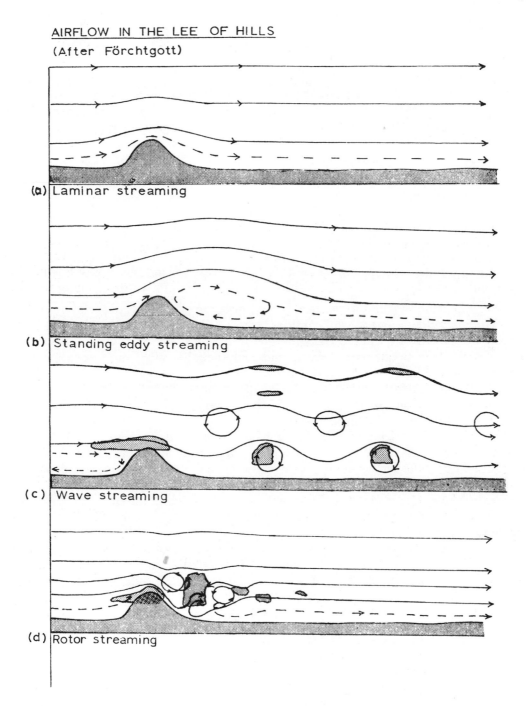

(a) Laminar streaming

(b) Standing eddy streaming

(c) Wave streaming

(d) Rotor streaming

5.29: *Four different types of flow in the lee of hill ridges. In the latter three, winds at the surface may be in any direction.*[24]

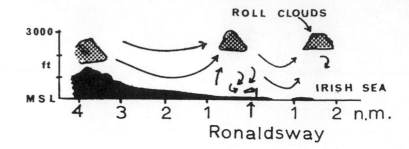

5.30: *To illustrate an actual example of wave streaming over the Isle of Man one of whose airports is Ronaldsway. The section is roughly orientated north-south.*

title. Once good examples of these lens-shaped clouds have been seen they are not forgotten, for their smooth whale-backed appearance is very striking. Such clouds will tell of standing-waves in lee of hills wherever they may be seen (Photos 4, 10 and 15).

Winds blowing over islands which have reasonable backbones of hills will produce rotor flow over the sea or coastal areas and can cause some curious wind situations. Thus an eye kept open for altocumulus lenticularis can discover why the wind is very variable and gusty. The rotor clouds and the altocumulus lenses remain largely stationary. They do not normally travel with the wind, although sometimes a most curious thing occurs in which a group of the lens clouds moves downwind and then literally jumps back against the wind to its original position.

At the same time a characteristic cloud called a helm may sit on the hill tops. Again it is stationary, but out of its lee edge (the helm bar) descends a wind which is often stronger than that in the valley beyond.

The fourth type of flow in the lee of a hill ridge is rotor streaming. As Fig. 5.29*d* shows, the roll cloud is larger, closer to the ridge and more turbulent than in standing wave streaming. The whole of the flow is stronger in its turbulent aspects, even producing a counter-flow at the surface of the windward side.

To give the reader some idea of the curious nature of wind under rotors the observations in the table on page 181 were made at Ronaldsway—the airport of the Isle of Man—on 28 July 1952 (see Fig. 5.30).

As the diagram shows, Ronaldsway had its roll cloud to tell why the wind was so utterly curious, and so did any luckless mariner in the Irish Sea presumably subjected to equally old puffs from all and every direction under the second roller of the wave pattern. As such turbulent wind zones remain more or less fixed (until the meteorological conditions change) the logical thing is to sail away from the roll cloud as quickly as the silly wind will allow.

Time	Wind at Control Tower		Wind at a wind-sock about half a mile to the east	
	Direction	*Speed*	*Direction*	*Speed*
0700	S	15 kt	—	—
0716	Calm	—	—	—
0728	A full cycle of 360°	8	—	—
0731	S.E.	14	N.	14 kt
0736	N.	10	S.W.	9
0741	S.W.	6	N.	14
0748	E.N.E.	14	N.	5
0752	Calm	—	N.	14
0754	W.	10	N.	9
0802	S.W.	10	N.	14
0808	E.	6	N.W.	9
0824	Calm	—	N.W.	9

CHAPTER SIX

Wind Shifts

THE wind will shift for many reasons, and the shifts may be small (10° or so) or large (as much as 180°). They may be permanent or temporary. By a permanent shift is meant one which persists for the rest of the race. A temporary shift is one where the wind is likely to revert to what it was before or change to something else during the course of the race. The shifts may also be general, that is affecting the whole fleet, or they may be local and only affect small sections of the fleet.

Therefore what is a permanent general shift to a dinghy race may be a temporary local shift to an ocean race. In the following summary what is and what is not a certain type of shift will depend on circumstances. To overcome this difficulty the probable time period before another shift occurs is given.

WIND CHANGES APPLICABLE TO RACING

Type of shift	Typical causes	Usual pattern	Typical time *before* next major shift
General and permanent.	Changes in the pressure pattern produced by (i) Depressions moving normally, *i.e.* west to east; (ii) Ridges moving west to east. When motion opposed to the normal then reverse back and veer in next column.	Wind backs ahead and to south of advancing depression. Veers as it passes. Cyclonic variation follows this pattern. Wind backs throughout if to north of centre. Wind backs if ridge apex is in northern quadrants. Wind veers if apex is in southern quadrants.	20–30 hrs.
	Passage of fronts and troughs.	Wind veers on passage. Wind often increases with small veers but may well decrease with veers greater than 45°.	Half a day or more.
	Passage of depression centres.	Wind goes down, with rain or drizzle occurring from low overcast. Picks up later from another direction.	An hour or so between loss of old wind and establishment of new.

Type of shift	Typical causes	Usual pattern	Typical time before next major shift
	Sea breezes.	Wind shifts more nearly onshore. Changes may be sharp or slow, total or partial. Breeze veers with the day.	Most of the day but thunderstorms, etc., can kill them.
	Land breezes.	Calm nights lead to flow off the land. Usually weak.	Midnight to dawn.
	Breaking of an inversion.	Wind picks up in the morning from new but permanent direction.	Most of the day unless a sea breeze replaces it.
Temporary.	Shower clouds.	Wind breaks ahead and veers behind.	½–2 hours.
	Big heat thunderstorms.	Wind light ahead of storm and often towards. Strong gusts under leading edge. Wind gradually subsides and veers.	Clear the air for a day or two.
Local and temporary.	Long eddies.	Wind veers as it gusts and backs as it lulls.	20 min to 3 hr recurrent.
	Medium eddies.	Wind veers as it gusts and backs as it lulls.	2–8 min recurrent.
	Abnormal eddy pattern.	Wind backs as it gusts and veers as it lulls. Direction changes are wide and speed often falls temporarily to zero.	5–10 min recurrent
	Thermals.	Shores in the sun produce thermals and slight wind towards shore results.	A few minutes.
Local but permanent.	Shore lines.	Wind tends to follow contours but oblique winds tend to flow straight off shores.	Shifts lasts as long as overall wind pattern lasts.
Very local.	Topographical. Trees, buildings, etc.	Wind strengthens in gaps weaker in lee. Tendency to flow parallel to obstructions.	Very short as one soon sails out of each individual influence.

ASSESSING THE POSSIBILITY OF A WIND SHIFT Knowing what weather feature will shift the wind is not of much help if the expected time is not known. Timing of the passage of fronts, etc., is the most difficult thing that the professional forecaster has to contend with, so the broadcast forecasts will usually leave hours of doubt in the mind of the listener or viewer. It is only on the spot that the vague timing given by the official forecasts can be tied down to useful proportions. In cruising yachts, whose navigators are on the ball, it may be possible from the shipping and other forecasts to draw useful weather maps and move on the existing fronts, etc., at the correct speed in one's own locality, thereby predicting wind shifts which other people are only vaguely aware of. Certainly ocean races can be won by the foreknowledge of major wind shifts. Or they may be lost if an unexpected shift does not turn up. Careful forecasting is of prime importance to ocean racing skippers and can make passage-making a faster and more comfortable pursuit than it might otherwise be.

The following is a summary of helpful pointers to wind changes.

Ocean racing and offshore cruising

Forecast period 10–20 hours.

Broadcast forecasts essential. Own forecasts very helpful.

Wind over the sea is purer than over the land. No diurnal variation unless under the land's influence.

Major changes of moderate to strong wind due to fronts and passage of pressure systems.

Calmer winds influenced within 15 miles of the coasts on hot afternoons by sea breezes blowing onshore. Wind found inshore.

Total calms in centres of North Sea, Channel, etc., due to sea breezes on summer days.

Day sailing

Forecast period 10 hours.

Radio forecasts helpful.

Own forecasts useful.

Quiet mornings with sun produce sea breezes near coasts and often evening calm.

Summer gales are rare, but an onshore wind in the forenoon of a summer's day can become strong in the afternoon when reinforced by sea breeze.

Diurnal variation will lead to wind increasing up to mid afternoon and then going down with nightfall.

In summer, winds tend to go onshore by day and offshore at night.

Coastwise sailing aided by avoiding shore during forenoon and hugging shore during afternoon of sea breeze days.

Calm overcast days tend to remain calm overcast days unless the sun breaks through, when wind appears.

Dinghy racing

Forecast period 2–4 hours.

Radio forecasts useful for general ideas.

Own forecasts of small changes paramount.

Remarks concerning day sailing also applicable, but summary of wind changes applicable to racing on pages 182/3 gives more information.

TACTICS FOR GUSTS AND LULLS The advantages of being on starboard in gusts and on port in lulls when the wind is at normal sort of unstable north-westerly (or a wind of that type) has been covered in Chapter Three. Due to the exigencies of a race such as strong pressure from close opponents, strong pressure from wind or strong pressure of some other kind it may not be easy to use the technique suggested there. The parallel dictum is

TACK WHEN HEADED

This rule is very like the gust-starboard, lull-port rule, but I believe it to be slightly less effective. It does however need less careful assessment of the wind field, and there is no doubt that it is of universal application.

In contributing a chapter to the collected experience of some of the most erudite International 14 sailors of North America, which goes under the title of *The Techniques of Small Boat Racing*, Stuart H. Walker comments on north-west winds. He notes their variability and how they swing back and forth about a mean direction over periods of minutes. This is in direct accord with the evidence of the anemograms of Chapter Three. He also confirms that there is periodicity in the shifting which can be usefully analysed before the race or even during it. Again American wind is no different from wind under the same conditions anywhere in the temperate latitudes of the northern hemisphere. All the helmsmen who mention the matter subscribe to the "tack when headed" rule in this very powerful book[17].

The two rules become the same providing the wind changes are sharp enough to be classed as headers and the advantageous tack has been assumed at the outset. Certainly to a port-tack dinghy the gust is a header which is sharp enough to force him about on the "tack when headed" rule. The more gentle sink into the lull, however, might not constitute a header, and therefore if this dinghy did not tack as the wind lulled and backed he could lose on an opponent who tacked to take advantage of the back. Further, the anemograms show how variability, borne on the back of the major gust-lull features, must not be allowed to panic one into hasty tacking before the time is ripe. Tacking purely on headers will not pay when these wind features are of short duration. In either technique the supreme difficulty is to recognise what is and what is not a major gust front. That useful precursor, the gust tongue, is a timely warning. Tacking on to starboard off a gust-tongue header produces precisely the same advantageous result as tacking on to starboard to take advantage of the veer in the gust. What knowledge of the micro-structure tells one is not to be rushed into almost immediately re-tacking as the wind backs behind the temporary gust tongue as might be the case if the "tack when headed" rule were blindly followed.

WHAT IS A HEADER? This is a difficult question to answer, because very little study has been made of such questions. The wind heads the craft—it seems an advantage to tack on its impulse—and how much the wind shifted ahead is never known. The technique pays off on the whole, so no one knows.

Perhaps a certain amount of estimation might be made. A dinghy sailed at 45° to the true wind, or a deep-keel yacht at 35° to it, must sail an undulating course at this angle (γ) to the true wind as it fluctuates. If you are sailing as close as practicable to the wind on starboard tack then rapidly backing winds are headers while veers will engender luffs.

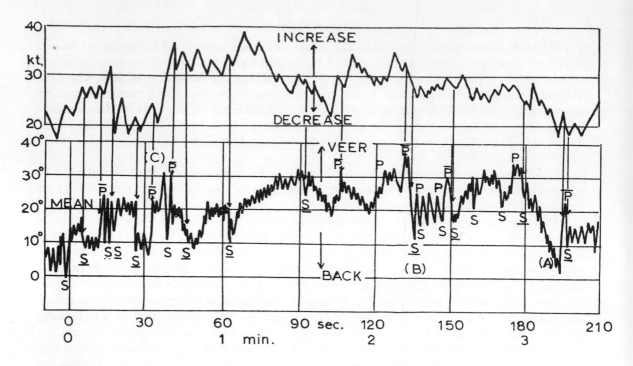

6.1: *What is a header? Potential headers on port tack (P) and on starboard (S) assessed from study of a typical gust-lull sequence of normal wind.*

Because "there's a luff in a puff" regardless of tack, a wind feature that backs sharply and increases sharply at the same time need not be a header, for a backing shift of 10° or less may be absorbed in the ability to point higher as the wind sharpens. On the other hand a backing shift as the wind suddenly lulls will appear as a header on starboard. All the points marked S in Fig. 6.1 are potential headers, being minor fluctuations of the wind field with a sharp back. However, only those underlined might appear as headers, for they are also accompanied by sharply decreasing speed. The portion marked A might not appear as a header as the wind goes back by a long way, but does so gradually, allowing plenty of time for slow reaction to the changing direction. Yet A is the biggest "header" of them all, and failure to react to it and tack on to port will lose valuable upwind way. Thus tacking only to immediate headers may be dangerous, for the sink into the lull is often slow like this, and only knowledge of the mean wind direction can yield the correct reaction of tacking on to port as the previously veered wind backs across it.

    If you stand on the shore and watch the antics of a wind vane, or the racing flag of a dinghy captive on its trolley, you can find the mean wind direction providing the place is open and not bedevilled by club premises or other impediments to the wind. Once this has been found then if you choose a land-mark many miles away, such as a church steeple or a clump of trees on a hill in the eye of the mean wind, you can use this point to determine the mean wind wherever you may be around the course. The change in the line of sight as you move about the course is often not great. For instance the end of the Isle of Wight in Photo 4 is some 11 to 12 miles from Pilsey Island where the photo was taken. The line of sight of such a landmark only varies by 10° either side of the mean line of sight wherever one sails in Chichester Harbour. This illustrates that, providing some landmark can be fastened on which is 10 miles away or so in the eye of the mean wind, then variation as one sails about a normal course is often small. Other useful delineators of the wind are cloud streets as in Photo 6. They will however define the gust direction when the wind is normal and the mean surface wind will be backed to their direction through the requisite angle.

One would imagine that a variation of 10° is, with a variable quantity like the wind, perfectly tolerable, and, if not, mental corrections can be made.

Now to return to the discussion of the tacking techniques. A rapid back of 10° or more can be a header to a starboard tack dinghy. Conversely a rapid veer of this magnitude can be a header on port, but should the wind increase at the same time then the ability to point higher in the stronger wind may cancel much of the heading quality of the veer. Thus again consulting Fig. 6.1 those features marked P might be headers, but those with bars might not be sufficient to call one about if tacking on headers is the rule.

The first three of them, however, are large enough changes of direction to be headers, and would perhaps call a helmsman about correctly on to starboard for the gust part of the cell, and the headers at B or A would perhaps bring him back on to port. The gust features can produce the same results on either technique, providing the micro-wind features play the game. I think that in winds which are unstable and Force 4 and above (so that they are not liable to change their direction appreciably during a normal race) one will enjoy the best of both worlds if one prepares to tack on heading shifts, taking care to be on starboard in the gust half and on port in the lull half of the gust cell sequence. Foreknowledge of the mean wind direction will help one to do so.

Perhaps now it is possible to begin to answer the question "What is a header?" A header would appear to be:

(i) On starboard tack: a wind feature which suddenly backs and decreases the wind, when the back is small. It may also be a feature which suddenly backs the wind and increases it when the back is over 10° from what it was immediately before the wind changed (example B in Fig. 6.1).

(ii) On port tack: a wind feature which suddenly veers and decreases the wind when the veer is small. It may also be a feature which suddenly veers and increases the wind with a change of over 10° from its direction just before the wind changed (example C in Fig. 6.1).

What is also interesting is that those features which might seem like headers on either tack are grouped away from the major part of the gust. In other words the lull is the time when potential headers are most prevalent whichever tack one is on, and they must be resisted. There are three major headers between 10 and 40 seconds to a craft on port tack. If he tacks and resists the starboard headers then he is correctly sited for the gust when it arrives at the end of that time. He must now resist the starboard tack headers which are in this example luckily minor (except for the one at 45 seconds) until the first really major starboard header hails him about at 135 seconds (B). Even then if he could have resisted until the wind went right back at A he would have extracted the maximum advantage.

Obviously this example is only one of the many whose minor fluctuations, while borne on the back of gust-lull waves, will always differ in detail. This is especially true in the type of lull which is surface air mucked about by surface features.

I think that careful assessment of this example will help to explain why "tack when headed" has been and remains one of the cornerstones of dinghy men's lore. Often, but not always, the wind structure is such as to communicate the correct reaction providing the correct tack has been assumed at the outset. The study of wind structure tells us that this tack is port in lulls and starboard in gusts in normal wind in the northern hemisphere. Those "down-under" can read veer for back and back for veer and remember that when they cross into our hemisphere, or we go into theirs, the wind is back to front in its micro-scale features.

TACTICS FOR GENERAL SHIFTS OF WIND
There are many instances of winds which shift by very significant amounts. Chief examples are the wide and sudden sweeps from offshore to onshore which accompany the onset of the sea breeze and the drastic wind changes which accompany certain types of cold front. On a lesser scale are the periodic changes associated with gust cells in an otherwise homogeneous airstream and changes which occur when inversions break under the upthrust of thermals. Greater again than any of these are the violent stabbing gusts which come with big thunderstorms. All these, and others, provide shifts of wind which can be wonderfully helpful if used properly and disastrous if not.

A simple rule which fits most situations is

ERR TOWARDS THE EXPECTED WIND SHIFT

What to do in the case of the gust and lull sequences associated with unstable air-streams is covered in Chapter Three leaving us here with the more major wind shifts.

Apart from stating the above principle the only way to illustrate the point and to show it to be true is to treat some examples.

SLOW CHANGE EXPECTED ON A WINDWARD LEG
If the wind is expected to change its direction slowly during a beat then err on the side towards which the wind is changing.

Such changes have been illustrated in the section on sea breezes, and these may be backs or veers depending on whether the wind before the sea breeze effect set in is blowing with components which have the main coastline on their left or their right.

The changes to expect when the morning wind is from the shoreward quadrants, and is stronger than a mean speed of about 10 kt, are summed up in Fig. 6.2. On a south-facing coast the tendency will be to swing an easterly to the south-east and a westerly to the south-west during the morning and early afternoon. As the day progresses, however, the wind slowly reverts. The example of 16 June 1959 (Fig. 5.2e, page 132), shows this very clearly.

Warm moderately windy days near the coast should produce slow changes towards onshore during the morning and slow changes back again during the late afternoon. Except on days with big showers or thunderstorms, this swing, once it has begun, can be expected to continue (1000–1100 and 1430–1500 in Fig. 5.2e).

The example cited shows that the wind may easily shift some 50° in half an hour.

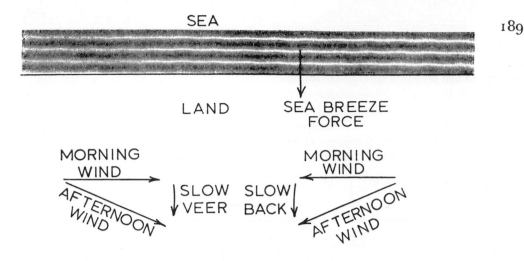

6.2: *What happens to winds along the coast when the sea breeze force is acting.*

Often a good beat against the tide can occupy half an hour. Or more correctly, what was a beat at the beginning of the leg becomes a close reach later on.

To illustrate that the principle "Err towards the expected wind shift" is true consider the beat from A to B in Fig. 6.3. During the beat the wind backs through 50° and so for the purposes of illustration the distance has been divided into six equal amounts, and in each the wind is considered to have a fixed mean direction which suddenly changes on the boundaries of the divisions. In fact we know it will change slowly and continuously, but this simplification will not upset the argument.

The craft S which hauls off on starboard, on the side towards which the wind is expected to change, becomes more and more windward craft as the wind shifts. If he hauls well out to the new windward he can then free off towards the end of the beat. The figures on the course lines give the speeds achieved taken from the Firefly performance chart. Craft P however who hauls off on the side of the mean course away from the wind shift must perforce beat all the time even though the wind is moving to bring his course more and more towards the mark B. It is obvious which is the faster course.

Thus for wind shifts, which are gradual and expected to be of the order of 40–50°, the fastest course is that which hauls out towards the expected wind shift—but not too far.

Slow swings of greater than 50–60° are relatively rare although they can and do occur. It depends on the allowed time scale. A westerly or even north-westerly wind will slowly back to south or south-east ahead of an advancing depression, and then the total wind change is 90° or more. However, the time period can be measured in tens of hours and not tens of minutes, so such extended changes are somewhat outside the present terms of reference.

SUDDEN CHANGES   When the wind shifts suddenly one of the following causes is normally to blame.

(i) passage of a front,

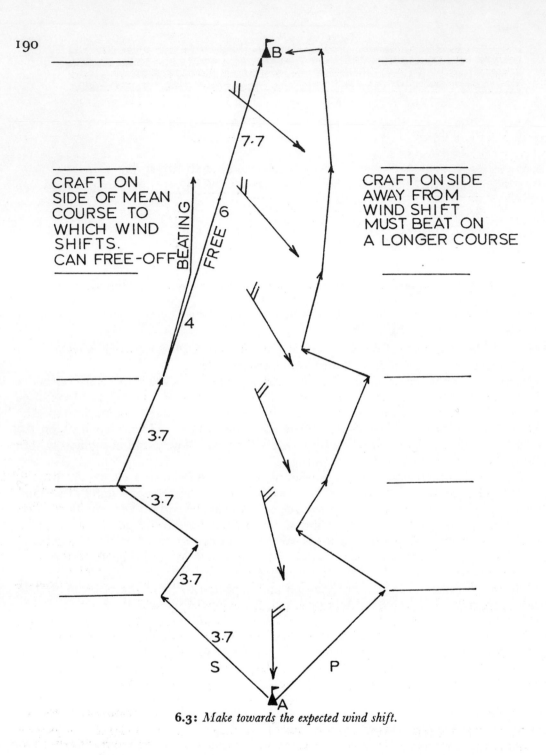

6.3: *Make towards the expected wind shift.*

(ii) passage of a sea breeze front,
(iii) sudden breaking of an inversion which allows the wind aloft to appear at the surface.

When warm and cold fronts pass the wind invariably veers. It veers most with sharp showery cold fronts, but these are less prevalent than diffuse frontal zones where the wind may take half an hour or more to change to its new veered direction. The veers, when warm fronts pass, are normally smaller than with cold fronts (see Chapter Two), but the one consistent thing about fronts and troughs which are revolving around depressions is that the wind will veer as they hurry damply by. This is just as true to the north of depression centres as it is to the south. Occluded fronts thread up through some low centres which have seen their best days, and troughs (which are not strictly fronts although they may look like them) appear in an otherwise homogeneous airstream. Ahead of such troughs the wind will probably back a little and then veer as the trough passes.

The line of division between the two different winds when it is sharp will often be revealed by a line of dark ragged cloud stretched across the wind. Abrupt change of direction is revealed by this lower cloud appearing to rapidly cross the cloud above. In any case a change in the cloud sheet which looks in any way like a break or a change of some kind often reveals a wind change as well. "A change of cloud means a change of wind" is often a true saying (Photo 13).

While fronts may produce sudden changes, they are not so sudden or so prevalent as those near our coasts, which occur when the sea breezes reverse an existing offshore wind. Such changes can produce a reversal of the wind from offshore to onshore in a few minutes. Taking a south-facing coast the wind may be 6 kt from the north one minute and 10 kt from the south the next. Again, such occasions are rarer than a slower change occupying tens of minutes, but the total change can be large enough to turn a run into a beat and vice versa.

Just inshore from the coast, therefore, any wind from the shoreward quadrants that is less than 8 kt mean speed is a likely source of a wind change some time during the day. When it will occur can be gauged from the section on sea breezes and so can the mode of onset. Here we can assume that such changes occur, and look at the previous advice to move towards the expected wind shift.

In general, as the sea breeze is often the stronger of the two winds in the period surrounding its onset, those who get into the sea breeze as opposed to the offshore wind will move faster on any given point of sailing. However the discussion is rather bedevilled by the very large direction change which often occurs. For instance, if you are reaching across a wind parallel to the coast, the arrival of the sea breeze from seaward will turn the reach into a dead run or force a complete change of course by coming dead ahead. The tactical situation alters in a few minutes. Hopeless positions find themselves miraculously transformed while the previous windward leaders curse the vagaries of the wind.

For instance in Fig. 6.4, before the sea breeze arrives, B is certain to make the mark M ahead of A, for they are the same distance from the mark, but B is on his fastest reach in a 5 kt wind, while A is on a slower broader reach.

A little later, when the sea breeze sets in from position 1, A can make the mark in one leg while B is forced into making two legs. The distances sailed by A and B now fall in the ratio 1 : 1·5, whereas before they were equal.

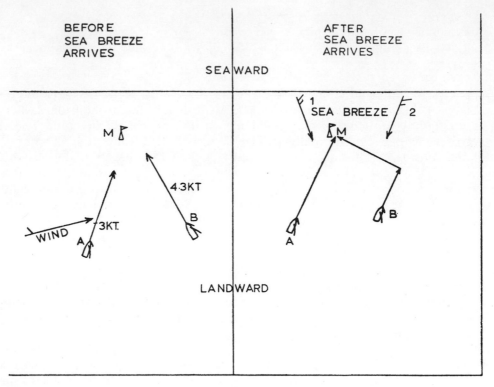

BEFORE
SEA BREEZE
ARRIVES

AFTER
SEA BREEZE
ARRIVES

SEAWARD

SEA BREEZE   1   2

M

4.3KT.

WIND   3KT.

A   B

M

A   B

LANDWARD

6.4: *If a sea breeze is imminent be on the side from which it will come.*

If the sea breeze had come in from position 2, B would have been the gaining craft. Once again erring on the side of the expected wind shift pays off.

It is usually only offshore winds above 5 kt mean speed which are suddenly reversed, and then this happens during the late forenoon or afternoon. The more normal state of affairs is for there to be a zone of transition between the offshore wind and the sea breeze. This is a strip of calm or light fitful airs separating the advancing sea breeze from the receding offshore wind. Thus the tactics to adopt when it is obvious that the calm zone is upon you will depend on whether the next mark is on the landward side or the seaward side. Considerations of tide and water will also impress themselves on any tactical considerations in small waters, but there are certain pointers to the correct procedure.

The immediate sign of the calm zone's approach is a lightening offshore wind. An eye should be kept to seaward for becalmed craft, vertical smoke, etc., and beyond them craft sailing in the onshore sea breeze. If there are any clear signs like this, every effort should be made to reach the new wind coming in. It will be moving towards the hinterland of the coast behind its calm zone, so sailing towards the coast will make the relative speed of approach larger than would be apparent. Days which are partly cloudy, with cumulus which has grown with the day, will induce a speed of approach of perhaps 3 kt. Running towards the calm area at say 3 kt will make the relative speed of approach 6 kt—that is,

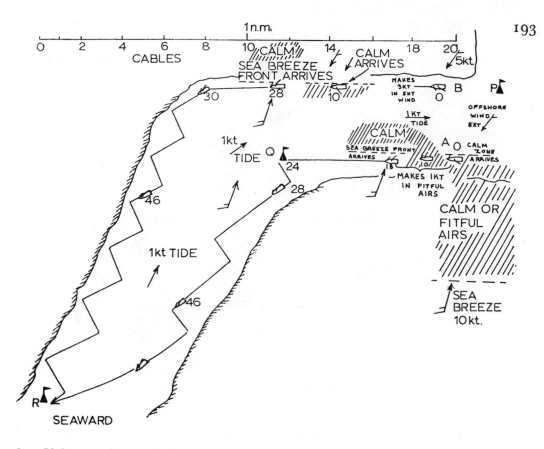

6.5: *If the course is towards the normal direction from which the sea breeze comes sail that way.*

while the offshore wind lasts. It is pretty certain to fail at some point for a while, so an adverse tide will indicate that to be on the shoreside is imperative.

To illustrate these points look at the composite diagram of a hypothetical race, Fig. 6.5. We look in on this race when the boats have come about the starboard-hand mark P and there is a choice of shore. The wind is 5 kt and from the opposite direction to that from which the sea breeze normally blows. It is warm and slightly cloudy with cumulus puffs here and there—time to suspect a sea breeze may be in the offing. As the turning mark R is on the same shore, B chooses the windward side so as not to cross the tide twice. A decides that a quick run across the tide will perhaps be worth it, for the disance sailed will be that much less. Also he thinks that should a sea breeze come in during the manoeuvre he will get it first. So we first come upon B apparently ahead of A who has just been smitten by the calm zone between offshore wind and sea breeze, which is assumed to be 6 cables wide and moving in at about 2 kt. So for the next 10 minutes A struggles along in little fitful puffs while B forges on at a good 3 kt leaving his rival far behind.

After 10 minutes, however, A, being a true sportsman, sees with some relief that the

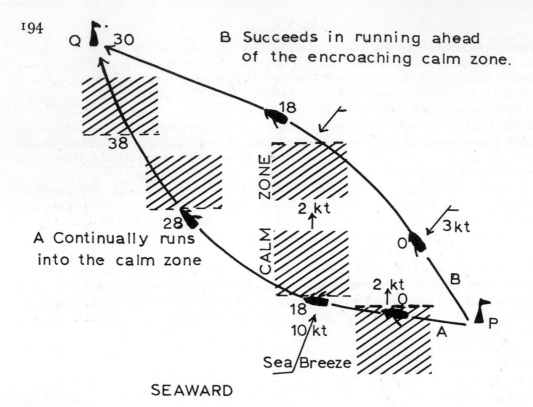

Q | 30

B Succeeds in running ahead
of the encroaching calm zone.

18

ZONE

38

2 kt

CALM

28

A Continually runs
into the calm zone

O

3kt

B

2 kt

18   O

10 kt   A   P

Sea Breeze

SEAWARD

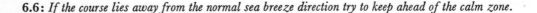

6.6: If the course lies away from the normal sea breeze direction try to keep ahead of the calm zone.

wind has gone out of B's sails and that he is in the stronger stream on the outside of the bend. Time for the tables to turn, and they do so as soon as A picks up the sea breeze some 18 minutes after first becoming becalmed. The sea breeze soon strengthens to 10 kt and by the time B gets the same sea breeze, A is round the port-hand mark Q and beating down towards R. The time mark 46 shows their relative positions some 18 minutes later and even though A has still to cross the tide he will beat B to the mark. Apart from the other tactical advantages A may have had over B he travels 1 nautical mile in the first 28 minutes whereas B only manages to make 8 cables. The reason is, of course, that they were becalmed for the same time but A did more than half the distance in a 10 kt wind while B did more than half in a 5 kt wind.

Therefore by making towards the new wind A gained over B.

Sailing in the same direction as the calm zone, however, produces some curious effects which can be illustrated by the tactics of craft A and B in Fig. 6.6.

This is a situation where the dictum "move towards the expected wind shift" does not pay off. To reach mark Q neither A nor B decides to sail the direct course. They have detected limp-sailed craft farther towards the main sea coast and, as we are depicting them sailing on water just inland from that coast, this is an indication of the incidence of the sea breeze calm zone. The breeze is moving in at about 2 kt so, although B has no way of knowing how fast the calm is approaching him, he decides he may manage to sail ahead of it in the 3 kt offshore wind. Thinking that this perhaps cannot be done A hauls off across the wind and soon finds himself in the doldrums (time O).

Assuming that the calm zone takes 18 minutes to pass, as in the previous example, B obviously gains hands down. The criterion is that, if the component of velocity in the direction of advance of the sea breeze can be maintained at greater than the rate of advance of the zone, sailing away from the calm zone is best.

However, should the sea breeze zone move in faster than this and overtake them, the loss of wind for an extended period can cause great loss of useful way on an adverse tide. Sailing off to wait for the stronger sea breeze is then likely to be advantageous. Criteria for a slow or fast onset are given in the section on sea breezes.

FORECASTING FOR BIG EVENTS There are times when personal prestige or national honour make it imperative to win or at least make it essential to leave no stone unturned to achieve the goal. The clime may be a foreign one either literally or metaphorically and this entails starting from scratch. In such cases the problem must be tackled logically.

The basic wind direction on which to hang changes is the wind above the friction layer which blows parallel to the isobars. Call this the isobaric wind. Its direction is either that of cloud whose base is around 1500–3000 feet (500–1000 m) or a more reliable estimate can be obtained from the local met. station. One can sometimes use a forecast to draw a weather map and if one is confident enough, deduce the lay of the isobars from this. The met. stations have at their disposal—and yours—records of winds found by radar wind-finding equipment, the first of which will be the wind at 3000 ft (1000 m). A recent one relevant to the area can be helpful in determining the isobaric wind. This will show whether the surface wind is a large-scale or local one.

The mean wind at the surface is backed to the isobaric wind in the northern hemisphere and veered to it in the southern. Also the sailing venue must be within the temperate latitudes or close enough to them for the geostrophic force to be appreciable; in other words for Buys Ballot's Law to hold (Chapter Two).

If the surface wind is doing this the wind is a large-scale one and will obey the large-scale rules. A normal wind will in general veer as it gusts and back as it lulls, the gusts and lulls appearing in a sequence every few minutes. Pointers to this state of affairs are surface winds whose mean speed is Force 4 or above and in which cumulus clouds have developed. If there are big shower clouds about one should expect a gust and lull sequence with a frequency of 20 minutes or more.

If the wind is Force 4 or less and there is a lot of sun one should expect that, near the coast but within it, the offshore wind may be abnormal in that it backs as it gusts and veers as it lulls (reverse the back and veer in southern hemisphere). Offshore expect this pattern along the shoreside strip of water reverting to normal farther out.

Next consider the possibility of a sea breeze. The isobaric wind will tell immediately if the present wind *is* a sea breeze, for the surface wind will often be at an impossible angle to the isobaric wind. If the isobaric wind is onshore then expect the surface wind to be close to the normal sea breeze direction for the coast and stronger than the isobaric wind.

This is about the only case where the surface wind will be stronger than the isobaric during the day.

Find out from the Admiralty Pilots the general state of wind on a strange coast. This is the basic sort of spadework which helps to produce a basis on which to hang details. The National Meteorological Library at Bracknell, Berks, can help with papers written by local weather men on the details of their local conditions. Such information is backed up by instrumental evidence and is more reliable than the lore of longshoresmen although this is by no means to be discounted.

Again, papers written on the breezes of a particular coast often exist and are very informative, as is evinced by the Great Lakes information included as an example in Chapter Five.

The next step to take is a look at the topography on a good contour map. If the area of the racing is overlooked by high ground one can sketch some streamlines for winds onshore, offshore and parallel to the coast. Use the rules in Chapter Four for the distance downwind at which the wind again becomes roughly equal to what it was before it was disturbed. Allow for sea breezes being shallow and having to flow round any obstacle which is more than a hundred feet high. Make the streamlines continuous and do not lose any, *i.e.* if ten lines start off shoreward from the open sea then those ten have got to escape somewhere. This will show local topographic cants and local increases of wind.

Allow for stability if you can. If the airstream is stable then winds pour off the cliffs and high ground like a water-jet out of a horizontal hose. They take a long time to get back to the surface. If the air is unstable then gusts will appear much closer to the cliffs than the $20h$ quoted in Chapter Four, as the air in them is already descending as it cascades over the cliff edge.

Allow for the $9h$ of roller cushion which extends to windward of leeward obstacles. A 100 ft cliff will begin to affect the wind some 300 yards out to sea from its foot, and so on.

These are the more or less ponderables of the situation. There are then large-scale moving systems which may cross the area during the racing. Fronts, for example, by whose agency the wind will veer in the northern and back in the southern hemispheres. These are almost impossible to time to closer than half an hour, and even then the change is more likely to be gradual than sharp. The passage of small lows may bring the wind all round the clock, but there is little that a pre-race prediction can do to forecast this.

CHAPTER SEVEN

The Wind and the Waves

WAVES cannot be just any height. Water is a known fluid with a definite density and viscosity, and waves in it are generated by viscous drag between wind and water and by the sheltering effect of any wave on the one ahead.

Ian Proctor has probably said all that it is necessary to say about the tactical use of waves in dinghy racing in *Sailing Wind and Current* and therefore nothing is said on that subject here. There is however something to be said on the subject of forecasting wave height for a passage or an offshore race.

FORECASTING WAVE HEIGHT The drag between wind and water slows the wind, which loses energy, and this energy is gained by the water. For a wave to grow the energy exchange must be sustained. So wave height is not only a function of wind strength, but also of wave "fetch" and the time for which the wind has blown.

CHARACTERISTICS OF WAVES

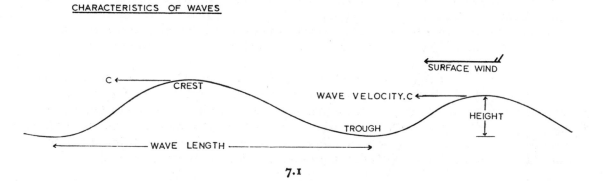

7.1

The shortest waves are generated first and they lengthen with time. Their characteristic features are shown in Fig. 7.1. The two most important attributes of a wave are its length (L) and its height (H). These are functions of the wind strength, the fetch, the depth of water, the length of time for which the wind has been blowing and the strength and direction of the tidal streams. Where the fetch and depth are to all intents and purposes infinite, as in mid-Atlantic, waves are called "free progressive" waves and are independent of fetch as they have travelled distances beyond which the effect of fetch is important. In the North Sea or Channel fetch is usually worth considering as these are both "narrow seas".

The effect of fetch on wave height is difficult to determine accurately, but for coastwise mariners the sheltering effect of the shore is very important. A simple and accurate

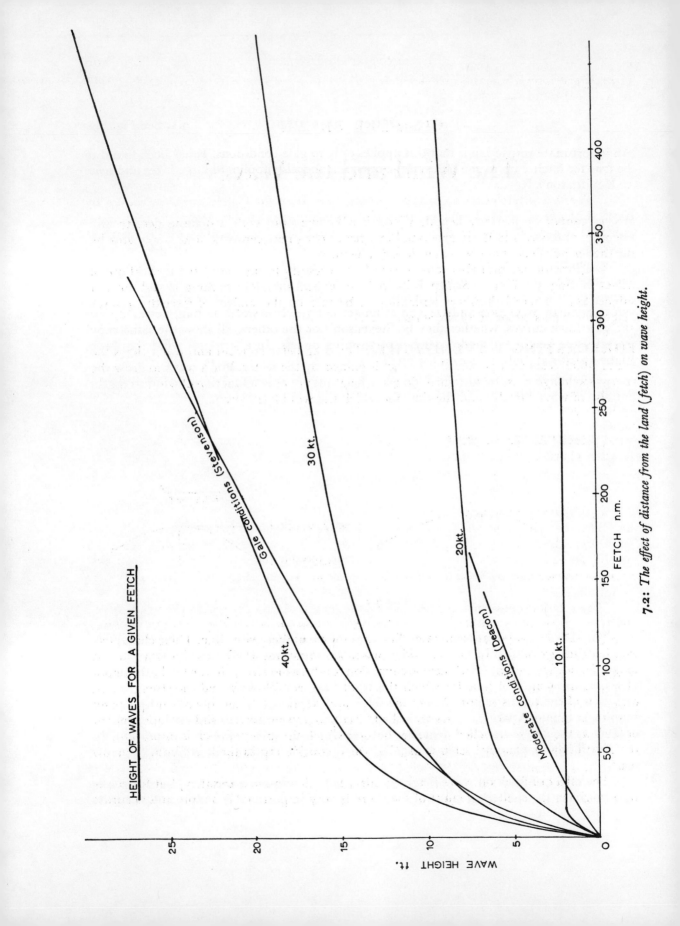

HEIGHT OF WAVES FOR A GIVEN FETCH

WAVE HEIGHT ft.

FETCH n.m.

Gale conditions (Stevenson)

40 kt.

30 kt.

20 kt.

Moderate conditions (Deacon)

10 kt.

7.2: *The effect of distance from the land (fetch) on wave height.*

formula given by Thomas Stevenson states the relation between wave height and fetch (F in nautical miles) as

$$H = 1 \cdot 5 \ \sqrt{F} \ \text{feet}$$

7.1. See Fig. 7.2.

An unfortunate restriction is that this applies only to gale conditions. It has been found to be true for fetches up to 200 miles in the open sea and also applies to large lakes and even to Kensington's Round Pond.

The effect of fetch in fresh to strong winds taken from the highest waves measured by Dr G. E. Deacon, in the Irish Sea is also plotted in Fig. 7.2. In the absence of more exact evidence it can be assumed that under these conditions of moderate wind, the highest waves increase in height by 5 feet for every hundred miles of fetch, but that they level out to the heights given in Fig. 7.3 over long fetches. Not all the measurements agree exactly, and another source gives the curves marked 10 to 40 kt for fetches up to 500 miles. They show more rapid rise in wave height with fetch in the first 50–100 miles but generally level out to confirm Stevenson and Deacon at longer fetches. It is worth noting, however, that the gale force curves, whether they be Stevenson's or the others, all show the same rapid rise of wave height for modest fetches of 20 miles or less. In a ten-knot wind the waves make about 2 ft high, whatever the fetch.

The height of a wave is related to the wind speed, but authorities differ as to which height and which wind speed to choose in the relation. One of the formulas is given by Commander Suthons, which relates the height (H_e feet) of the simple wave which has the same energy as the resultant of the actual waves (which vary in height) to the gradient wind velocity (U_g knots). The latter is obtained from the distance apart of isobars on a weather chart. Suthons' relation is

$$H_e = 0 \cdot 01 \ U_g^2 \ \text{feet}$$

7.2

The maximum wave height is about $1 \cdot 4$ times H_e.

Thus entering Fig. 7.3 the height of the biggest waves can be obtained (neglecting fetch) providing a weather map covering the area of the passage can be drawn. This is not as difficult as it sounds and, as the wind at yacht level is about $0 \cdot 8$ of the gradient wind speed a knowledge of the gradient wind is useful in assessing both wind and wave conditions.

The relation between wave height and the length of time for which the wind, which generates them, has been blowing is summed up in the curves of Fig. 7.4 (due to Sverdrup and Munk). Care must be exercised when using this sort of information as, during the passage of depressions, for instance, the wind will often change direction appreciably over a given area in a matter of hours. However, situations where Fig. 7.4 will be applicable are not difficult to find. For example the westerly or north-westerly that blows for days over our western seaboard in the rear of depressions which are filling up over Scandinavia; or when the weather situation is stable and winds blow for extended periods down the North Sea or up the Channel with, to all intents and purposes, infinite fetch.

To illustrate the use of Fig. 7.4 let us predict the wave height in a moderate breeze which it is estimated has been blowing for four hours. Entering the graphs at A it is seen that the waves will be a little less than three feet high at their highest. The estimated passage time in this same wind and water is four hours. What will the wave height be then?

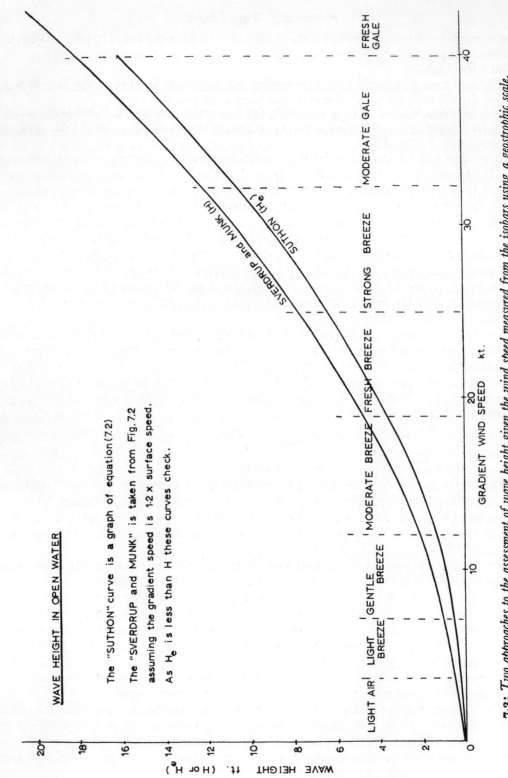

7.3: *Two approaches to the assessment of wave height given the wind speed measured from the isobars using a geostrophic scale.*

Re-entering the graphs at B the highest waves will be $3\frac{1}{2}$ feet high. However, should the wind (as is suspected) increase to 20 knots the highest waves must be expected to grow to at least 6 feet high.

These curves give some help in assessing the probable heights of the largest waves allowing for the time for which the wind has been acting on the waves.

It is said that "every seventh wave is a big one", but any seaway will be the result of the superposition of many different trains of waves. Where the crests coincide there will be a bigger wave than the others, and as Ovid considered that every *tenth* wave was a big one there will never be any chance of agreement on this question. This is understandable as so many factors go to make up an observed sea. The idea however of superposition, that is of a "spectrum" of simple waves superimposed on one another making up the observed seaway, is an idea analogous to the "quality" of a musical note. Both are one or two basically simple waves with many other waves (overtones) superimposed on them. The seaway may be the result of many different wave trains—swell from a storm which has passed or is yet to come, plus a general wave-form due to the wind which is now blowing, to which may be added reflection from a nearby shore.

The seaway *must* in general be a confused jumble of waves as wave velocity (C) depends on wavelength. The relation between these quantities is

$$C = 2 \cdot 26 \sqrt{L} \text{ in feet per second} \qquad \textbf{7·3}$$

Thus the longest waves travel fastest. The long swell from a distant storm can arrive on our western coasts as much as a week after the storm which originated it. By timing the period of the swell and the shorter waves, which arrive later, the oceanographers can estimate the distance of the storm centre. In fact in California waves have been detected which had travelled from New Zealand some 8000 miles away. The practical use of this sort of knowledge is to provide suspicion if a swell arrives which is out of keeping with the prevailing wind conditions. The few extra-tropical cyclones we experience can give their presence away by the curiously confused swell which runs on ahead of them.

Therefore, one should keep an eye, when in exposed offshore areas, on any swell running under an established seaway. It may have a better prognostic value than a weather report.

Table 7.A

Approximate height of swell in feet at various distances from storm areas.

Distances in nautical miles

0	500	1000	2000	3000
40	25	20	12	8
30	19	14	8	5
20	12	8	5	3
15	8	5	3	2
10	5	3	2	1
5	2	1	0·5	—

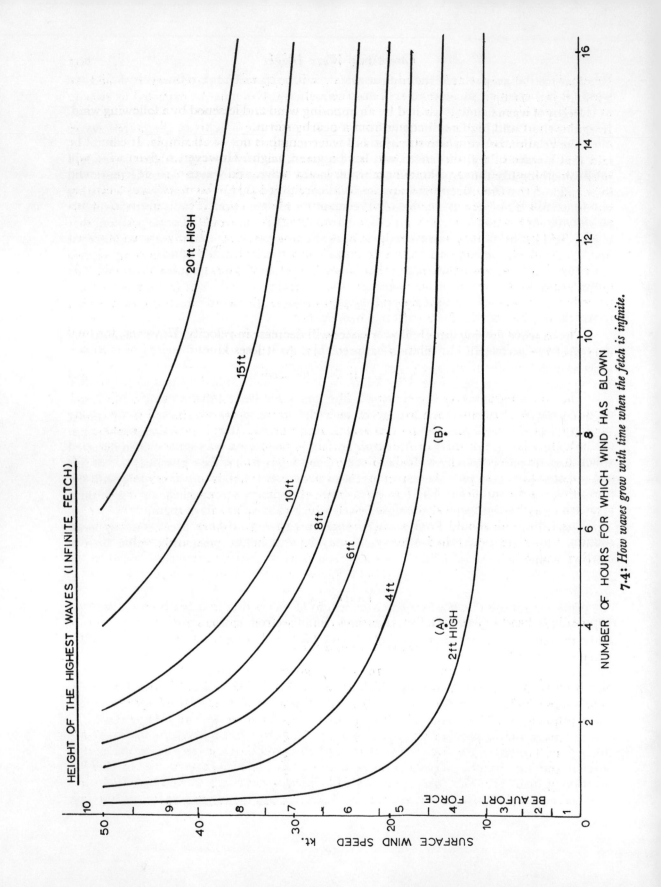

HEIGHT OF THE HIGHEST WAVES (INFINITE FETCH)

20 ft HIGH

15 ft

10 ft

8 ft

6 ft

4 ft

2 ft HIGH

(A)

(B)

BEAUFORT FORCE

SURFACE WIND SPEED kt.

NUMBER OF HOURS FOR WHICH WIND HAS BLOWN

7·4: *How waves grow with time when the fetch is infinite.*

Example: Waves which are 20 ft at storm centre (0) will have reduced to 8 ft. after travelling an unimpeded 1000 miles of deep ocean.

Decay of wave height is assisted by an opposing wind and lessened by a following wind. Irregular short and high swell comes from a nearby storm.

The relation between wave height and wave length is not at all simple. It cannot be said that a wave of a given length will have a given height. However, a given wind will raise something like the same amount of water in any wave, and waves of short length tend to be tall and therefore steep, while waves which are long may not be of sufficient height to be noticeable. This is certainly true of the longest sea waves which can only be detected by instruments.

A further fact about wave height is that the shortest, steepest waves are generated first. Under this head comes the short steep sea associated with wind against tide.

The velocity of a wave in shallow water is governed by the depth of water (D fathoms) and is given by

$$C = 4\cdot88 \ \sqrt{D} \text{ feet per second} \qquad\qquad \textbf{7.4}$$

Thus a wave flowing into shallower water will decrease in velocity. However, the total energy of the wave will not diminish appreciably. As it loses kinetic energy of motion it must gain potential energy by steepening. Anyone who has been too far inshore, or over a bar or sandbank in a moderate wind knows how true this is. It is only true in a qualified way, however. For instance the waves begin to steepen only when the ratio of D to L becomes less than 0·055. Thus waves whose length in deep water is 100 feet will begin to steepen at about the one-fathom line and then increase in height until they break.

The last factor which is worth consideration is the way waves grow when the wind starts to blow and continues to blow under the same conditions for some hours. How the wave height increases with time can be gauged from Fig. 7.4 when the fetch is very great. The effect can be studied over a short fetch when a sea breeze sets in. Here is a wind which starts at a more or less definite time. At first very short low waves are produced, but by the afternoon these waves are longer and steeper and produce quite a crop of crashing breakers. By evening, as the sea breeze dies away, the waves revert to a hardly audible sluicing as they sidle on to the sand. Anyone who cared to notice the average height would have found it to be increasing even though the wind was a *steady* 10–14 knots for most of the afternoon.

One cannot use Fig. 7.4 to predict the height of waves due to a sea breeze, however, as the fetch is very limited (10 miles or less), but they can be used with some assurance when the fetch is 200 miles or more and are useful for predicting the growth of wave height when on passage.

MAKING A WIND AND WAVE FORECAST
Wave height and length depend on the fetch, the wind strength, the length of time for which the wind has blown and the depth of water. This information can be used when planning an intended passage.

Let us assume a passage is to be made from the Solent to Le Havre, a matter of 100 miles or so. The passage will take most of the 24 hours, and thus it is essential to ensure that there is nothing unpleasant cooking in the weather pot. An idea of what the weather has been doing is of prime importance if probable developments are to be assessed. In this connection study of the weather charts to be found in certain daily papers for the few days before is well worth while. Noting where the high and low centres have moved to over a sequence of charts can very often help in deducing what tomorrow's weather picture will look like. Pressure centres do not move just anywhere, and their movements can be followed. The moving on of a weather sequence is one of the chief pieces of evidence upon which the professional forecaster deduces the chart of tomorrow's weather. That is what appears in the newspaper, of course: a forecast chart of the weather as the forecasters expect it to be, and the chart for midday today was based on the actual chart at midday yesterday. Thus present weather prospects gained from the shipping and land area forecasts must be used in conjunction with the newspaper charts to correct the picture in detail and warn of fresh and unexpected developments. When the weather tends to be unsettled the greatest risk to the accuracy of any official forecast lies in the development of an unexpected secondary depression. Modern methods have meant that fewer of these wind-filled secondaries escape the forecasting noose, but some are still unforeseen.

By the use of Fig. 7.3 the probable wave height can be obtained if the gradient wind is known. At the end of the five minute shipping forecasts "actual" weather reports are given from coastal stations. These are full of clues to the latest weather situation if interpreted properly. They include statements of the sea-level pressure in millibars and the "tendency" of the barometer, *i.e.* falling rapidly, rising slowly, etc. If one knows the weather picture as it ought to be, and uses these pressures, isobars can be drawn and the gradient wind obtained.

USING WEATHER CHARTS TO FORECAST WAVES   In co-operation with the Royal Meteorological Society, the Royal Yachting Association has produced a form called "Metmap" which is specifically designed to aid in taking down the shipping forecasts and then drawing a passable weather map from the information. With the pressures from the coastal stations given at the end of the longer shipping forecasts, and one's own pressure taken from an aneroid which has been checked for accuracy, this can be done more easily than is normally thought. The specific aids which the Metmap has, and which have not to my knowledge been found on any previous similar forms, are geostrophic wind scales which enable the distance apart of isobars to be marked on the map when the surface wind speed is known. The usual spacing of isobars on relatively large-scale maps (such as this one of the British Isles and surrounding waters) is 2 mb. With a little practice one can sketch in the correct number of isobars between stations, and their given surface winds plus the geostrophic scale will help in this. For wave height prediction it may not be necessary in some cases to draw an isobar at all. Given a south-westerly up the Channel, the actual winds at Scilly, Portland and Royal Sovereign will be true ones off the sea, and if they are 15 kt or more they will not be greatly affected by disturbing influences like sea breeze forces. Making the assumption that the gradient wind U_g is $1.25 \times$ mean surface wind speed over the sea, Fig. 7.3 can be entered and the wave height predicted.

A word of warning must be sounded to those contemplating drawing weather maps using the surface wind as a guide to isobar direction. In spring and summer, coastal stations are especially likely to be affected by sea breezes, and, if they all were, some very curious weather features could be drawn on the home-made chart, with all the isobars coming to a heap in the middle of England. It is necessary to allow for this and rely as far as possible on the actual pressures given for the stations to draw the few isobars which may be required.

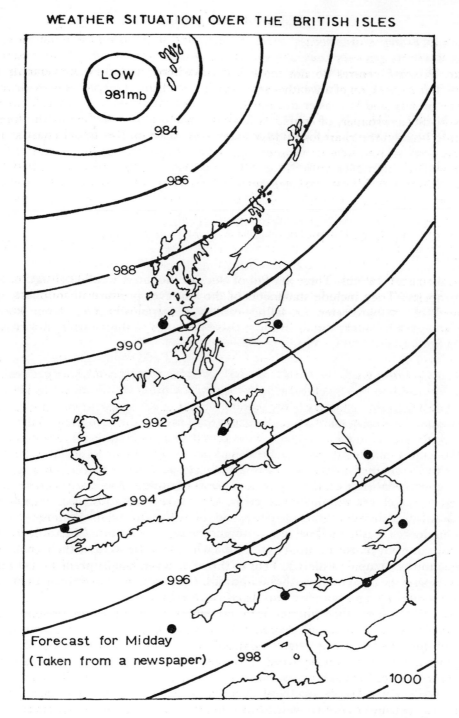

LOW
981mb

984

986

988

990

992

994

996

Forecast for Midday
(Taken from a newspaper)

998

1000

7.5: *Forecast for today was made and issued to the press yesterday. Is it right?*

Also the isobars will be veered to the surface wind in the northern hemisphere by the angle of about 10° over the open sea and 30° or more over the land. More details of the difference in speed and direction between the surface and the wind at isobar height are to be found in Chapters Two and Four.

THE GEOSTROPHIC WIND SCALE The very name of this device tends to put people off using it, but once it has been used, its long name is of little consequence, for it is simplicity itself.

A scale of the correct size for the chart in question is appended to chart blanks issued by H.M. Stationery Office. The two useful ones for the British Isles and surrounding waters are:

(i) Chart of Weather in North-West Europe (Form 2214).
(ii) Chart of Weather in British Isles (Form 2216), the extent of which is shown by Fig. 7.6.

The Royal Meteorological Society's chart "Metmap" has its geostrophic scale in Beaufort Force for use directly with the shipping forecasts. Because warm fronts travel more slowly than cold fronts there are also different scales for moving on warm and cold fronts. These are features helpful to the amateur which are not considered necessary on the more professional Stationery Office publications.

The form of the scale is shown at the foot of Fig. 7.6. As isobar spacing × wind speed is a constant quantity so, as the measured wind speed becomes greater, the spacing becomes smaller. The method of use is to sketch the isobars at 2 mb intervals and then lay the scale with its left-hand edge on one isobar, reading off the wind speed where the other isobar cuts the scale. This wind speed gives the strength of the wind above the friction layer, *i.e.* at around 2000 ft aloft. The surface wind speed can then be assessed for the locality where the wind is measured, using the relations between wind at the surface and at isobar height given in Chapter Two or as given in Fig. 5.17 on page 157.

The effect of latitude on the size of the scale is not marked so that it can be used over the whole of the charts without much error. Only if there is wide variation in latitude, especially towards the equator or the poles, will the scale become misleading.

When depressions are following one another across the British Isles the weather may deteriorate (or even improve) more rapidly than it is possible to forecast. Passage making in these conditions may be a matter of running between the lows, and the decision to go or not may depend on an actual weather report of nicely rising pressure and clearing skies at Scilly or a plummeting barometer and drizzle at Valentia.

A situation where something is definitely wrong with the forecast weather chart is depicted in Figs. 7.5 and 7.6. The forecast for midday today is a simple picture of a low centre off the Faeroes and an uncomplicated set of isobars covering the British Isles, leading to mainly south-westerly winds and some showers. The 1355–1400 shipping forecast (which gives the weather situation *and* the actuals) reveals that while the forecast was extraordinarily correct over Scotland, something is very amiss over the South-West Approaches. Instead of a south-west wind of Force 3 at Valentia and perhaps a shower, there is a light north-easterly with drizzle and fog. At Scilly the barometer is tumbling and the wind is south-easterly Force 4, whereas south-west Force 2–3 was expected. It is also raining. In the Solent our own barometer is falling, not very fast, but significantly, and the

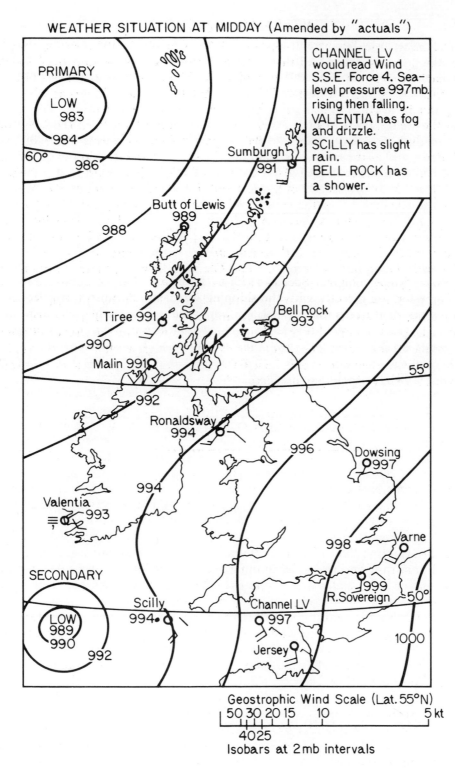

WEATHER SITUATION AT MIDDAY (Amended by "actuals")

PRIMARY

LOW
983

984

986

60°

Sumburgh
991

CHANNEL LV
would read Wind
S.S.E. Force 4. Sea-
level pressure 997mb.
rising then falling.
VALENTIA has fog
and drizzle.
SCILLY has slight
rain.
BELL ROCK has
a shower.

Butt of Lewis
989

988

Tiree 991

990

Malin 991

Bell Rock
993

55°

992

Ronaldsway
994

996

Dowsing
997

994

Valentia
993

998

Varne

SECONDARY

Scilly
994

Channel LV
997

999
R. Sovereign

50°

LOW
989
990

992

Jersey

1000

Geostrophic Wind Scale (Lat. 55°N)

50 30 20 15   10   5 kt

40 25

Isobars at 2mb intervals

7.6: *Today's picture is correct over most of the country but something is brewing in the south-west. The actual weather reports from the south-west confirm it. The wind scale has been adjusted to give surface wind speed over the sea.*

wind is freshening from the south-south-east. On drawing the isobars a "dog's-leg" appears in the 994 mb isobar. All this suggests a secondary depression over the South-West Approaches, and that one can be scribbled in. It may not be just there, but at least one knows that something is brewing. This immediately produces doubts as to whether to go or not, and is worth a consultation with the nearest forecast office. The forecaster thinks that the secondary is rather farther away than would have been thought from the rough and ready home-made chart and they expect it to move across the Irish Sea with winds of Force 5 and at the most Force 6 in the Channel. So the decision to go is made.

This is based on the following considerations. The gradient wind is at present about 13 kt which leads to a wave height of 2–3 feet and this wind has changed direction within the last 6 hours. The new waves thus created will be limited in fetch, and this will limit their height. The wind is expected to increase and veer as the secondary moves into the Irish Sea, but the increase is a limited one and will take some hours to become effective. It follows that a relatively quiet beat is to be expected for some hours during the shake-down period. The wind being largely across the mid-Channel tideway, there is little likelihood of a nasty unpredicted wind-against-tide chop setting in.

Allowing for the wind to increase to 20 kt, Fig. 7.4 shows that the waves would be 7 feet high after 12 hours if the fetch were unlimited, but even if the veer of wind to south-west takes place within this time, one can expect to be in the shelter of the Cherbourg Peninsula for most of the passage. One can thus weigh anchor with the confidence that the greatest wave height can only be 5–6 feet (Fig. 7.3), and this is across a swell from the south-west which it will help to dissipate.

CHAPTER EIGHT

Conversion Diagrams

ON the following pages are three nomograms, which will enable the reader to make certain conversions very easily. They are between feet and metres, thousands of feet and nautical miles and kilometres, and miles and kilometres. In every case a ruler is laid through the figure to be converted and the centre spot. It is then possible to read off the answer on the opposite scale.

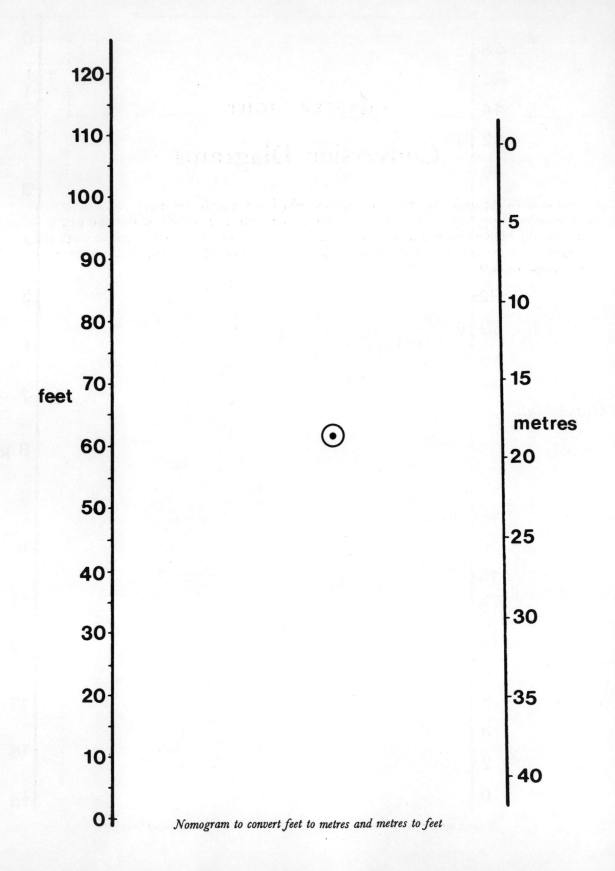

Nomogram to convert feet to metres and metres to feet

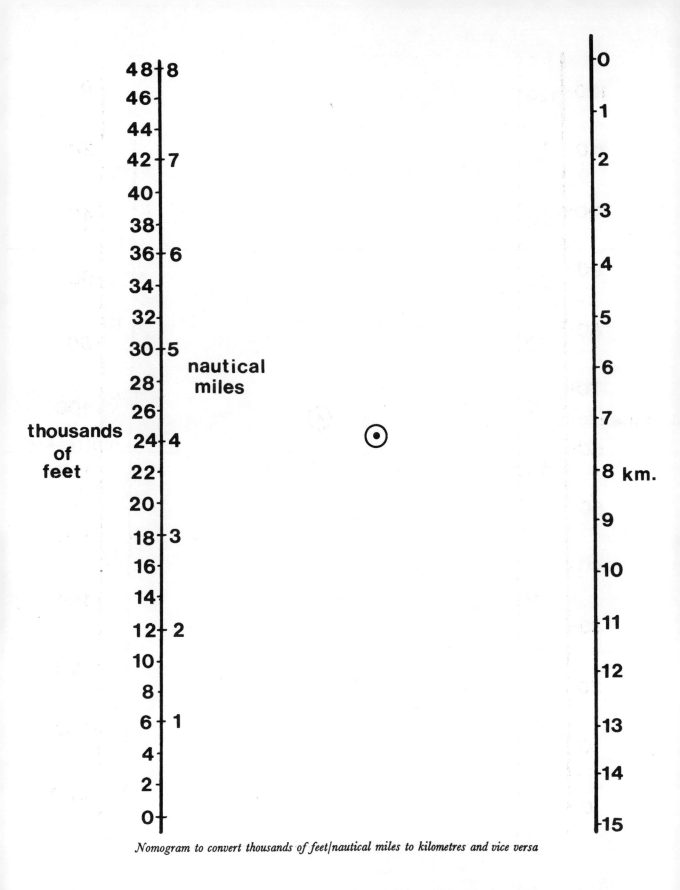

Nomogram to convert thousands of feet/nautical miles to kilometres and vice versa

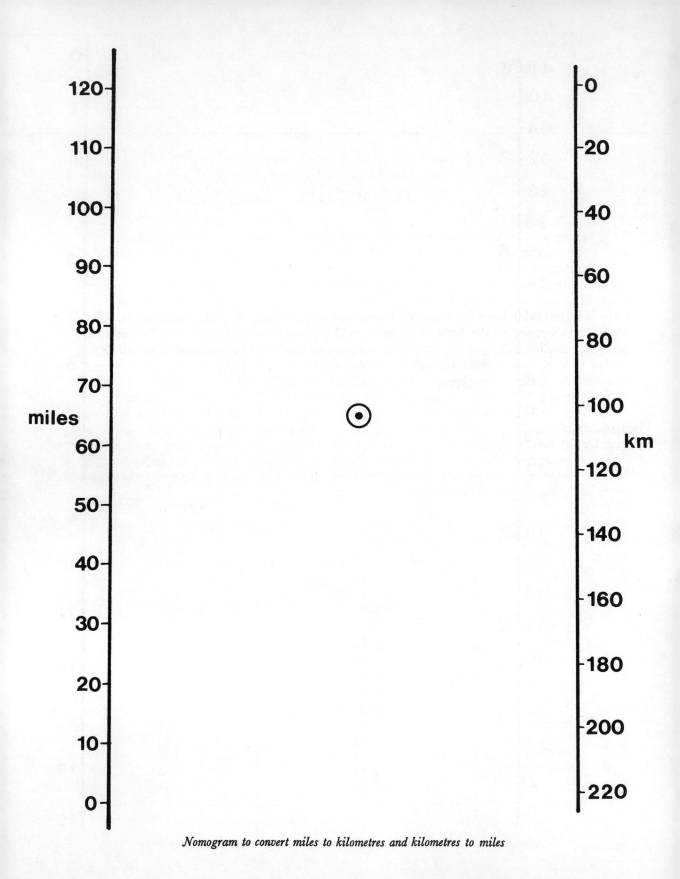

Nomogram to convert miles to kilometres and kilometres to miles

Appendix

The Beaufort Wind Scale. Wind strength is notoriously difficult to assess, especially at sea, where the seaway and the addition of heel due to gust, and heel due to waves, makes the wind seem far stronger than it is. The most practical scale is based on the idea which was initiated by Admiral Beaufort in 1806 and which still bears his name. His criteria were directed at the men o' war of his day and are obviously not applicable today. The sea criteria in the table have been agreed by international meteorological organisations since 1939 and amended in the light of experience. The landsman's criteria are of more antiquity, having been devised by Dr. G. C. Simpson in 1906 and having since then stood the test of time without material change. Alongside these have been included the dinghy helmsman's criteria given by Ian Proctor in his book *Sailing: Wind and Current.*

The symbols used on plotted charts as given below do not exactly fit the accepted convention for Beaufort Force, namely that half a barb means one Beaufort Force. Thus there is the anomaly that on the Daily Weather Report and other official charts issued or used by the meteorological offices an arrow with two long barbs and a short one is not as would be imagined Force 5 but Force 6. Therefore care must be taken when looking at weather maps to see which convention is being used. The symbols denoting Beaufort Force are given in the Beaufort Wind Scale Tables.

Symbol	Speed	Beaufort Force
	Calm	0
	1–2 kt	1
	3–7	2
	8–12	3–4
	13–17	4
	18–22	5
	23–27	6
	28–32	7
	33–37	8
	38–42	8–9
	43–47	9
	48–52	10
	53–57	10–11
	58–72	11–12

THE SCALE OF WIND SPEED
Taken from the author's *Instant Weather Forecasting* with amendments

Beaufort number	General description	Limit of mean speed (knots)	Land signs	Dinghy criteria
0	Calm	less than 1	Smoke rises vertically. Leaves do not stir	Sails will not fill. Racing flag will not respond. Flies and tell tails might just respond
1	Light air	1 to 3	Smoke drifts. Wind vanes do not respond	Sails fill. Racing flag may not be reliable. Flies and tell tails respond. Crew and helmsman on opposite sides of craft
2	Light breeze	4 to 6	Wind felt on the face. Leaves rustle. Light flags not extended. Wind vanes respond	Useful way can be made. Racing flag reliable. Helmsman and crew both sit to windward. Spinnakers may fill
3	Gentle breeze	7 to 10	Light flags extended. Leaves in constant motion	Helmsman and crew sit on weather gunwale. Spinnakers fill. Fourteen-footers and above may plane
4	Moderate breeze	11 to 16	Most flags extend fully. Small branches move. Dust and loose paper may be raised	Dinghy crews lie out. Twelve-foot dinghies may plane; longer dinghies will plane. The best general working breeze
5	Fresh breeze	17 to 21	Small trees in leaf sway. Tops of tall trees in noticeable motion	Dinghies ease sheets in gusts. Crews use all weight to keep craft upright. Genoas near their limit. Some capsizes
6	Strong breeze	22 to 27	Large branches in motion. Whistling heard in wires	Dinghies overpowered when carrying full sail. Many capsizes. Crews find difficulty in holding craft upright even when spilling wind
7	Near gale (American usage: Moderate gale)	28 to 33	Whole trees in motion. Inconvenience felt when walking against wind	Dinghies fully reefed. Difficult to sail even on main alone. This is the absolute top limit for dinghies – other than *in extremis*
8	Gale (Fresh gale)	34 to 40	Twigs broken off trees. Generally impeded progress on foot. Rarely experienced inland	Dinghies may survive if expertly handled in the seaway on foresail alone
9	Strong gale (Strong gale)	41 to 47	Chimney pots and slates removed. Fences blown down etc	Not applicable
10	Storm (Whole gale)	48 to 55	Very rare inland. Trees uprooted; considerable structural damage	Not applicable
11	Violent storm	56 to 63	Once in some hundreds of years. Forests flattened	Not applicable
12	Hurricane	Over 63	Not experienced in Europe. Occasionally in Caribbean and USA	Not applicable

Deep keel criteria	State of sea	Local wind criteria near shore and on landlocked or inland water
Boom swings idly in the swell. Racing flags and anemometers will not respond. Flies and tell tails might just	Sea mirror-smooth. Calm enough to preserve shape of reflections of sails, masts etc	Local wind-making forces totally dominant. Seek shores for thermals
Sails just fill, but little way made. Racing flags and vanes may respond but cup anemometers may not. Flies and tell tails respond. Spinnakers do not fill	Scaly or shell-shaped ripples. No foam crests to be seen on open sea	Local winds still dominant. Sea breezes will set in in forenoon. Nocturnal winds at night. The wind may already be a local one. On lakes, rivers etc anabatic or katabatic winds
Wind felt on the cheek. Controlled way made. Spinnakers and sails generally fill. Racing flags and anemometers respond and are reliable	Small short wavelets with glassy crests that do not break	Local winds can easily influence this wind speed. Sea breezes set in by midday. Usual upper limit to nocturnal winds. Mountain and valley winds achieve this speed and more
Good way made. Light flags fully extended	Large wavelets. Crests may break but foam is of glassy appearance. A few scattered white horses may be seen when wind at upper limit	Sea breezes set in against this speed but usually not until afternoon. Allow earlier time in southern latitudes. Nocturnal winds do not often modify a gradient that is blowing at this speed in evening and early night
Best general working breeze for all craft. Genoas at optimum	Small waves lengthen. Fairly frequent white horses	Stronger local winds influence this speed. Sea breezes may set in in late afternoon. Too strong normally for nocturnal winds to modify greatly. However, allow for effects of high ground near the shore
Craft's way somewhat impeded by seaway. Genoas near their limit. Spinnakers still carried. Yachts approach maximum speed	Moderate waves. Many white horses	Upper limit to winds that can be modified by local influences except in southern latitudes. Sea breeze effects only serve to shift the direction of the winds of this strength – if at all
Edge of 'yacht gale' force. Cruising craft seek shelter. Reefing recommended to meet gusts when cruising	Large waves form and extensive foam crests are prevalent. Spray may be blown off some wave tops	Not normally influenced by local wind effects
Yacht gale force when most cruising craft seek shelter. Racing yachts may just carry spinnakers. Reefing essential	Sea heaps up and white foam from breaking waves begins to be blown in streaks along the wind direction	Not applicable
Gale force in anybody's language. Only necessity or ocean racing keeps craft at sea. Set storm canvas or heave-to	Moderately high waves of greater length. Edges of crests begin to break into spindrift. Foam blown in well-marked streaks along the wind	Not applicable
Unless ocean racing – and sometimes even then – craft seek deep water. Run towing warps etc. This may be survival force for most	High waves. Dense streaks of foam along the wind. Crests begin to topple, tumble and roll over	Not applicable
Almost the ultimate for yachts. Only chance in deep water and with sea room to run before it or possibly lie to a sea anchor	Very high waves with long overhanging crests. The whole surface of the sea takes on a white appearance. Tumbling of sea heavy and shocklike. Visibility impaired	Not applicable
Survival conditions	More intense form of above	Not applicable
As above	As above	Not applicable

Wind on Weather Maps. As pointed out in Chapter Two and elsewhere, the isobaric tramlines define the wind direction above the earth if Buys Ballot's Law is applied in the correct way, depending on the hemisphere. Wind arrows are usually plotted on to station circles, although on TV summary charts they are just drawn vaguely for an area. The arrows fly with the wind and the barbs indicate speed in knots up to 50 kt which is a solid triangle. Half a barb is 5 kt. Thus a conversion is required into Beaufort Force.

Wind speed units. In days gone by miles per hour was the accepted unit in this country. Now it is the knot, one nautical mile per hour = 6080 ft/hr = 1·69 ft/sec.

The metric unit is metres per second. Roughly 1 m/sec = 2 kt. So to convert knots to m/sec divide the knots by two.

Wind direction. Measured in degrees from 360° (north) clockwise and always expressed as a three-figure number, *e.g.* east is 090°, etc.

Precision in wind direction tends to be unnecessary when it is taken to a degree or two, but even the men of sail boxed the compass to quarter points, *i.e.* to less than 3°. Where general direction is adequate then cardinal and half-cardinal points are used.

A quadrant is one of the 90° divisions of the compass. The northern quadrants would mean the span from 270° to 090° through north.

An octant is half a quadrant, *e.g.*, south-east to south or 135°–180°.

Mean wind speed and direction. These are the averages taken over a sufficient period of time. The period depends on the circumstances. Figure 3.3 (page 000) provides an example. The mean direction over the fifty minutes of wind depicted is 003° whereas the true mean over a longer period of time was 007°. In general the longer the wind can be sampled the truer the mean, but there are limits. In increasing or decreasing wind the longer the sampling period the less true the mean for the immediate future. The best period would appear to lie above 10 minutes, with half an hour being necessary if it is imperative to know the true mean. Of the two the direction is the most likely to be wrongly assessed (see Chapter Three).

A gust is a period when the wind speed is increased substantially above the mean speed.

A lull is a period (often following or preceding a gust) when the wind speed is substantially below the mean.

Backing is changing direction against the clock, *e.g.* a westerly backs to south-east ahead of an advancing depression.

Veering is changing direction with the clock, *e.g.* winds may sometimes veer from south-west to north-west on the passage of cold fronts.

Temperature scales and conversions. Celsius (or Centigrade) scale (°C). A scale with 100 grades or degrees between the temperature of melting ice (ice point) and the normal temperature of boiling water (steam point).

Absolute (or Kelvin) scale (°K). A scale whose zero is the lowest possible temperature. Ice point is 273°K above absolute zero but the degree size is the same as the Celsius scale.

Fahrenheit Scale (°F). The domestic scale in use in the British Isles. It marks ice point as 32°F and steam point as 212°F.

CONVERSION SCALE

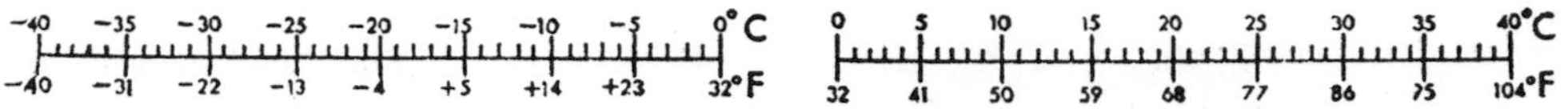

Pressure is force exerted over unit area. In air columns the air pressure at any height is the force due to the weight of that column above that point when measured over unit area. If the average temperature of a column is T° Absolute then the density, d, of the column is governed by this temperature, and d is inversely proportional to T.

If d_o is the density of air at the temperature of melting ice (273°K) then $d = d_o \dfrac{273}{T}$

The pressure P due to height Z of air of density d is $P = gZd$ where g is the acceleration due to gravity (32 ft/sec² or 981 cm/sec²).

Thus a cold column whose density is greater exerts a higher pressure at any level than a warm one. High pressure areas are therefore colder aloft than low ones.

Pressure units

Millibar (mb) = 1000 dynes per square cm = 750·062 mm of mercury = 29·53 in of mercury.

Standard pressure = 1013 mb = 760 mm of mercury = 15 lb/in². The usual range of pressure experienced in temperate high latitudes is between 970 and 1030 mb.

Isobars are lines which connect places with equal pressures at any height.

The power of the wind. Power is defined as the rate of working. That may be taken either as work done in unit time or kinetic energy destroyed in unit time.

Taking the definitions one stage further, work or energy is measured by the product of a force and the distance through which that force acts (assuming force and distance to be in the same line).

For an air column of cross-sectional area A and density d moving at velocity v then in unit time a volume of vA arrives on any area A presented to the airstream. The mass of air which arrives is this vAd as d is the mass of unit volume.

The kinetic energy of mass m moving with velocity v is
$$E = \tfrac{1}{2} mv^2$$
Thus the kinetic energy destroyed on area A in unit time
$$W = \tfrac{1}{2} vAdv^2 = \tfrac{1}{2}Adv^3$$
The kinetic energy destroyed on unit area in this time is
$$W = \tfrac{1}{2}dv^3$$
Thus the rate of working of an airstream of velocity v increases as the cube of the airspeed.

The pressure exerted is defined as the force exerted on unit area of the rate of change of the air's momentum per unit area. The latter is mass × velocity destroyed per unit time on unit area.

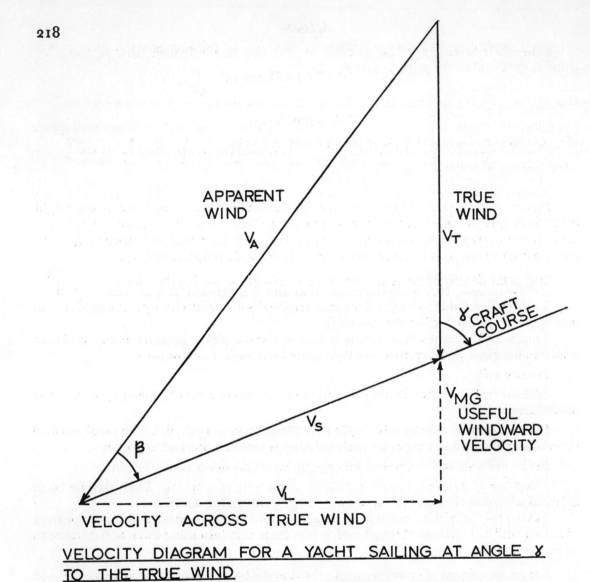

APPARENT
WIND

V_A

TRUE
WIND

V_T

γ CRAFT
COURSE

V_{MG}
USEFUL
WINDWARD
VELOCITY

V_S

β

V_L

VELOCITY ACROSS TRUE WIND

VELOCITY DIAGRAM FOR A YACHT SAILING AT ANGLE γ TO THE TRUE WIND

A.1: *A vector diagram to compute the true wind and to show the angles and other notation referred to in the text and the "made good to windward" component of the craft course vector* (V_{MG}).[10]

The force exerted $F = vAdv$ on area A

$$\text{Thus } p = dv^2$$

Hence the air pressure varies as the square of the wind velocity.

To calculate the true wind strength when on the wind

Consider Fig. A.1 where a craft is travelling at velocity S at 45° to a true wind of velocity T leading to an apparent wind velocity of A. The relation between these quantities is given by the cosine rule

$$A^2 = S^2 + T^2 + 2ST \cos 45°$$

$\cos 45° = \dfrac{1}{\sqrt{2}}$. Divide through by T^2 and let $\dfrac{S}{T} = n$ then $\dfrac{A^2}{T} = n^2 + \sqrt{2}\,n + 1$

Simplification swiftly follows when it is realised that for winds of 20 kt or so and craft speeds of 3–5 kt then $n = \frac{1}{7}$ to $\frac{1}{4}$ and n^2 becomes 0·0205 to 0·0625.

Thus neglect n^2 leaving $T = \dfrac{A}{\sqrt{1·414n + 1}}$

Example. If A is measured as 22 kt and S is assessed to be 5 kt it transpires that little is lost by taking n to be not $\dfrac{S}{T}$ but $\dfrac{S}{A}$ whence $n = \dfrac{5}{22} = 0·227$ and $T = \dfrac{22}{\sqrt{0·32 + 1}} = 19$ kt.

The value obtained by careful drawing is 18·3 kt and the difference is really not significant being much less than the variations in speed of normal airstreams. The percentage error amounts to a little less than 4 per cent.

Another example. If A is measured as 10 kt and S is assessed as 3 kt then

$$n = \dfrac{3}{10} = 0·3. \therefore T = \dfrac{10}{\sqrt{1·425}} = 8.4 \text{ kt}$$

The actual value is 7·8 kt. The percentage error in this case is about twice as great, namely 8 per cent. Therefore the approximate method is more accurate as the wind speed increases.

Note. The vectors S, T and A are the same as V_S, V_T and V_A in Fig. A.1 while the angle γ of the latter figure is 45° in the above examples.

The true wind speed on other points of sailing

The difficulty encountered when the angle γ is something other than 45° lies not only in the complication of finding the cosine but also in the much larger changes in craft speed which occur with craft heading to the true wind. The performance chart for the Firefly (Fig. 3.17, page 67) shows the variation in performance as a dinghy sheers off the wind. Thus the only practical computer is a vector diagram.

The procedure is:

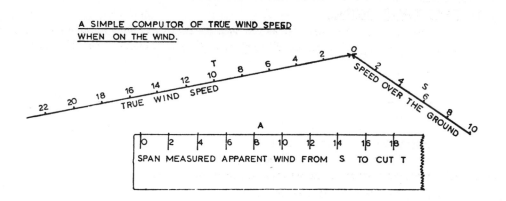

(i) Draw a vector S representing craft speed and direction.

(ii) From its tail end draw a vector representing the apparent wind A reversed.

(iii) The true wind vector T is that which joins the arrowhead of A to that of B.

A useful scale is 1 cm = 1 kt, and for windward work a permanent computer can be made consisting of S marked in knots and a line T at 35–45° also marked in knots up to 25 say. The apparent wind speed is laid on a transparent rule marked in cm from the tail of S to cut T and the speed of the latter read off (Fig. A.2).

Obviously it is impractical in small dinghies to draw vector diagrams to assess the true wind, and the approximate but more easily memorised rules which can be deduced from performance charts are given in Chapter Three.

References

Bracketed numbers appended to captions on the diagrams show that they are based on ones appearing in the publication referred to.

1 *Elementary Meteorology*, Meteorological Office, H.M.S.O.
2 "Nocturnal Winds", E. N. Lawrence, *Prof. Notes Met. Off. London* 7. No. III, 1954.
3 "An Introduction to Lee Waves in the Atmosphere", C. E. Wallington, *Weather*, August 1960.
4 *Land and Sea Breezes*, S.D.T.M., No. 58, Meteorological Office.
5 *Monthly Mean Temperatures for Home Waters*, M.O. 447, H.M.S.O.
6 "The Nocturnal Wind at Thorney Island," B. J. Moffitt, *Meteorological Magazine*, September 1956.
7 "Some Observations of the Effects of Precipitation Downdraughts", C. E. Wallington, *Weather*, February 1961.
8 *Royal Aircraft Establishment Report*, B.A. 1505, October 1938.
9 *Sailing Wind and Current*, Ian Proctor, Adlard Coles.
10 *Sailing Yacht Performance*, J. C. Sainsbury, John Trundell.
11 "The Sea Breeze at Thorney Island", A. J. Watts, *Meteorological Magazine*, January 1955.
12 "Sea Breeze Fronts in Hampshire", J. E. Simpson, *Weather*, July 1964.
13 "Some Effects of Shelter Belts and Wind Breaks", R. W. Gloyne, *Meteorological Magazine*, No. 999, Vol. 84.
14 "The Structure of the Sea Breeze as revealed by Gliding Flights", C. E. Wallington, *Weather*, August 1959.
15 *The Structure of Wind over Level Country*, M. A. Giblett and others, Geophysical Memoir No 54, Meteorological Office.
16 "Tacking Down Wind", M. Lindstrom, *Yachting World*, July 1956.
17 *The Techniques of Small Boat Racing*, edited Stuart Walker, Hodder and Stoughton.
18 "The Tide Wind", J. P. Whitehead, *Yachting World*, August 1954.
19 *The Vertical Profile of the Mean Wind Velocity in the Surface Layers of the Atmosphere*, E. L. Deacon, Porton Technical Paper No. 39.
20 "The Wind Goes Down With the Tide", A. J. Watts, *Yachting World*, December 1961.
21 "Winds over the Great Lakes", F. Lemire, Great Lakes Institute-University of Toronto Cir.—3560 TEC—380, 2 November 1961.
22 "Wind Tunnel Studies of Shelter-Belt Models", Woodruf and Zingy, *Washington Journal of Forestry*, 51, 1953, pp. 173–8.
23 "Wave Currents on the Leeward Side of Mountain Crests", J. Förchtgott, *Bull. met. tchécosl*, Prague, 3, 1949, p. 49.
24 "Zur Theorie der Hangewinde, nebst Bemerkungen zur Theorie der Berg und Talwinde", F. Defant, *Arch Met.*, Wien 1, Series A, 1949.
25 "Forecasting the Lake Breeze and its Effects on Visibility at Chicago Midway Airport", Clifford D. Hall, *Bulletin of American Met. Society*, March 1954.

Index